Everyday Examples

Everyday Examples

An Introduction to Philosophy

DAVID CUNNING

B L O O M S B U R Y

LONDON • NEW DELHI • NEW YORK • SYDNEY

Bloomsbury Academic

An imprint of Bloomsbury Publishing Plc

50 Bedford Square	1385 Broadway
London	New York
WC1B 3DP	NY 10018
UK	USA

www.bloomsbury.com

BLOOMSBURY and the Diana logo are registered trademarks of Bloomsbury Publishing Plc

First published 2015

British Library Cataloguing-in-Publication Data
A catalogue record for this book is available from the British Library.

ISBN: HB: 978-1-47257-464-0
PB: 978-1-47257-463-3
ePDF: 978-1-47257-465-7
ePub: 978-1-47257-466-4

Library of Congress Cataloging-in-Publication Data
A catalog record for this book is available from the Library of Congress

Typeset by Newgen Knowledge Works (P) Ltd., Chennai, India
Printed and bound in India

CONTENTS

PREFATORY REMARKS

This book is intended as a supplement and tool for university courses and for individuals in the broader public who are curious to explore philosophical views and arguments. An assumption throughout is that philosophy is best learned by doing. The philosophers of history supply a treasure trove of views and arguments, and I attempt to offer accessible and illustrative examples to help students to engage the material and make it their own.

A few prefatory remarks are in order. The first is that although philosophy is an important subject matter, students are sometimes reticent to engage the issues, out of a sense that it is not their turf. My hope is that students are able to bring philosophical issues to life by using accessible examples as a starting point. Students can engage the various views and arguments, and there can be discussion of where there is disagreement and why. Accessible examples are already considered in many classroom discussions, but part of the idea for the book is to help students to work through examples outside of class, as a way to generate further engagement still.

I do not utilize a structure in which arguments are presented in premise-conclusion form, or lay out every possible objection. Part of my concern is that a structure like that can incline the student just to memorize the views and arguments, and to memorize the critical thinking maneuvers by which problems might be raised for them. The views and arguments are instead presented more colloquially. I am attempting a project in which students would confront the ideas for themselves, sort out the different motivations behind them, and then think through the consequences and complications firsthand. Note also that students can proceed in whatever chapter order is fitting, and students can focus on particular sections within a chapter as well.

As befits an introductory discussion, there are details and complications that are bracketed for treatment later on, once the students have a sense of the lay of the land. For example, in the sections on externalist theories of knowledge, there is little treatment of the many different versions of externalism that have been proposed. Instructors might want to expand some of these discussions on their own. By the same token, not every philosophical view or argument or topic is treated, but instead there is a cross-section of material that students will hopefully be excited to dive into and tackle and engage. An aim again is that students get a lot of firsthand practice at doing philosophy.

The text incorporates a number of everyday accessible examples. In a few cases the examples are from popular culture, especially television and film, but those of course have a shelf life. Instead of supposing familiarity, I take steps to flesh out the larger context and then explain their significance to the philosophical issue at hand. Philosophical discourse often operates at a very stratospheric level. I try to fashion the everyday examples to achieve accessibility without compromising rigor.

The book also has a web component, with YouTube videos, comics, songs, newspaper clips, a discussion board and blog, suggested readings, and other resources. The appropriate places in the text are marked by an asterisk (*), with a corresponding link at www.everydayexamples.net. There will be regular updates and additions.

I have attempted to include a broad cross-section of philosophical perspectives, and I have also attempted to include a cross-section of the work of philosophers who are not white men. I try not to make too big a deal of this; it's just that a lot of philosophy is done by people who are not in that category. Instead of having a single chapter devoted to these different perspectives, I have interspersed the various discussions throughout the book as topically appropriate.

The book attempts to lay out important arguments that have been offered by the great philosophers of history, but there can be disagreement about the proper interpretation of these arguments. I do not want to suggest that the interpretations that I suppose are the only ones that are legitimate, and I invite students to take issue with my interpretations, and to actively engage in any other way that would be fitting. If some of my interpretations turn out to be controversial (or even mistaken), I hope that they might still help to lay the ground for the discussion of an important philosophical thesis or point.

A number of different philosophical issues are considered in the book, along with a number of different views and arguments that philosophers have presented on the many sides of each issue. I attempt to motivate each argument in a way that highlights the reasons why it is compelling to the side in question. Enough different views and arguments are presented that of course many are not my own, and to be honest I am not sure what to say in the case of a number of the issues that are treated. I am also assuming that my own particular views do not matter much here and that what does matter is taking on the arguments and reasons.

Finally, the structure of the text is unorthodox. There are a number of short sections (around 40 to 50) in each chapter, and each is supposed to be a separate nugget—either a premise, or an argument, or an objection, or an example. The everyday language of the text invites this sort of structure, and the structure also allows for each point to be finite and manageable. An additional benefit is that students may be assigned an individual section in advance of class, and be resident expert for the day. In some cases I introduce a view or argument that a student might find highly problematic, and I hope the student will take it on directly. That is a very important part of the project here. Each chapter also contains a set of discussion questions for students to address—they might write on one of these at the start of class, as the basis for discussion, or students might discuss the questions in a group. An implicit proposal in each of the study questions is for the student to illustrate their response with an example.

ACKNOWLEDGMENTS

I am indebted to a number of people for their extremely helpful comments as the textbook was in progress. These include Matthew Drabek, Michael Eng, Peter Fosl, Seth Jones, Tammy Nyden, Simone Renault, Samuel Taylor, and Emily Waddle.

I am also very grateful for the assistance and support of Liza Thompson, Colleen Coalter, Mat Nichols, and Chloe Shuttlewood at Bloomsbury Academic Publishing. And I am grateful to Srikanth Srinivasan at Newgen for his extremely careful and generous editorial work.

I also need to thank Naomi Greyser and Mira Grey Cunning. Their support is constant and unwavering.

Finally I would like to express gratitude to my father, Robert Cunning. He passed away as the book was in press, but I was very lucky to be able to share draft chapters with him. Our conversations were always lively and illuminating. I am grateful for his insightful feedback and for his many other influences.

CHAPTER ONE

The nature and existence of the external world

Abstract

This chapter will consider: whether or not our perception of the external world might be a massive hallucination; commonsense responses to skepticism; internalist versus externalist views of knowledge; the view that our experience of reality is heavily shaped by contributions from our own end; the impact of technology and social media on perspective; and standpoint epistemology.

Skepticism about the external world—is it all just one big dream?

1

The philosopher René Descartes introduces a famous worry at the start of his *Meditations on First Philosophy*.[1] He notes that some of his dreams are just as vivid as his waking experiences and then concludes that, if so, he cannot be certain that the outside world is as he perceives it. The idea is this. When he dreams, he is having perceptions of dragons or monsters or perhaps a clear blue day, but in fact he is lying in bed—his brain is being stimulated to have perceptions that do not reflect the configuration of the bodies that surround him. If dreams are sometimes just as vivid as waking experiences, he cannot be certain which of his vivid perceptions is a dream perception and which is a perception that he is having while awake. That is, he cannot be sure which of his perceptions is giving him information about what the world is actually like:

> How often, asleep at night, am I convinced of just such familiar events—that I am here in my dressing-gown, sitting by the fire—when in fact I am lying undressed in bed! Yet at the moment my eyes are certainly wide awake when I look at this piece of paper; I shake my head and it is not asleep; as I stretch out and feel my hand I do so deliberately, and I know what I am doing. All this would not happen with such distinctness to someone asleep. Indeed! As if I did not remember other occasions when I have been tricked by exactly similar thoughts in sleep. As I think about this more carefully, I see plainly that there are never any sure signs by means of which being awake can be distinguished from being asleep.[2]

Our beliefs might be based on extremely vivid perceptions. For example, we have a belief about a favorite piece of clothing, or a nearby park, or the details of our commute to school or work, or a belief about something that we perceived long ago. Such beliefs are based on perceptions, but we can never be certain that a vivid perception is not a dream, and so we can never tell if it (or the belief that is based on it) is getting at how things really are.

2

Descartes summarizes the argument later in the Sixth Meditation:

> [E]very sensory experience I have ever thought I was having while awake I can also think of myself as sometimes having while asleep; and since I do not believe that what I seem to perceive in sleep comes from things located outside of me, I did not see why I should be any more inclined to believe this of what I think I perceive while awake.[3]

Here he is putting the skeptical worry a bit differently. In the First Meditation he was suggesting that dream perceptions are illusory and that waking perceptions are not, but that we cannot tell which of our perceptions is which. The thought there seemed to be: if we could only tell which of our perceptions was a waking perception, we would have knowledge of the outside world. Now he is saying that we have no reason to think that our waking perceptions tell us about the outside world either. When we dream, our brains are stimulated to have perceptions that are illusory. When we are awake, our brains are stimulated to have perceptions as well. We can never compare our perceptions to the external objects that are stimulating the brain—to see if they are a match—because all that we would be doing in such a case is comparing one set of perceptions with another. For example, if we have a perception of a tree, our brain is being stimulated, and when we try to approach the tree that we think is causing that perception—in order to confirm it—we are just being stimulated to have another perception! As Descartes puts it, our sensory perceptions do not by themselves provide any reason or evidence for thinking that waking perceptions are produced by objects that resemble them.

3

This is the skeptical worry that is borne out in movies like *Total Recall* and *The Matrix*. In both, the main characters have supposed for their entire lives that their sensory perceptions have been delivering a more-or-less accurate picture of reality. In *The Matrix*, Neo comes to learn that all along he has been imprisoned in a chamber: he is hooked up to a machine that makes him have seamless perceptions of (what he thought was) real life.* In *Total Recall*, the main character Quaid enters a virtual reality machine, with the aim of getting away from it all: he wants to have the experience of being a secret agent on Mars.* Moments after he enters the machine (at the headquarters of Recall), he finds himself desperately attempting to break out of it. He insists that he *is* a secret agent. The rest of the movie is an adventure indeed. Quaid cannot tell if his experiences from that point are all part of the virtual program, or if in fact he broke out of the machine. At 59:41 of the movie, he is in his bedroom on Mars, when he hears a knock at the door.[4] A scientist from Recall has come to help—Quaid is told that he is still in the machine, but that he has had a schizoid embolism, and that he needs to take a pill as a symbol of his desire to return to reality. Quaid deliberates: he cannot tell if he is in fact a secret agent on Mars, and if his visitor is trying to poison him, or if he is actually in the machine. Quaid's wife appears: she says that she loves him, and that he needs to take the pill. He does not know what to do. Shortly after the start of his adventure at Recall, he had a vivid experience that his wife was his enemy all the while, and a secret agent herself. So he cannot tell if she is really on Mars, helping the visitor to administer the poison, or if instead she was never his enemy at all, and is holding his hand at *Recall* as he sits motionless in the machine. At the pivotal moment in the scene, he puts the pill into his mouth. He almost swallows it, but he notices the visitor begin to sweat. Quaid shoots him in the head, assuming that the person would only be nervous if he was really in the room. The secret-agent adventure continues, with a bloodbath that is unmitigated Schwarzenegger. The problem of course is that the virtual reality machine would also be able to make its occupant have the perception of a bead of sweat. No matter what happens—if Quaid's grandma tells him he is back at Recall, or Mother Theresa—he cannot be sure what is happening in the external world.

4

There is presumably a fact of the matter about whether or not Quaid is in the virtual reality machine. If he is in the machine, then he is being caused to have a bunch of perceptions, but his perceptions do not accurately represent the world around him. If he is not in the machine, and is really a secret agent with dealings on Mars, his perceptions of the people and objects on Mars are caused by those people and objects, but Quaid is none the wiser. His beliefs about these people and objects might well be true, but the worry that Descartes is highlighting in the First Meditation is that from Quaid's perspective it is just a matter of luck that they are true. As Descartes says in his own words:

[T]here was something else which I used to assert, and which through habitual belief I thought I understood clearly, although I did not in fact do so. This was that there were things outside of me which were the sources of my ideas and which resembled them in all respects. Here was my mistake; or at any rate, if my judgment was true, it was not thanks to the strength of my understanding.[5]

If we cannot confirm that our sensory perceptions are caused by objects that resemble them, then simply put—we do not know that the external world is as we perceive it.

5

Part of Descartes' goal in offering the dream argument is to try to get us to entertain a surprising idea—that what we know best of all we do not know through our senses. Descartes thinks that there is room to doubt claims like that there really is a piece of paper in front of me, but that there is no room to doubt claims like "I think, therefore I am," or that something cannot come from nothing.[6] For example, we try to think of the prospect of there existing nothing, and then of something all of a sudden coming into existence, and we just get a brain cramp. That . . . can't . . . happen. Nor is this result known through the senses, Descartes thinks, for it is not as though we would accept any observations in which something happened to come from nothing. We would just insist on looking harder for the cause that we did not see.

The experience machine

6

One response to Descartes' dream argument is that the argument is irrelevant: it does not matter if we cannot tell that our perceptions correspond to reality, because we could never know the difference. All that we know is our experience, and it is the same to us whether we are in a virtual reality machine or if the things that we perceive are really there. But people might be pulled in very different directions here. On the one hand, we might say: we cannot demonstrate once-and-for-all that the external world exists as we perceive it, and indeed all that we have ever known is our perceptions, so there is no important difference. We might say that all that we can know is our experience—and so all that can matter is our experience—and that is that. On the other hand, we might try to conjure scenarios in which we care about more than just our experience. For example, a person might want to know the truth about whether their spouse is having an affair: the person would prefer to have their life turned upside down and learn the truth, rather than live a happy deception. Or we might imagine a more science-fictional example, along the lines of *Total Recall* or the *Matrix*. We are ordered to enter a virtual reality machine for the rest of our lives, in which we would think that everything is perfectly real, but we have a choice between two options: one, where we prosper and have the greatest experience imaginable, but back in reality our loved ones suffer and are sad and miserable; and another, where we have a horrible experience, in part because we experience our loved ones as suffering and miserable and sad, but in real life they flourish.[7] I know what I would do in this case; or I would like to think that I do.

7

It is interesting to ask whether our preference would change at all if we specified the case a little differently: suppose that we *began* our lives in an experience machine, and later on (perhaps in our twenties) we are removed from the machine and told that we can either return to our "family" and our former "life," or start over in a largely foreign world. We would presumably miss all the "people" and "situations" that were so orienting to us, and the new world might seem cold and dark. Perhaps our preference would depend on how old we are and on how long we would have left to live— and whether or not we would have much prospect for building a life in the real world.

A commonsense response to skepticism

8

One line of response to Descartes' dream argument is to say it is cheating: it cannot call into question our perceptions of the external world without assuming that for the most part those perceptions are trustworthy after all. More specifically, the objection to Descartes is this: the dream argument only gets off the ground if we assume that sensory perceptions are due to neuronal firings in the brain, but the reason we accept *that* assumption is that we take our sensory perceptions of brains to be evidence that brains exist and are stimulated to have perceptions. To be sure, we do not trust perceptions of brains that are had in suboptimal viewing conditions. But the dream argument is making assumptions about how brains work, presumably on the basis of observations of brains in good lighting. Presumably we should be entitled to trust any other sensory perceptions that are had in circumstances that are similar.

9

The philosopher G. E. Moore offered a refutation of external-world skepticism along these lines. He pointed to his hands and said: here is a hand; here is another hand; therefore, there now exist two hands. Therefore, there is an external world.[8] It is tempting to regard Moore's thinking here as a little dense: he does not seem to be understanding the skeptic's argument at all. Moore was a brilliant philosopher, however, and so it is important to ask if he might be doing more than meets the eye. He is dismissing the skeptic—there is no question about that—and he is refusing to grant the skeptic's argument any force. Moore interpretation is a matter of some controversy, but his point would seem to be that if we think about it the skeptic's argument does not *have* any force. More precisely, he is calling attention to the fact that the argument is not effective unless it provides us with some reason for thinking that it is possible that our sensory perceptions are misleading. And Moore would say that the argument does not do that. If the argument tries to do it by specifying that our brains work in such a way that they could be stimulated to have perceptions even if the perceived objects are not there—for example, in dreams or hallucinations—then we are taking for granted the trustworthiness of perceptions that tell us that we sleep in beds, or that inform us that we have brains. If so, we are committed to trusting any other perceptions that are had in conditions that are just as good. We are entitled to assume that we have hands, and we are entitled to assume that there are beds and trees and tables and chairs.

10

A proponent of the dream argument might respond that we *can* get skepticism off the ground—without advancing any claims about neurons or brains or dreams or beds. In fact, we do not need to presuppose anything at all about what external bodies are like; we just need to put forward some obvious claims that fall out of our definitions and concepts and ideas. And claims of this sort are wholly uncontroversial. We do not need to assume that there are basketball teams in order to put forward the claim that part of what it is for something to be a basketball team is to have five position players, and we do not need to know that there are scissors to be entitled to put forward the claim that a pair of scissors is the sort of thing that is good for making a cut. We know these things from the concept or definition of scissors and basketball team. We can also put forward a claim about the nature or definition of knowledge: namely, that we do not really know a result if as far as we can tell it is possible that it is false. From this claim, skepticism about the external world follows quite easily. We just need to add this: it is imaginable that our sensory perceptions are not produced by things that resemble them, and hence it is *possible* that our sensory perceptions are not produced by things that resemble them.

11

So the skeptic might say that there are claims that the philosopher is entitled to put forward and that do not require that we make any assumptions about what is real or exists. Skeptics have to be entitled to put forward at least some claims; otherwise they would not be able to draw any conclusions. In particular, they would not be able to draw conclusions about whether our beliefs live up to the definition of knowledge. It seems that we can know a priori[9] what something has to be in order to be knowledge, and we can also know what is and what is not imaginable or possible.

12

Here Moore (or his advocate) would take issue with the idea that the definitions or claims of the philosopher are on firmer ground than the claims of common sense.[10] The latter include the following: there is a computer in front of me; many of the people in the world are currently eating food; some of the people in the world are thinking about the problem of philosophical skepticism. So a question is which claims should be privileged—the conceptual theses of the philosopher, or the deliverances of daily life. Skeptics proceed as though they are not presupposing anything that is very contentious, but Moore would say that they are presupposing quite a bit. So perhaps both sides are making use of presupposition. Moore would add that upon reflection it is the second sort of claim in which we have more confidence and that when we put forward that sort of claim instead, the results that follow are not in the least bit skeptical. However, the definition of knowledge has been contested for over 2,000 years, and is still contested today!

13

There is a story (perhaps apocryphal) about Moore giving a lecture at UC Berkeley and pointing to two windows at the back of the room, exclaiming, "Here is a window; there is a window; there are two windows." But the "windows" were at the very back of the room, and they were just painted on the wall.

"Externalist" responses to skepticism

14

Another response to Descartes' dream argument is to agree with the skeptic—up to a point—and grant that we can never confirm that our perceptions are produced by objects that resemble them. But we might insist that nonetheless we have knowledge about the external world. If so, knowledge must be something short of what Descartes had in mind. A simple analogue is this. A person might insist that (by definition) friendship is a matter of being totally selfless toward another human being—and always putting that person's interest first. If we remark that there has never been such an individual in the history of human civilization, the appropriate response might be that there has never been a single instance of friendship. That would be one response, but another would be to say that the stated requirements on friendship are too strong. We made up the word "friendship" to name a phenomenon that we actually encounter, and hence friendship is *that* phenomenon and not a thing that has never existed. If there are and have been friends, then friendship is not a matter of being totally selfless toward other human beings or always putting their interest first.

15

Another example is where a person might insist that by definition a "perfect day" is a day that involves no flaws whatsoever—not in any of the objects that surround us, nor in any of the people. In that case we should take issue with, and argue against, any individual who describes a given day as perfect. There are many other analogies of course, but the main idea (to return to the discussion at hand) is that if "knowledge" is a word that we invented to talk about something that actually confronts us and that is part of the landscape, and if we can never secure a guarantee that our perceptions are caused by objects that resemble them, then knowledge is something different from what Descartes assumed it to be.

16

One sort of case where we might be inclined to identify a person as having knowledge is the case in which a person always seems to come to the right view, or offer the right advice, even if the person cannot articulate exactly how they settle upon it. The person might tell us exactly the thing to say to negotiate a conflict at work; or they might be really good at recognizing what to say to diffuse an awkward social situation; or they might be a genius or savant who can solve a complicated problem in mathematics without running through the steps of the calculation. There is, for example, the kind of case that is featured in movies like *Rain Main*, where an autistic individual is able to determine the number of sticks in a box of matches immediately after it spills onto the floor. Of these people, we feel the pull of saying that they know things—that somehow they know things—even if they do not quite understand how they know things, and even if we do not understand it either. The mathematical savant might seem like a special case—where she is magically interfaced with the domain of numbers in such a way that she just gets it right every time—but there are plenty of cases that are more mundane. On an everyday basis, we seem to form beliefs that track the facts about our surroundings. We know that the traffic light is about to turn green, or that a cup of coffee is just what the doctor ordered, or that a certain thought is going to keep us awake all night if we entertain it right before bed. We know a lot of things like these even if we do not have what Descartes would count as proof or confirmation.

17

We might further motivate this conception of knowledge by noting that we often attribute knowledge to animals, even if they are not in a position to confirm their beliefs or put them to any rigorous test. We say that "Spot knows that he is about to be fed," for example, and presumably we say it because we suppose that Spot's beliefs about his food are appropriately tethered to the details of his immediate environment. A Cartesian would argue that in such cases we are using the word *know* in scare quotes and do not really mean it.

18

Some are very compelled by this intuition—that if we have true beliefs in a certain domain of inquiry (e.g. matchsticks or mathematics), and if the reason why we have these true beliefs is that we have a cognitive mechanism for getting things right, then we have knowledge in that domain of inquiry. The mathematical savant knows the results that her mind presents to her, even if she does not perform the calculations that would confirm that they are true, and indeed even if she does not ever perform such calculations. Somehow, she knows. The same applies in the case of a person who in fact is not dreaming and who is surrounded by the objects that the person takes to be there. If the person's mind forms the belief that there is a table in front of her when in fact there is a table, and not when there is a plant, etc., or a massive computer simulation, then the person is a knower. She is a knower as long as her mind happens to form true beliefs reliably. At the end of her life, God might do a retrospective and show her that she was in fact perceiving the objects that she thought she was, and she would exclaim—"Yes!! All along, I was a knower!"

19

Descartes would worry that these are less instances of knowledge than they are instances of luck. The mathematical savant does not *know* the results that his mind presents to him, even if his mind presents the right result every time. The person who is not in a Matrix machine does not *know* that she is surrounded by trees and cars and people and pets; it just turns out that she is surrounded by these and by other real things. Descartes is (what is often called) an *internalist* about knowledge. He thinks that in order for a mind to know about objects, it is not enough that it reliably forms true beliefs about those objects. The mind has to form true beliefs about the objects, but it has to be able to see for itself—on the basis of evidence of which it is aware—that its beliefs are true. The *externalist* disagrees. The externalist holds that all that we need for knowledge is for our minds to be hooked up to the world in the right way, whether we know it or not. That is, we are knowers even if we do not take the steps to confirm that our minds are hooked up to the world in this way: we know even if such confirmation is external to our awareness, and is not available to us. That is a good thing, the externalist would note, because it seems to be impossible to meet Descartes' requirement of confirming that we are not in a dream.

20

It may be a matter of luck to have a mind that tracks the details of the world around it, but if we have such a mind, it is not a matter of luck that we get things right. An analogue is the person who has outstanding athletic genes and becomes an Olympic gold medalist at track and field. The person is lucky to have the genes that they do, but it is not an accident every time they win a race. It is probably an accident when they lose.

21

A famous and relatively early version of an externalist view of knowledge is in the work of the current-day philosopher Alvin Goldman—what he calls the causal theory of knowing.[11] Goldman begins by describing other cases of cognition and noting that they seem to be uncontroversially externalist. For example, when we make the distinction between a person that sees an object and a person who just hallucinates the object, the important difference is that in the case of the first person the object is actually before them. The person does not need to confirm that the object is before them, but still we can say (and say accurately) that they see the object. Goldman also notes that we say from a third-person perspective that a person remembers something so long as the things that they call to mind actually happened. A doctor might be checking to see if a patient has overcome their amnesia, and if the patient is able to offer faithful descriptions of events—and events that are part of the patient's past—the doctor would be right to say that the patient remembers, and is cured. The patient may not be in a position to say that he remembers, but it is a fact that he does remember, as long as the things that he calls to mind actually occurred and in the way that he lays out. Goldman then considers examples of yet another kind of cognition—knowledge. He presents the case of a person who observes a sea of lava surrounding a volcano and who concludes that there has been an eruption.[12] Goldman takes it to be intuitive that if the person is actually seeing lava, and if the lava was in fact caused by an eruption, then the person knows that there was an eruption. If (instead) the lava was placed at the foot of the volcano as part of a prank, and there was no eruption, the person would still believe that there was an eruption, but he would not know it. Goldman then argues (with a few qualifications) that we know something so long as we believe it and so long as the thing itself is the cause of our belief. That is to say, we know something if we believe it and if the cause of our belief is the fact that that is how the world actually is. We do not need also to *confirm* that that is the cause of our belief, and indeed we do not need to have any reason at all for thinking that that is the cause of our belief.[13] That is one of the things that makes Goldman's account externalist.

22

Another way that philosophers have attempted to motivate the externalist picture of knowledge is through a comparison between the human mind and a thermometer. According to the externalist, we know something so long as our mind is hooked up to the world in the right way. If our minds reliably form true beliefs about the world and consistently get things right, then we are knowers. A thermometer is similar in this regard. It tells us the current temperature, and when the temperature changes, it offers a new reading to reflect the change. The thermometer has a mechanism for getting the temperature right, and if it works correctly it gets the temperature right every time, and not by accident. But it is not aware of whether or not its mechanism works accurately. That is not relevant to the question of whether it is a well-working thermometer. Similarly, if a mind forms true beliefs about its environment, and if it adjusts its beliefs in line with changes in that environment, it is doing all that we could ask of a cognitive system.[14] It has knowledge.

Internalism versus externalism

23

It is possible to have very different reactions to the thermometer analogy. Some find it pretty unintuitive. The philosopher Lawrence Bonjour has pointed to it to highlight that, according to an externalist view of knowledge, we can know something without having any reason whatsoever for believing that it is true. We consider, for example, the case of Norman the clairvoyant. All of a sudden Norman forms the belief that the president of the

United States is in New York City today. Norman has no reason for holding this belief: he has not seen any reports on television; he has not looked at the paper; he has not heard anything about it from his friends. When pressed, Norman cannot give any reason for his belief. It turns out, though, that his mind is so constituted that it tracks the president's presence in New York City. For example, as soon as the president leaves, Norman will believe that he is no longer there. The externalist is committed to saying that Norman knows that the president is in New York City today, and to some that is an odd thing to say indeed.[15]

24

It is difficult to know how to weigh intuitions here, and some might insist that Norman *does* know. He does not know *how* he knows, and we do not know how he knows, but if he always has the right view about whether or not the president is in New York City, then somehow he knows. We might vary the case a little. Imagine that Norman finds out that he is always right when he forms beliefs about whether or not the president is in New York City, and as a result he (Norman) has some assurance that he is equipped with a reliable belief-forming mechanism. Norman is certainly welcome to have this assurance, Armstrong and Goldman would say, but it is not a part of what it is for him to have knowledge. It is just a bonus. Indeed, it is not even relevant to knowledge, for a person can have psychological assurance for terrible reasons that have little to do with the truth of the thing that they believe. For the externalist, Norman has knowledge as long as he has a reliable belief-forming mechanism, whether he is aware that he has it or not.

25

We might vary the case a bit more. Imagine that there is a fortune-teller who lives deep in the forest and never ever receives confirmation about whether her predictions are right. She does not *want* to know whether her predictions are right, and she has isolated herself accordingly. People come from all over the world to seek her counsel; they are more than happy to make the long and difficult trek. The fortune-teller makes 500 predictions a year, and 500 are correct. The newspapers report on it. In the world beyond the forest, she is regarded as a phenomenon. But again, she does not know her success rate; she refuses to hear anything about it, and she puts anyone on a blacklist who even attempts to bring it up. She has no information about her success rate, and she is not in a position to regard it as a reason for increased confidence that her predictions will be true. In some cases she only has a feeling of 60 percent confidence that any given prediction will be true—and we might still call this arrogance, if she has absolutely no reason to think that she is right—but in fact she will get things right 100 percent of the time. Some might have a strong inclination to say that this is a person who somehow knows.

26

One of the worries about both the Norman case and the thermometer case is that they appear to suppose that knowledge is not especially cognitive. That is, something is a knower so long as it cranks out the right answer in a reliable way. It does not need to be in possession of any reasons for thinking that it is getting things right. Part of the issue here is what it means exactly to call a process or system "cognitive." One might argue that for a process to be cognitive it must involve conscious awareness of information and ideas. It must also engage in calculation and reasoning, where these are also understood to be a matter of consciousness and reflection. On this view, the behavior of a calculator or computer is not cognitive because calculators and computers are (presumably) not conscious. Nor does a cell engage in behavior that is cognitive, even though scientists use locutions like that cells communicate with each other, or that viruses are smart.

27

But someone—in defense of the thermometer picture of knowledge, for example—might argue that cognition is often far below the threshold of consciousness and that, even though cognition is often conscious and reflective, it often is not. For example, we might point to processes that occur in sleep and that would appear to be cognitive—when we fall asleep thinking about a problem, and we have a solution to the problem as soon as we wake. We might also consider the sort of case in which we are able to recognize a person's face right away, but without consciously running through a list of their facial features and how they are different from the features of someone else. If there are processes that are cognitive but that do not involve conscious awareness, perhaps it makes sense to say that knowledge is not a matter of having inner accessible states. There is further discussion of this issue in Chapters Three and Five.

28

Descartes agrees that our minds have to get reality right in order to be knowers, but he does not think that that is enough. We also have to *know* that our minds are getting reality right. According to the externalist, we know about reality even if we do not know that our minds are tracking it. Still, the externalist would be wary about using Descartes' language here. That is, the externalist would be reluctant to give *this* response to Descartes: we do not need to know that our minds are tracking reality if we are to know things about it. This is because the externalist has a different understanding of what knowledge is, and hence a different understanding of what it would mean to know that our minds are tracking reality. For the externalist, what it is to know that our minds are tracking some aspect of reality (e.g. the truths of mathematics) is to have the belief that our minds are tracking truths of mathematics, and also a mechanism whereby that belief changes if and when our minds stop tracking truths of mathematics—perhaps because of a brain trauma or some such. The externalist applies their view of knowledge across the board—even to the question of whether we know that we know. To know that we know, we do not need to confirm that we know.

29

If a person can be a knower without ever needing to confirm that her mind gets reality right, Descartes' skeptical scenario falls by the wayside. So long as a person happens to be consistently and reliably correct with respect to their beliefs, then she has knowledge. Some have argued that an externalist account is best able to make sense of other kinds of knowledge that we appear to have as well. For example, we take ourselves to know things not just on the basis of the testimony of the senses, but also on the basis of the testimony of other human beings. The philosopher Jennifer Lackey has pointed out the many ways in which an externalist account allows us to capture that we can know things on the basis of testimony, even if we do not go to the work of confirming that the witness or reporter is telling the truth.[16] We would know hardly *anything* on the basis of testimony if we had to confirm—in the extreme Cartesian sense—the reliability of the testifiers that we trust, but instead we appear to know quite a bit. We might raise the objection—in the context of legal testimony—that if we are voting to convict a defendant, we are supposed to believe that he is guilty "beyond a reasonable doubt." Since much of the evidence in a trial is testimonial, we might think that we would never meet this standard if the externalist was right: we would know facts about the case, but without being sure, and without eradicating all of the doubt that we find to be reasonable. Here the externalist might respond in a number of ways. For example: we can be sure of a person's innocence or guilt "beyond a reasonable doubt," but that might have little to do with the facts of the case and a lot more to do with our presuppositions going in. Another response is that there is a way in which all evidence is testimonial, where the testimony of human reporters is just one instance. We also trust the reports of the senses.

30

A worry for the externalist is that it is not clear how we would be able to tell that anyone ever has knowledge. Any time that we try to confirm that someone has a mind that is getting things right, we would need to check to see that their mind is hooked up to reality in the right way and form true beliefs about it. We would need to be able to say what reality is like, so that we can check to see that the mind in question is getting things right. But for all we know *we* might be dreaming, or in a Matrix machine. The externalist might come back and say that in fact we *can* know who has a reliable mind and who does not. We know, so long as we form beliefs about who has a reliable mind, and so long as the mechanism for producing those beliefs is reliable itself. But that is not to say that we can *tell* who has a reliable mind! If Descartes is right and we can never confirm that our perceptions are produced by objects that resemble them, it seems that we are never in position to determine if others have knowledge or if we have knowledge ourselves.

31

A related worry is that a theory of knowledge that is worth anything would presumably give us some guidance on how to acquire knowledge, but externalism seems to rule that out from the start. If we cannot tell who has knowledge, or that our own belief-forming mechanism is reliable, then we appreciate what the target is but we have little sense of where to aim.

32

A response on behalf of the externalist is that it is the internalist who leaves us with no hope for securing knowledge. For the internalist, our minds need to get reality right (if we are to have knowledge), but we also need to be sure that our minds are getting reality right. On this view, it looks as though we can know nothing about the external world, or how best to navigate it. We can know things like "I think, therefore I exist," or "I am in pain, right now," but it is not clear how such knowledge is supposed to help us to get around.[17] So the externalist can argue that it is the internalist who keeps us from knowledge of the external world, and that he does so straight out of the gate. At least the externalist is leaving us a chance. Furthermore, if the externalist is correct, knowledge-acquisition is more inclusive and pluralistic and egalitarian, as there are a lot of different ways to get to the point where our beliefs track reality. We could study, or do science or philosophy, or we could simply attempt to pick up the habits and skills of expert mentors. We could look around at people who appear to have beliefs that track reality, and who just seem to get things right, and we could emulate them. Or perhaps there will someday emerge a surgical procedure that will make us like Norman, but in respects that are tailored to our own cognitive concerns.

33

A problem of course is that the internalist could respond that all of this would be just one big roll of the dice. We cannot be sure which people around us are getting things right, and we cannot even be sure that there are people.

34

Some philosophers have felt the pull of intuitions on both sides of the internalism-externalism debate and have argued that there are two kinds of knowledge. The philosopher Ernest Sosa has argued that *animal knowledge* is of the externalist sort where our minds are hooked up to the world in the right way—whether we have reasons or evidence for believing so or not—and *reflective knowledge* is of the sort where we do have reason for thinking that our beliefs are true.[18] Sosa can respond to the skeptic that a lot of the beliefs that we identify as knowledge are in fact knowledge and that any of these that we cannot confirm to the satisfaction of a philosopher like Descartes are instances of animal knowledge. A full-blown externalist might worry that on this view almost all of our knowledge would be seen as somehow base or inadequate or deficient, and so a case would have to be made for the view that animal cognition is impressive and something to write home about.

Is reality a mental construction?

35

A final response to Descartes' dream argument is that it is simply hinting at what we already know. That is, the argument is not especially worrisome, because modern science tells us that there is a radical divide between our sensory perceptions of the world and what the world is like in itself. What is really out there are things like electrons and quarks and waves; there is not even the empty space that we perceive between objects, and what we call "empty space" is just fields of gravitational energy.[19] The colors and tastes and sounds and smells that seem to be so ubiquitous, and that help us to discriminate among the objects that we know and love, are not really out there, at least not in the ways that we experience them. Accordingly, one might argue that waking experience is so divorced from reality that we *should* be skeptical about the existence of the objects that we perceive. That is, Descartes' dream argument is not raising a worry as much as it is reflecting a fact of life. The everyday objects with which we are familiar are things like tables and chairs and coffee cups and shoes and flowers and mountains and the sun. But in reality, the sun is not yellow; coffee is not dark or tasty; there is no empty space and no blue atmosphere; and flowers do not have an odor. We encounter a world of sensible objects, but what is out there is something different entirely. A version of this view was in place as far back as the seventeenth century. Some even argued that the reason why we experience colors and tastes and other such qualities is that a benevolent God wants to make it easier for us to get around:

> Though it was not the intention of God or nature to abuse us herein, but a most wise contrivance thus to beautify and adorn the visible and material world, to add lustre or embellishment to it, that it might have charms, relishes, and allurements to it, to gratify our appetites. Whereas otherwise reality in itself, the whole corporeal world in its naked hue, is nothing else but a heap of dust or atoms, of several figures and magnitudes, variously agitated up and down. So that these things, which we look upon as such real things without us, are not properly modifications of bodies themselves, but several modifications, passions, and affections of our own souls.[20]

On this view, the world of everyday experience exists almost entirely in our thought. What is outside of us right now is just particles and gravitational fields; what was out there 5 minutes ago was particles and gravitational fields; and the same applies to what was out there all of last year and well before our birth. We string together our experience of present sensory objects with our memory of past sensory objects, as though it is these that have persisted across time. What has in fact persisted across time is particles and gravitational fields, and also the thinking minds that work to produce the sensible world and that help to maintain its integrity.

36

Kant had something like this view in the eighteenth century, though he went even further and argued that not even particles and gravitational fields are mind-independent. He argued more generally that space and time do not exist outside of our thought and hence that things that are spatial or temporal owe their spatiotemporal features to our thinking as well. Part of Kant's motivation is the worry that space and time would be really weird beings if they were real—they would be things that objects exist in, but at the same time they would not be things at all.[21]

37

One argument that he offered (for space) is this: we are absolutely certain in advance of encountering an object that we will encounter it in space, but the only way we could be so certain is if spatiality was just a subjective way of perceiving things. He put it like this:

> Space is a necessary representation, *a priori*, which is the ground of all outer intuitions. One can never represent that there is no space, although one can very well think that there are no objects to be encountered in it. It is therefore to be regarded as the condition of the possibility of appearances, not as a determination dependent on them.[22]

It is conceivable that there be empty space, but it is inconceivable that we encounter an object that is not in space. That is to say, we know in advance of encountering an object that it will have the feature or determination of being spatial. We do not have to wait until we experience the object, but as Kant says, we know that it will be spatial a priori. He concludes that

> Space represents no property at all of any things in themselves nor any relation of them to each other, i.e. no determination of them that attaches to objects themselves and that would remain even if one were to abstract from all subjective conditions of intuition. . . . Space is nothing other than merely the form of all appearances of outer sense, i.e. the subjective condition of sensibility, under which alone outer intuition is possible for us.[23]

Kant's thinking appears to be this. We can think of other things that we are very confident about: that our team will win the game tonight, or that there will still be a soda can in the driveway when we go outside and look, or that a car will be parked beside it, or that next week our mailbox will be blue. We cannot be *totally* certain about such things; or as Kant says, we cannot be apodictically certain about them.[24] Instead, we have to wait and see how things turn out. We have to wait for the world to tell us about itself. Our team might lose, or the soda can that we left in the driveway might have been moved, or someone might paint our mailbox as a prank.

38

If we *were* apodictically certain, it would be because we saw to it that the things occurred: we encased the soda can in a sturdy shell, or we stood guard by the mailbox all night long. But even then, there is a chance that things would go awry. The only way that we could be infallibly certain about our belief is if we could succeed in seeing to it that it was true.

39

Kant seems to be arguing that we are apodictically certain that any objects that we encounter will have the feature of being spatial and that the only way that we could be so sure is if we projected spatiality onto objects as we encounter them. If we did not see to it that objects appeared spatially, we would have to wait until we experienced them before we weighed in. But we don't have to wait. The same applies, Kant thinks, to time. We know certain features that are had by time without having to experience it. He writes,

> It [time] has only one dimension: different times are not simultaneous, but successive (just as different spaces are not successive, but simultaneous). These principles could not be drawn from experience, for this would yield neither strict universality nor apodictic certainty. We would only be able to say: This is what common perception teaches us, but not: This is how matters must stand. These principles are valid as rules under which experiences are possible at all, and instruct us prior to them, not through it.[25]

We could not know that moments are necessarily successive if time was really out there and we had to wait to encounter it.

40

A more familiar example might help to make Kant's point. Imagine that we encounter someone at the office who has always behaved like a jerk, and who we expect will behave like a jerk today. We cannot be apodictically certain, however. Perhaps the person has gone into therapy; or perhaps they have been a jerk because they have always gotten very little sleep, but now the cause of their sleep deprivation is absent. Now Kant is asking—what if we actually were certain that our coworker was going to be a jerk?—as certain as we are about claims like that two and three add to five. Kant thinks that we could only be that certain if there was something taking place on our end that guaranteed that the person would come off as a jerk. Perhaps we are very defensive, and behavior that shows up to others as confident or quirky shows up to us as obnoxious and rude. What this would mean of course is that the person himself is not a jerk, but that is to make Kant's point. If we experience reality to have a feature, and we know that we will experience it to have that feature before we encounter it, that means that it is not a feature of reality but a part of the way that we are constituted to perceive it.

41

Or to consider a different example, my wife has issues with blood circulation and, as a result, often has cold extremities. When she puts her hand on our daughter's forehead to check her temperature, she suspects (almost invariably) that our daughter has a fever. We double-check with a thermometer and the temperature is (almost invariably) normal. First I thought my wife was just imagining the alleged temperature. Only recently, when our daughter was 5 years old, did we realize that our daughter did feel warm to my wife, but only because of things that were happening on her end of the perception.

42

Part of what is interesting here is not just whether or not Kant is right, but how he is getting so much out of what is apparently so little. He is making some fairly minimal assumptions about our experience of objects and about the kind of knowledge that a person can have of an object before encountering it. Kant is exhibiting some of the ways in which the philosopher goes about looking for gold.

Technology and social media

43

A final issue is one that Kant might be shocked to see mentioned in the same neighborhood: technology and social media, and their influence on the way that we experience the world. The philosopher Martin Heidegger benefitted from the many conveniences of technology, but he worried that the more we are surrounded by efficient machines, the more we become satisfied by efficiency and the less we become satisfied by anything else.[26] He contrasted our current-day immersion in technology with an earlier time in which human beings engaged in what the Greeks called *techné*—a slower process in which we were willing to proceed in a more exploratory manner, allowing a situation or activity or relationship to develop spontaneously and at its own speed, without the nagging sense that we are wasting our time if our efforts do not result right away in a tangible product. Techné is the human equivalent of *physis*—the productive activity that appears in nature. Examples of physis are the blossoming of a plant, the growth of a fetus in utero, the healing of a wound. Heidegger's umbrella term to cover both kinds of skillful production is *poesis*, and he is concerned that poesis has become endangered. His worry specifically is that the more we are immersed in our machines, and the more we get a rush out the satisfaction that they deliver, we still start to develop complementary habits: we will not take time to really get to know people; we will be uninterested in developing creative skills that take time to come to fruition; we will only want to do what can be done quickly, to the point where we do not find ourselves doing (or wanting to do) anything else. The term that Heidegger uses to describe the process by which a person's perspective becomes so narrowed is "Enframing."[27] This is a phenomenon in which our perspective is framed: we only notice or care about or pay attention to what can be done quickly or results in an efficient and further useable product.

Standpoint epistemology

44

Presumably there are other enframers in addition to technology, Heidegger would admit. In that case we might use the term *Enframing* in cases where our perspective is made to see things through the lens of efficiency, and the term *enframing* in cases where our perspective is framed and we notice some things to the exclusion of others. Some recent epistemologists—for example, those who work in standpoint epistemology—have argued that there are aspects of the world that individuals miss, and also aspects that individuals notice, as a function of their membership in a specific gender, race, or class. The philosopher Charles Mills offers a number of examples: women report that there are contexts in which they feel that the threat of rape is imminent, but men do not have a similar experience, and they might say that women's concerns are overblown; oral histories capture that whites responded so negatively to black assertiveness, especially black male assertiveness, that a practice emerged in which blacks would be overly deferential as a survival tactic, but whites did not appear to know that this was going on; and other examples as well.[28] Part of what is driving the development of these more recent varieties of epistemology is the thought that we do not want to wait until we refute Cartesian skepticism to be able to say that we know that there is social injustice or that we have a good idea how to eradicate it. The philosopher Sally Haslanger has argued that the discipline of epistemology has focused a disproportionate amount of energy on the attempt to secure Cartesian indubitability, with the result that other questions and concerns go uninvestigated. For example, there are questions about gender and race and class and about who is deemed an authoritative knower and why. There are also questions about why, if there are different kinds of knowledge— absolute certainty, pragmatic knowledge, know-how, etc.—some are taken to be more important and fundamental.[29]

45

Some epistemologists have argued that race and gender biases extend even to the sciences. This would be important to point out if science is otherwise taken to be neutral and objective. The philosopher Sandra Harding has argued that historically the research questions of natural science and social science have been formulated by men and that the answers to these questions have incorporated male bias. We might not be as surprised that this happens in the case of social science, but Harding argues that it applies in the case of the natural sciences as well:

[N]atural science is a social phenomenon. It has been created, developed, and given social significance at particular moments in history in particular cultures. Many of the claims made by feminist critics about how white, modern Western men of the administrative/managerial class tend to conceptualize social phenomena can be directly applied to the story of natural science as it is handed down in the history and philosophy of science, in science texts, and by the "greats" of modern science. If gender is a structure in the most formal variables of beliefs about the boundaries between nature and culture, or the fundamental constituents of socially constructed realities, why should we assume that the formal structures of natural science belief are immune?[30]

To take an example from social science, a predominant male view is that men are active and women are passive, and this has crossed over into our understanding of the early distinction between men as hunters and women as gatherers.[31] Harding discusses how even in their capacity as gatherers women were quite active in the invention of tools and other creative adaptations. But the notion of a gatherer is fairly passive—the notion of someone who follows the work of another—and so perhaps it should be dropped. Perhaps if men were not the social scientists telling the story, women would have been featured not as gatherers but as *closers*—the individuals who completed all the essential steps after the initial kill, to the creation of actual food. An example from natural science is that male human sperm has always been regarded as active and the female egg as passive, but recent research has supplied evidence that the female egg is highly energetic and active both before and after the sperm reaches it.[32] Again, if men had not been telling the story, the female egg might have come down in history as creative and sophisticated, a being so exalted that sperm has to come to *it*. Early in this chapter the discussion was focused on the question of what knowledge is and whether we can know anything about the external world. Then the discussion shifted to questions about how we take in information and about how much of our experience is due to what is happening on the side of the perceiver. The latter questions bracket a number of important skeptical worries, but they would appear to be very timely and practical. There is a further discussion of these and related issues in Chapter Seven.

Technology and social media, continued

46

Heidegger uses the word *Enframing* to name the process whereby technology affects our perspective. He fleshes out the process in a discussion of Aristotle's fourfold classification of causes.[33] A material cause is literally the material out of which a product is made—for example, the silver that composes a cup or chalice. A final cause is the purpose for which the product is made—for example, a ritual in which a chalice is a central element. A formal cause is roughly the idea of the product and its purpose, something like the blueprint by which the material is guided into shape.[34] An efficient cause is then the being that has the idea and puts it into effect. Heidegger says that, in one way or another, the four kinds of causality enter into the creation of any product and that all four are threatened by Enframing. Final causality is affected in that we become restricted to purposes that result immediately in a product, and other purposes fall by the wayside. Formal causality is affected (in our thinking) when we stop at the ideas that come to us most quickly, and at ideas of purposes that can be achieved right away. If Heidegger is right, ideas with a longer gestation period would not have an opportunity to arrive on the scene. Material causality is affected in that materials start to become less available if they are harder to store efficiently on a shelf, or harder to ship or transmit. Efficient causality is affected also. Although we are free to enjoy the comforts of technology, we are no longer free to choose between as many creative ideas and possibilities, and we are no longer free to enjoy things that take a lot of time.

47

Heidegger is worried that one of the initial motivations for adopting technology was to give us more leisure time, but an inadvertent effect is that the only leisure activities that interest us are activities that can be done in a rush. Historically, human beings have gotten mileage out of a much wider range of activities, and the concern is that these are no longer available to us. A more recent commentator has raised the concern about social media in particular. Sherry Turkle started out as an enormous fan of the possibilities of social media—and was even featured on the cover of *Wired* magazine, along with a story about the positive social aspects of chat rooms and video games. Fifteen years later (in 2011) her book *Alone Together* argued that in fact we are becoming more and more isolated as the result of our use of technology and social media.

There is a wonderful TED video in which she explores the various themes of the book, although the irony cannot be overlooked that the video (at a mere 20 minutes) is a more tempting draw.* The themes include: instead of getting to know a few people very deeply, we skim the surface and get to know a lot of people hardly at all; we speak in (what we hope are) memorable sound bites on the assumption that we will only have so much time to get a word in; we structure our day into efficient and regimented slots with the result that nothing unstructured can happen, and if something unstructured *almost* happens, we say, "I've gotta run." Turkle also worries that there is a significant amount of self-knowledge that we will pass over—when and why we are sad or anxious or mad, what drives our habitual behaviors, or even what those behaviors are. We will miss important bits of self-knowledge if the signals are not immediately obvious or if they do not point to an immediate and happy result. A more humorous representation of these themes is in the work of the comedian Louis C. K.*

48

Turkle is also worried about the institution of friendship. She pokes fun at the notion of a Facebook friend and says (in the video) that if she has a thousand friends then she does not really have any friends at all. Part of her concern is that we do not have the opportunity to get to know others except in a superficial and piecemeal way, and others do not really get to know us. But we like the feeling of being known. If I am to everyone else just like most everyone else is to me—a being with just the most superficial of features—then I am isolated, and we are (as her books states it) together alone.[35] Turkle might add to the list of ways in which efficient causality is affected: there are skills and capacities that might go undeveloped, with a diminished ability to pick up on cues.

49

If Heidegger and others are right about the impact of technology and social media on our perspective on the world, there is a lot happening around us that we do not notice. There is information that we do not take in—about people and situations and problems and objects—with the result that our perception of these is much less complete than we are prepared to admit. This is not to say (along the lines of Kant, for example) that what we experience is not really out there, but instead that we only experience a small part of what it *is* out there. An example is this: a billboard in the distance has alternating horizontal stripes of red, white, and yellow, but the yellow stripes are very thin and hard to see; we look at the image quickly and from a distance, and we experience the flag of the United States of America. We get closer and notice that there is no blue in the top left corner, no stars, and quite a bit of yellow. If we had not confirmed this up close, our experience would have remained fictional. Heidegger and Turkle and Louis C. K. are worried that much of our experience is fictional in this way and that there is no impetus to double check. A danger is that the concern applies more globally—to the way that we understand political events and history, the behavior and needs of friends and loved ones, and the behavior and needs of people who are more distant. Heidegger is especially worried that we will become so Enframed that we will not even notice that any of this is happening—we will not notice Enframing, and we will say "What Enframing?," and quickly move on to the next thing.

50

A flipside of course is that technology, the internet in particular, has made possible a massive increase in the amount of information that is available. They have also made possible an increase in the number perspectives that are able to get exposure.[36] Heidegger would probably worry about the likelihood that we take the time to process such information critically. He is trying to highlight the irony that technology might increase our freedom and our leisure time, but at the same time it might have an impact on our psychology and keep us from enjoying the things that our freedom and leisure time were supposed to make possible in the first place.

Possible discussion exercises

1 Have you ever had a dream or hallucinatory experience that seemed so real that you were sure that it *was* real?

2 Do you think that there are legitimate reasons for thinking that it is possible that our sensory perceptions are produced by objects that do not resemble them?

3 Do you think that Moore is right that the claims of common sense are less controversial than the conceptual claims of the philosopher?

4 Consider the fortune-teller example—where the person always gets things right. Do you think that the fortune-teller *knows*? Suppose that the fortune-teller is presented with fabricated newspaper stories that report that her predictions are false, and she has no proof that the stories are fabricated, but her reliable mind tells her that they are. Does she still know?

5 Does it make a difference if we are in an experience machine our entire lives? Would you be hooked up to such a machine? Would it be more enticing if your loved ones were also hooked up to the machine, and you were "interacting"?

6 Imagine the scenario in which you exit the experience machine, and it turns out that you have been in it since birth. The "loved ones" in the machine do not exist, and you are now surrounded by a world of strangers. Would you want to return to the machine?

7 What is the outside world like when we close our eyes? What evidence is there for this view?

8 What are some perennial philosophical questions (about the beginning of the universe, for example) that Kant's view would allow us to forever bracket? Is that a good thing?

9 Is there another (and more plausible) explanation for our expectation that objects will be spatial?

10 Are there any specific ways that you experience the world (or situations or people) that you suspect have a lot to do with factors at work on your own end?

11 Are there everyday examples of political debates that are affected by Enframing?

12 Do you think that Heidegger is right that even though we use technology voluntarily, it might have an impact on us that we did not intend? Bracketing technology for the moment, are there other examples of things that we do (or have done) voluntarily, but that have an unwelcome and unintended impact on us?

13 Assume for the moment that Heidegger is right that technology Enframes us and takes away our desire to do things that take a lot of time, or that do not result in a tangible product. In that case, we only want to do things quickly. If that's what we end up wanting, and we are able to satisfy our desires on a daily basis by doing things that are quick and efficient, is Heidegger right to object?

14 Do you think that Turkle is right that we are together alone?

15 How does it feel when we are without our cell phone for a day, or if the internet is down, or if we are using an old dinosaur computer that takes 5 minutes to start up? Are these feelings relevant to the thesis that technology has an impact on how we stand toward people, situations, objects, history?

16 Does technology have an impact on our curiosity?

17 Does technology help to spur our curiosity?

18 Should Heidegger be required to give up his typewriter and his car?

19 Come up with your own everyday example for one of the views or arguments or objections presented in this chapter.

Notes

1 Descartes was a French philosopher and mathematician who lived in the first half of the seventeenth century. He is famous for the x-y coordinate system in geometry, and (in philosophy) for arguing that the things that we know best about reality are abstract and insensible, for example, "I think, therefore I am." His *Meditations on First Philosophy* is composed of six separate Meditations that he intends us to work through sequentially, one per day.

2 The First Meditation, CSM 2:13.

3 The Sixth Meditation, CSM 2:53.

4 This is in the original 1990 version with Arnold Schwarzenegger. A remake came out in 2012.

5 The Third Meditation, CSM 2:25. Here I have used "understood" and "understanding" in place of "perceived" and "perception." Descartes himself alternates freely between talk of intellectual perception and understanding, and the latter language makes better sense in the current context.

6 Descartes, *Second Replies*, CSM 2:106.

7 See, for example, Robert Nozick, *Anarchy, State and Utopia*, New York: Basic Books (1975), 613–14. Professor Nozick was a philosopher at Harvard University in the second half of the twentieth century. He wrote extremely influential books and articles in political philosophy, epistemology, and decision theory, among other areas. He was very interested in the power of philosophy to explore the logical space of different possible explanations for pretty much any phenomenon.

8 G. E. Moore, "Proof of an External World," in G. E. Moore, *Philosophical Papers*, New York: Collier Books (1962), 144–8. Professor Moore was a philosopher at Cambridge University for most of the first half of the twentieth century. He defended extremely influential views in the fields of epistemology (the theory of knowledge) and ethics, among others. He was a founding figure of the analytic tradition of philosophy, a tradition that is predominant today.

9 Not all philosophers agree on how this term should be used, but historically it tends to refer to items of belief or knowledge that are known through intellectual reflection and not through the senses.

10 I am being a bit speculative here; for systematic reasons, Moore would rarely engage his skeptical opponent directly. Commentators have attempted to reconstruct Moore's thinking however. See,

for example, Barry Stroud, *The Significance of Philosophical Skepticism*, Oxford: Oxford University Press (1984), ch. 3.

11 Alvin Goldman, "A Causal Theory of Knowing," *Journal of Philosophy* 64 (1967), 357–72. There is no single externalist view of knowledge, so here I am considering some different views that are under a common externalist umbrella. Professor Goldman is a philosopher at Rutgers University. He focuses on issues in epistemology, most recently in social epistemology, a field of which he is a founder. He also works on the many issues that are interconnected with these.

12 Ibid., 361.

13 Ibid., 370.

14 D. M. Armstrong develops the thermometer conception of knowledge in *Belief, Truth and Knowledge*, ch. 12. David Armstrong is Emeritus Professor of Philosophy at the University of Sydney. He is famous for a number of influential views in epistemology and metaphysics—for example, his investigations into what it is for something to be a law of nature (above and beyond the entities that follow a law of nature).

15 Laurence BonJour, "Externalist Theories of Empirical Knowledge," *Midwest Studies in Philosophy* 5 (1980), 53–73. Professor Bonjour is a philosopher at the University of Washington. His views are at the center of the debate on the nature of knowledge and the nature of justification.

16 See, for example, Jennifer Lackey, "Testimonial Knowledge and Transmission," *The Philosophical Quarterly* 49 (1999), 471–90. Jennifer Lackey is Professor of Philosophy at Northwestern University. She works primarily in epistemology and philosophy of mind, and has written numerous books and articles on such issues as testimony, epistemic luck, norms of assertion, and the epistemic significance of disagreement.

17 The Second Meditation, CSM 2:16–21. This is one of Descartes' most famous arguments—that it is impossible to doubt our own existence because if we attempt to doubt it, we have to assume that we are there doing the doubting.

18 Ernest Sosa, *Reflective Knowledge: Apt Belief and Reflective Knowledge*, ch. 7. Ernest Sosa is Board of Governors Professor of Philosophy at Rutgers University. He has written numerous books and articles in epistemology, philosophy of language, and related subareas of philosophy. He has received fellowships from the American Council of Learned Societies, the National Endowment for the Humanities, the National Science Foundation, the Exxon

Educational Foundation, and the Canada Council. He has also
participated in sessions featuring Hispanic/Latino philosophers at
meetings of the American Philosophical Association.

19 See, for example, Albert Einstein, Foreword to Max Jammer,
    Concepts of Space, Cambridge: Harvard University Press (1954).

20 Ralph Cudworth, *A Treatise Concerning Eternal and Immutable
    Morality*, ed. Sarah Hutton, Cambridge: Cambridge University Press
    (1731/1996), 148–9. Cudworth was a philosopher at Cambridge
    University in the seventeenth century and an opponent of materialist
    philosophers like Thomas Hobbes. Cudworth had unshakeable
    commitments as a philosopher, and indeed his other central book
    was the mammoth *True and Immutable System of the Universe*, but
    as a political activist he preached religious toleration.

21 Immanuel Kant, *The Critique of Pure Reason* trans. and ed. Paul
    Guyer and Allen Wood, Cambridge: Cambridge University Press
    (1998), 167–8. Kant was a professor of philosophy at the University
    of Königsberg in the latter half of the eighteenth century. He is
    famous for the view that we cannot know what reality is like in
    itself and also for the view that what matters about an action is
    the intention or volition behind it, and not its consequences. An
    interesting fact (and a surprising one given his fame) is that for his
    first 15 years of teaching he was paid directly by his students; only
    afterward (at age 46) did he secure a professorship.

22 Ibid., 158.

23 Ibid., 159.

24 Ibid., 158.

25 Ibid., 162.

26 A nice example is from the television show, *The Simpsons*.*

27 Martin Heidegger, "On the Question Concerning Technology,"
    in William Lovitt (trans. and ed.), *The Question Concerning
    Technology and Other Essays*, New York: Harper & Row
    (1962/1977), 17–19, 25, 27. Heidegger was a German philosopher
    who worked in the first half of the twentieth century. He was
    interested in a number of issues in metaphysics and philosophy of
    mind, but also wrote and theorized about poetry and literature. He
    had a problematic relationship with the Nazi party; that is not a
    debate I will attempt to settle here.

28 Charles Mills, "Alternative Epistemologies," *Social Theory and
    Practice* 14 (1988), 241–7. Charles W. Mills is John Evans Professor
    of Moral and Intellectual Philosophy at Northwestern University.
    He specializes in social and political philosophy, with a focus on the
    issue of race.

29 See, for example, Sally Haslanger, "What Knowledge Is and What it Ought to Be," *Philosophical Perspectives* 13 (1999), 459–80. Sally Haslanger is Professor of Philosophy and Women's and Gender Studies at Massachusetts Institute of Technology. She has written numerous articles and books on issues in metaphysics and epistemology, ancient philosophy, social and political philosophy, feminism, and critical race theory.

30 Sandra Harding, *The Science Question in Feminism*, Ithaca, NY: Cornell University Press (1986), 84–5. Sandra Harding is Distinguished Professor of Education and Gender Studies at UCLA and Distinguished Affiliate Professor of Philosophy at Michigan State University. She has written many books and articles, focusing on philosophy of science, feminism, epistemology, and postcolonial theory. Her PhD is in Philosophy (from New York University), but many of her appointments have been in other units.

31 Ibid., 92–102.

32 For example, Athena Beldecos, Sarah Bailey, Scott Gilbert, Karen Hicks Lori Kenschaft, Nancy Niemczyk, Rebecca Rosenberg Stephanie Schaertel, and Andrew Wedel, "The Importance of Feminist Critique for Cell Biology," *Hypatia* 3 (1988), 61–76.

33 Heidegger, "On the Question Concerning Technology," 6–8.

34 The qualification "roughly" is to track that for Heidegger ideas are not always of the highly conscious variety, and indeed he seems to allow that ideas are in play even in the teleology and order that is found in physis. This is an unusual view in contemporary times— the view that ideas and intelligence are ubiquitous in nature—but it was standard during the time of Aristotle (roughly the fourth century BC) and for many centuries after.

35 There is a terrific song by Sia that speaks to the desire to be known—to be breathed in.* There also are worries that if we end up being "alone together," we will have to seek connection in virtual reality machines.*

36 For an interesting discussion, see Hubert Dreyfus, *On the Internet*, London: Routledge (2008). Hubert Dreyfus is Professor Emeritus of Philosophy at UC Berkeley. He has written numerous books and articles on phenomenology, existentialism, philosophy of psychology, philosophy of literature, and artificial intelligence. He is a leading expert on Heidegger.

CHAPTER TWO

Morality and value

Abstract

This chapter considers the following: whether there is a connection between morality and the existence of God; whether human beings are motivated by anything other than self-interest; whether morality is objective; whether we have any reason to obey the dictates of morality, if it is objective; and whether or not morality is instead subjective or based on sentiment.

Morality and God

1

It is very tempting to think that if God does not exist, then nothing matters. That would be bad—if nothing that exists, and nothing that we do, has any value. Or it wouldn't be *bad*; it would just be disappointing in a certain way. One issue is whether or not a person's brief earthly existence is of any consequence if that is all there is—a brief earthly existence. Another issue is whether or not there are any such things as morality or value if God does not exist.[1]

2

The ancient philosopher Socrates offered a number of controversial views. He was put on trial for corrupting the youth, and unfortunately for him and for us, he was sentenced to death by hemlock.[2] One of his controversial views was that goodness and morality are not dependent on the existence of God. If God is good, Socrates argued, then He acts in the light of standards of goodness and morality, and hence these must already exist before God does anything that is good. On the alternative view, Socrates thought, God is the author of standards of goodness and morality, pretty much like He creates everything else, but in that case He has no criteria on the basis of which to create the standards, so they would be arbitrary. God would just say—here are some standards that I am making up, so obey them, or else! Socrates' thought was that God would not proceed in this way. We might imagine alternately a very powerful playground bully, or a dictator, who makes up some rules and then uses all due force to make sure that they are followed. Socrates is thinking that neither of these would be God. Instead, God is *good*.

3

Socrates presses this question: are things loved by God because they are good, or are they good because they are loved by God?[3] He thinks that the answer is that God loves things because they are good. In the dialogue *Euthyphro*, he offers an analogy to motivate his case:

> I shall try to explain more clearly: we speak of something being carried and something carrying, of something led and something leading, of something seen and something seeing, and you understand that these things are all different from one another and how they differ? . . . Tell me then whether the thing carried is a carried thing because it is carried, or for some other reason. . . . And the thing led is so because it is being led, and the thing seen because it is seen?[4]

Perhaps the analogy is not a lot clearer than the point that Socrates intends it to elucidate, but he seems to be thinking something like this. A thing that is carried has the property or feature of being carried, but it does not have that feature until someone picks it up and carries it. The same applies in the case of a thing that is seen or led; it is not as though a thing first has the property of being seen, and then we look at it and see it. Instead, it is seen after we look at it, and *because* we look at it. Socrates wants to argue that the relationship between God and the property of being good is very different from the relationship between a seer and the property of being seen. A thing is good not just because of God's stance or attitude toward it. Instead, if God loves a thing, He loves it *because* it is good, which would mean that it was good already. That is, God would not love just any old things, but only things that are worthy. If things *were* good because God loved them—in the same way that a thing has the property of being seen because someone sees it—there would be no reason behind God's preference. God would happen to prefer some things, and then He would order us to act in the light of His preferences. Being all-powerful, He could enforce His rules firmly and without exception.

4

Socrates is not questioning the existence of God—he appears to think that it is uncontroversial that God exists[5]—but in effect he is asking which feature of God it is more appropriate to emphasize: His power, or His goodness. If God is maximally powerful in such a way that He is in control of *everything*, then He is even in charge of defining what counts as good, bad, right, or wrong. If there were facts about these which were not set by God, and which could not be changed by God, then there would be a limitation on His authority and power. Socrates' worry though is that the more that God's power is emphasized, the more we would have to downplay His goodness. If He creates standards of goodness and value arbitrarily and then enforces them, He starts to sound more like a tyrant and less like a being that is omnibenevolent.[6] To emphasize God's goodness is to emphasize that there is already such a thing as a criterion of goodness and that God acts in accord with it.

5

Another way of cashing out the concern is to imagine Moses arriving at the bottom of Mount Sanai with the Ten Commandments, but his people question why God has offered *these* commandments and not some others. Moses climbs the mountain again and asks God—"Why these?" God responds—"No reason." He takes the tablets back from Moses and says, "Here is a different list instead."[7]

6

Another objection to Socrates is that if God exists, He is supremely perfect and hence would be infinitely powerful *and* infinitely good. He would be completely good, and at the same time there would be no limitation on His power.

7

Part of what Socrates is trying to argue is that, given what we mean by "power" and "goodness," we do not have a coherent idea of a being that is fully omnipotent and also omnibenevolent. A useful analogy here might be the equalizer knob on a stereo. We could imagine that one of the knobs is for God's power, and that another is for His goodness. Socrates is arguing that both knobs cannot be moved to the top. If the goodness knob is at the top, the power knob has to remain lower down, and vice versa. We might respond that an omnipotent being would have enough power to put both of the knobs at the highest setting, even if that would be contradictory or incoherent. Socrates would worry that such a being is not thinkable and is not a possible object of discussion.

8

One of Socrates' concerns is that if God is the author of standards of morality and value, then God could have decided that killing and torturing innocents was perfectly acceptable. An objection to Socrates is that God would never do that: after all, God is *good*. Here things get very tricky. The supposition is that God would not have defined the torturing of innocents to be acceptable because God is good and a good being would not do that, but in that case God would not be *deciding* the standards of goodness, but living up to them.

9

Socrates presents two options for making sense of the basis of goodness and value—that things are good because they meet an independent standard of goodness, and that God makes up standards of goodness that are thereby arbitrary. A third option is to say that there is nothing that is independent of God, not even standards of goodness, but that that does not mean that standards of goodness are arbitrary. Instead, goodness might just be identical with God's nature. God just is what is good, not because He meets the criterion for being good, but because He *is* the criterion for being good.

10

A worry for this third option is that if there is no independent standard of goodness, it is not clear that it amounts to anything to say that God's nature is identical with goodness. There are a number of ways to flesh out the worry. One is to highlight that if what it is to be good is just to be God, then we are not saying anything descriptive or additive when we say that God is good. We are just saying that God is God. If a person does not know anything about some entity X, one way to inform the person would be to tell them some of the characteristics that the entity has. We might say that it has the feature A, for example. If it turns out that all that it means for a thing to have A is for it to be X, then the claim that X has A is just the claim that X is X. Talk of A would not really add anything.

11

A more concrete example to flesh out the worry is the sort of case where a mother describes her child as beautiful. When I was very young, I would go to school looking frumpy and disheveled, my hair a mess, but my mom would say that I looked terrific. I was also overweight to the point of being unhealthy. The reactions that I got at school were not so positive, and at a certain point I asked my mom what was going on. She told me that I was beautiful and that I should not pay attention to what the kids were saying. They did not know anything, and someday when I got older I would appreciate that. But the insults started to become difficult to take. I was young, and I craved at least some level of respect and attention from my peers. After a particularly bad day of taunting, I locked myself in my room and refused to come out. My mom finally got me to talking, and she explained again that I was beautiful. She added this time that what she meant by "beautiful" is that I was me. I did not quite appreciate the philosophical relevance of her point, but I did get the sense that it was little consolation. I wanted to have the property of beauty that everyone else was talking about when they identified things as beautiful. I know that I have the property of being me, but I wanted to have the other property as well. I was obese and unhealthy, and not particularly attractive, and I was not going to become beautiful by decreeing that beautiful is just whatever I happened to be. To be sure, I wanted a parent who would be supportive, but I wanted a parent who would help me to identify my strengths and encourage me to build on them.

12

That is not a very good example perhaps. We should not call a kid fat and ugly, especially given all of the unhealthy body-image stuff that is going around. I used this example in class once, and the response was negative. The irony of course is that my dear mother, bless her soul, would have said that it is an outstanding example. And she would add—"By outstanding example, I just mean any example that is given by you!"

Morality and its authority over us

13

Another objection to Socrates is that the standards of morality and value would not have any weight if they *were* independent of God. After all, if the standards of morality and value were independent of God, and were just a fixed and objective part of the universe, there would be no further reason or explanation for those either. They would just be sitting there, as brute facts. We might consider this analogy: we wake up one day in a clubhouse and see a list of rules on the wall that specify how we are to behave; we ask someone why those are the rules, and where they come from, and we are told that they have just always been. We might not feel any allegiance to these rules, and the question is whether things would be any different if we found ourselves plopped into a bigger clubhouse—the universe—and we encountered a set of rules that likewise has no further justification and has always been. If the clubhouse includes a rule to the effect that the rules of the clubhouse should be obeyed, that just pushes the problem back a notch. The same would seem to happen if one of the tenets of morality was that we ought to do what is moral. Or, if the ground of morality is somehow *outside* of morality, the question is why we should pay heed to that. The philosopher Phillipa Foot has argued that morality is a system of imperatives that are not automatically binding on us.[8] We obey the specific rules of etiquette if we are already invested in the larger institution of etiquette, but we might also choose to opt out. A question is whether the dictates of morality are any different, or if these are optional as well.

14

The philosopher Linda Zagzebski has defended the view that if goodness is identical to God's nature, and not something external to God and to which God is subordinate, then we still have reason to be moral. She writes,

> On this approach we have to give up any idea that God aims to create in the world something he independently considers to be good. His motivation cannot be explained by saying that he does something because it is good. God does what he does because it is expressive of his nature. God's actions are like those of the artist who creates works of beauty, but hardly can be said to create these works because they are beautiful. He simply creates out of a desire to create, a desire which expresses the inner beauty or aesthetic value of his own inventive imagination. Similarly, God does not create because his creation is good. It is not as if God sees in thought that such a creation would be good and

then goes about creating it. The created universe is good because it is the expression of the desire to create of a perfectly good being whose inventiveness is a component of his omniscience and omnipotence.[9]

Part of the idea appears to be that if goodness is a fixed and not-further-explained aspect of God in the same way that (on Socrates' view) goodness is a fixed and not-further-explained aspect of the universe, then a God-bound morality would have no less claim on us than an objective morality that was independent of God. A problem that Zagzebski's view brings out, however, is that it is not clear why either kind of morality would have a claim on us. A problem for Zagzebski's view in particular is that we seem to be able to rule out from the start that a God-bound morality would have any bearing on the earthly pursuits of human beings. The standards of morality and value would appear to have little to do with the activities and behavior of human beings if they are pegged to the behavior of a divine being, assuming that earthly beings are very different.

15

A final wrinkle from the *Euthyphro* dilemma is that if morality and goodness and decency are objective, it would appear that the reason for doing the right thing would have nothing to do with God's feelings about us, or with a possible reward in the afterlife. If our reason for doing the right thing is that we want to be rewarded by God, that would just be a matter of looking out for our own skin.

16

There is a very tense moment in the jailhouse interviews with Jeffrey Dahmer, when he opens up about the faith that he found in prison.* Dahmer was a bad man. He would pick up his victims at a bar or similar venue and invite them home for a nightcap; he would lock them in a cage or freezer, and then he would eat them. One of the things that Dahmer says in the jailhouse interviews is that it is good that he now has faith in God, and that it is good that he fears punishment for the horrific things that he might want to do, otherwise there would be no reason not to do them. The reason not to kidnap and terrorize and eat people, Dahmer says, is that it is not in his self-interest.

17

The philosopher Friedrich Nietzsche talked a lot about the connection between the lack of a belief in God and *nihilism*—the belief (at least as he is using the term) that nothing is of any value or importance. Nietzsche did not think that the loss of the belief in God could bring about nihilism on its own. Another cause had to be present—the belief that morality and value are God-dependent. He writes,

> The nihilistic question "for what?" is rooted in the old habit of supposing that the goal must be put up, given, . . . by some *superhuman authority*.[10]

> Extreme positions are not succeeded by moderate ones but by extreme positions of the opposite kind. Thus the belief in the absolute immorality of nature, in aim and meaninglessness, is the psychologically necessary affect once the belief in God and an essentially moral order becomes untenable. Nihilism appears at that point. . . . One interpretation has collapsed; but because it was considered *the* interpretation it now seems as if there were no meaning at all in existence, as if everything were in vain.[11]

We might think, for example, of a person sitting next to us on the bus who says that if God does not exist, there is no reason not to kill everyone. We might want to move a couple of seats over. The twentieth-century philosopher Bertrand Russell echoes Nietzsche. He writes,

> More and more people are becoming unable to accept traditional beliefs. If they think that, apart from these beliefs, there is no reason for kindly behavior the results may be needlessly unfortunate.[12]

If we lost our belief in the existence of God, but we did not think that the existence of God had anything to do with whether or not there is such a thing as morality or value, nihilism would not follow. To decipher what is valuable and what is not, we would need to have a kind of moral sense or moral cognitive faculty that enables us make the relevant discriminations.

18

We might worry though that we do not have such a faculty and that the way that we uncover what is or is not valuable is through our knowledge of God and revelation. Here a terrific chicken-egg problem emerges, one that returns us again to the *Euthyphro* dilemma. Imagine that we are at a religion fair, and we have a procedure for choosing a religion and for ruling out the others as objectionable. At the fair, each faith is represented by a table that advertises its central tenets. According to one, it is obligatory to perform an annual sacrifice of a human innocent. Another announces (on its banner) that human beings have no free will. Another might have as one of its tenets that if a woman is raped, the woman's family is required to kill her to extinguish the shame that it would otherwise bear. Another might have as a tenet that we should not lie. Another might say that fairness is bad. Different people are going to have different reactions to the doctrines presented at each booth, but if a person dismisses a religion because she thinks that a good God would not endorse its tenets, the person is taking a side in the *Euthyphro* dilemma.

19

So a question is whether it is by means of a moral sense or moral cognitive faculty that we tell what is good or bad or right or wrong, or if it is by means of a faculty for deciphering God's word that we make these discriminations. There is also a question of which faculty we have reason to believe would work better. There is no question that historically people have made skewed and self-serving assumptions about the nature of God, but we could raise the same worry about a cognitive faculty for detecting value—that it does not work as well as faculties like hearing or sight. The philosopher Sarah McGrath has argued that the existence of disagreement on matters of ethics—especially disagreement among those we could plausibly identify as experts—is at least some evidence that our moral judgments are not tracking moral facts. Part of the problem is "the lack of an independent check."[13] McGrath offers as an analogy the case of unique green—which is the single shade of green that is not too close to blue and not too close to yellow. Human beings are asked to identify which shade of green is unique green, and the answers are quite varied. It is not clear who (if anyone) should be identified as an expert who is getting it right because there is no independent check that tells us which shade is unique green. With so much variation, we start to suspect that there is no such shade of color and thus that none of the "experts" is actually tracking anything.

20

If we side with Socrates, we would still have to admit that there are important connections between morality and God. Presumably morality specifies that we respect those who are moral exemplars and that we should have tremendous gratitude to those who have been extremely generous to us. If so, we are under significant obligation to God if He created us and is letting us reside in His space. The subjects of a king would owe him a lot of gratitude and respect for the protection that he offers, for example, as we would also presumably owe something to our parents. In addition, a divine being would have an important role to play as the enforcer of morality—as the ultimate police authority and judge. Human beings do not have the resources to notice what anyone is doing all of the time, but an omniscient and omnipotent being has no such limitation. It would be able to hold us accountable, and without error. If there is no God, but there is freestanding objective morality, people would be able to get away with quite a bit. Perhaps we could be on alert as much as possible, and punish people in cases that are clear-cut, but that would not be the same as the coverage provided by God. A being that is omnipotent and omniscient would know the law and how it applies in each and every instance.

Is morality objective?

21

It can certainly seem that morality and goodness are objective. It seems that there are truths about what is good or bad or right or wrong and that these truths are independent of what anybody in particular happens to believe is good or bad or right or wrong. For example, it is bad to eat innocent babies. Anyone who does not recognize this—it is not clear what to say to them if we are to get them to see what they are missing. We would have to get them to recognize a truth that is even more simple and obvious and that entails that innocent-baby eating should be avoided. But it is not clear what this more simple truth would be. Other examples of uncontroversial ethical truths might include that Hitler did things that were horrific, or that Jeffrey Dahmer should have done otherwise, or that it is bad to bury puppies while they are alive. To say that a moral claim is an objective truth is not just to say that our community believes and affirms it, or even that the whole world believes and affirms it. The idea is more that entire communities and even all of humanity could have certain settled beliefs about what is moral, but still be wrong. We might imagine the (thankfully fictional) scenario in which Hitler and Nazi Germany won World War II and then took over the world. Suppose also that all of their opponents are exterminated on earth, but we somehow escaped individually in a rocket to outer space. The idea is that we could look down at earth and say that the actions of Hitler and his followers are bad, no matter what anyone thinks. The idea is that we could think that even if we died 10 minutes later, it would still be a fact that the actions of Hitler and his followers are bad, with no one around to believe it.

22

Some might object to the whole idea that there is such a thing as objective morality. The objection might continue: there are facts about how things are, but not in addition facts about how things *ought* to be. We do make statements about how things ought to be, but these are a reflection of the values and interests of a given culture, and perhaps there is no sense to the notion that a particular culture could itself be right or wrong. The philosopher John Mackie offered a famous defense of the view that there is no objective morality. One of his arguments is that, historically speaking, people of different societies have different beliefs about what is good or bad or right or wrong, and these beliefs do not seem to be tracking facts that are external to them. We all live in the same world, and we all form pretty much the same beliefs about mountains and lakes and tables and chairs—that is presumably because those things are out there, and all of us are mutually detecting them. Moral codes seem to be different. It is not clear what we would even be detecting, and indeed the formation of our moral beliefs seems to be much more traceable to our education, our family, our culture, our tradition, our history.[14] Morality would appear to be a set of rules that are relative to the traditions and practices and concerns of the particular culture in which it incubates and develops. When an individual objects to a Hitler society, the individual is simply struggling to get outside of the framework in which she is immersed. There can be shouting and yelling, but moral disagreement is not a disagreement of *fact*.[15] It is different from disagreement about, for example, the age of the universe, or about who had the highest batting average in the 2013 World Series, or about how many coins are in a given jar. There is a fact of the matter about these, even if we do not know it, and not all of the disputants can be right.

23

Some philosophers have attempted to describe a very detached perspective from which even horrific actions seem banal and mundane. Such a perspective might give us a sense of what it would mean for the universe to contain no objective value—where things just happen, and that is that. Thomas Nagel argues that although our pursuits and concerns mean a lot to us, there is a perspective from which we can see them as not mattering.[16] For example, we can calmly witness the destruction of an ant colony, and think that it is just one of those things, and then not give it a second thought. We are not taking account of the well-being or interest of the ants, and perhaps there are beings who are larger than us and who would view our demise with the same level of indifference. We would no doubt protest, as would the ants. However, a question that would always remain is whether our lives *matter*, or if it's just that we care about them a lot.

24

The philosopher Hannah Arendt also attempts to capture a perspective from which actions that we take to be horrific are just a neutral part of the lay of the land. She wrote *Eichmann in Jerusalem: A Report on the Banality of Evil*, an account of the trial of the Nazi official Adolf Eichmann. Arendt considers testimony in which Eichmann says that when he oversaw the death of Jewish prisoners, he was doing what a soldier is supposed to do—following the orders of his superiors, and doing what he assumed was necessary to further the projects and pursuits of the German state and its people. People had to die, but people die all the time, he seemed to be thinking, and the world of German culture was not going to be sacrificed instead. We could imagine witnesses holding up evidentiary photos in the courtroom, attempting to observe or point to the wrongness in the acts of which Eichmann was accused, where he insists that all that he sees is bodies and weapons and blood, and not anything like right or wrong. To every one of the 15 charges against him, Eichmann pleaded—"Not guilty in the sense of the indictment."[17] Arendt and Nagel are attempting to present us with a perspective from which all the fuss about human life appears to be overblown, even if it is hard to take such a perspective without becoming ill. That might just be a further fact about us (and the kinds of things that make us feel sick), but let's hope not.

25

A second argument that Mackie offers is that if objective moral properties existed, in such a way that wrongness was really a property that inhered in an act of incest, for example, it would be very different from the other properties that we typically identify as real. Moral properties would be very different from properties like size and shape and mass—the kinds of qualities to which we can point, the kinds of qualities that we can measure. Moral properties would be out there in the world, telling us to act in certain ways, and they would not be visible or detectable in the way that other qualities tend to be. In short, objective moral qualities would be really weird, and so they do not exist.[18]

26

Moral properties can come across as weird and unusual, and the worries that are presented by Mackie are going to be shared by anyone who is sympathetic to moral relativism. But the worries do not arise without the help of some additional assumptions. One is an assumption about what it is for a property to be weird. The other is an assumption to the effect that reality wouldn't be weird, and so it isn't.

27

Sometimes what we mean by weird is just "unusual." If that is what it is for a property to be weird, then an objection to Mackie is that moral qualities are not weird at all. We take them for granted on a daily basis. They are as much a part of our discourse as anything else. It would be weird if wrongness did *not* attach to the killing of an innocent as one of its objective properties. The philosopher Diane Jeske has argued that moral qualities are sui generis—or qualities of their own kind—and that they are quite different from qualities like size and shape. They are also perfectly familiar, and so in the end they are just different from things from which they are different.[19] We might also ask about other unusual things: like the unevenness that is common to even numbers, or the green that is common to, and shared by, all green things. We might ask if the color blue is darker than the color yellow, without talking about any particular shade of blue or yellow. We would just be talking about blue and yellow *in general*. Or we might talk about laws of nature, as entities that exist over and above the things that act in accord with them. Historically, philosophers have referred to such entities as "universals" and have argued that, even though they might seem weird, our story about the contents of the universe is incomplete if they are left out.

28

Or we might think that moral properties are weird in the sense that they are not visible or tangible. If so, there is a "companions in guilt" retort that could be leveled against Mackie. We are very much inclined to admit that minds exist, and *they* are not sensible or tangible, and there are also things like empty space, superposition, and numbers. For example, the philosopher Penelope Maddy has argued for a realist understanding of numbers according to which numbers are real entities—to be more specific, they are properties of sets, where sets are things that we know and encounter. She writes,

> [N]umbers are properties of sets, analogous to physical properties, and in particular, to physical quantities. . . . Just as the perception of physical objects includes the perception of their properties, so the perception of sets does the same.[20]

Professor Maddy's account is subtle and sophisticated, and numbers do not turn out to be the same sort of thing as a table or pen or tree, but presumably there are more than just these kinds of being. In addition to numbers (and superposition and space), other weird entities or properties might include time, context, gravitation, trust, and the ability to detect humor. Morality is certainly different from all of these, as they are different from each other, but presumably they all exist.[21] Mackie appears to be forced to say that the weirdest of these do not exist and that moral properties do not exist either. Or he might try to argue that some of these things only seem weird but in fact are constituted by entities that are normal and familiar.

29

Perhaps it is unfair to call moral properties "weird." If we do want to identify them as weird, we would have to point to ways in which their existence is more unlikely than the existence of other things that are weird but that we are prepared to identify as real. If we think that moral properties are even weirder, we would need to isolate a reason for thinking that reality is not weird itself. A big part of the evidence for thinking that morality is objective is that we are just as certain that Hitler was bad as we are that we are surrounded by the world of external objects (and are not in a Matrix machine), and we do not seriously consider giving up our belief in the latter. Perhaps reality is weird, and we have a cognitive faculty for detecting weird things, and numbers and space and time and minds and morality are just par for the course. We would then use this cognitive faculty to detect what has nonmoral value as well: a great piece of art, a chess championship, a sophisticated maneuver in football or gymnastics or dance, a language, a friendship, a cultural practice like singing an anthem or shaking hands or baking an apple pie, an invention, and presumably countless other things in addition.[22] If we are suspicious that these have value, maybe we do not think that we have the cognitive faculty in question.

30

It seems that no matter what, we are going to have to say something weird. To say that there are objective moral properties that are out there even if no human beings are around to detect them, that might sound weird. That would be to hold that in something like the way that there are tables and mountains and planets outside of us, there are things like goodness and value, where there is an objective fact about which behaviors are right or wrong, and where a person can be mistaken about these and be called to task. But it also seems weird to deny that there are behaviors that are objectively right or wrong. For example, it seems weird to say that Hitler was just reflecting the value system of his culture, and that we adhere to a different value system. It also seems weird to say that we cannot step outside of both value systems and say that one is accurate and the other is not.

31

Still another worry about the prospect that there are such things as objective value and objective morality is that even if there are these things, we do not have any obvious reason to believe that they would give a lot of weight to human concerns. We might ask about some of the other ways that the universe makes provision for its creatures. Animals slaughter each other in the wild. People get cancer or AIDS. There are not enough resources available for everyone to have all that they want or need. Food that tastes delicious tends to be unhealthy, and instead it is broccoli and Brussels sprouts that make us strong. In many cases we do not have the talent or skill or wherewithal to do what we find interesting or fulfilling, or we *do* have the talent and wherewithal to do things that we find to be a bore. If there is such a thing as objective morality, there is a distinction between the way that things are and the way that morality specifies they should be. A problem is that if the universe does not make any provision for us in so many other cases, there is little reason to believe that it would make provision for us in the case of morality either. It may be that a human being acts in the light of objective morality and objective value, but these have nothing to do with our fulfillment or well-being.

32

We might think of the example of a will that is left by a person who has passed away, and of whether or not a given individual is named in it. If we are not particularly significant in the life of the person who has died, it is likely that we would not be included in the will. Perhaps the universe contains objective moral properties and objective values but makes no provision for us either.

33

If there is such a thing as objective morality, we cannot automatically conclude that it takes us into account or is relevant to us. That is, if there is such a thing as objective morality, then moral properties would just be some properties among others, tacked onto objects and situations, like size and shape and the color blue. For all we know, they would have nothing in particular to do with us. If we learned that by taking them seriously we would not benefit in any way, or flourish or become fulfilled, we would do well to ignore them. So perhaps there is no reason for us to do the right thing just because it is the right thing to do. Perhaps the only reason for us to do the right thing is if it in fact contributes to our well-being and happiness.[23]

Is morality just based on sentiment?

34

A final view to consider on the origin and status of morality is in the work of the philosopher David Hume. Hume was famous for a number of philosophical doctrines, one of which is that every idea that we have is copied from experience—either experience of the outside world, or experience of the workings of our own psychology.[24] We might do some creative sculpting and craft ideas of things that we have never encountered or that do not exist, but the simple elements of our ideas are all derived from experience. In part, Hume is declaring his hand as an empirically and scientifically minded philosopher who holds that the only way that we are informed about things is by observing them.

35

Hume confronts a puzzle when he attempts to locate the observations that give rise to our ideas of qualities like goodness, justice, and virtue. On the one hand, he acknowledges that we have ideas of these things. On the other hand, he looks to the outside world to locate exactly where and when it is that anyone has seen or experienced goodness or badness, and he comes up short. We are at a crime scene, for example, and we can point to the victim, and some blood, and a knife, but we cannot similarly point to the quality *badness*. Hume has the resources to say that there is another source from which our ideas of ethical qualities are copied, however. Since we *do* have ideas of ethical qualities, and these ideas are not copied from "outer" experience, they must be copied from "inner" experience. In particular, they are copied from our feelings and sentiments. Hume writes that even though many of our desires are self-interested, it is also the case that to some degree

> [E]very thing, which contributes to the happiness of society, recommends itself directly to our approbation and good-will. Here is a principle, which accounts, in great part, for the origin of morality.[25]

> How, indeed, can we suppose it possible in any one, who wears a human heart, that, if there be subjected to his censure, one character or system of conduct, which is beneficial, and another, which is pernicious, to his species or community, he will not so much as give a cool preference to the former, or ascribe to it the smallest merit or regard? Let us suppose . . . a person ever so selfish: let private interest have engrossed ever so much his attention; yet in instances where that is not concerned, he must unavoidably feel *some* propensity to the good of mankind, and make it an object of his choice, if every thing else be equal. Would any man, who is walking along, tread as willingly on another's gouty toes, whom he has no quarrel with, as on the hard flint and pavement?[26]

For Hume, ethical qualities are not out in the world, and in the end they amount to sentiments and feelings that we have in response to people and situations. He thinks that for various reasons that we cannot fully explain—perhaps some of them having to do with the long-term survival of the species—we have sentiments of benevolence and sympathy, and these are the primary basis of morality.[27]

36

One of the things that Hume thinks is so plausible about locating the foundations of morality in our sentiments is that there would be a clear explanation of why we feel the pull of morality in our behavior. Morality does not always trump in our deliberations, to be sure, but even when it doesn't, we (or most of us) still feel a tug in the direction of doing what it specifies. If we are late for a movie or a class or a date, but we encounter someone suffering on the way, we feel at least some inclination to stop and help. Hume thinks that if it wasn't our sentiments and feelings that were driving such inclinations—but instead something like ethical facts or qualities that we were somehow deriving or detecting—it would be very hard to make sense of why we would be motivated. He writes,

> Philosophy is commonly divided into speculative and practical; and as morality is always comprehended under the latter division, 'tis supposed to influence our passions and actions, and to go beyond the calm and indolent judgments of the understanding. And this is confirmed by common experience, which informs us, that men are often govern'd by their duties, and are deter'd from some actions by the opinion of injustice, and impell'd by others by that of obligation. . . . Morals excite passions, and produce or prevent actions. Reason of itself is utterly impotent in this particular. The rules of morality, therefore, are not conclusions of our reason.[28]

We might think of a number of examples in which we use our skills of reasoning to draw a conclusion about something, but where the conclusion does not incline us to act one way or the other unless we also have a corresponding passion or desire. We might conclude that a certain brand of ice cream is the least expensive and is of the highest quality, or that a team has scored the most touchdowns in history, or that a particular combination of molecules is able to kill cancer. If we do not have some antecedent interest in these, however, they are just facts among others, and we would be as indifferent to them as to the fact that the Pythagorean Theorem is true, or the fact that there are certain kinds of rock on the moon. Hume is thinking that it would be too much of a coincidence if ethical qualities were really in objects, and our passions and sentiments were also responsive to them. We can explain the correlation very easily if we say that morality has its origin in our sentiments to begin with.

37

An interesting question, though, is whether or not there *are* certain facts that are in some way intrinsically interesting or exciting. For example, a person might bracket all of their own interests and concerns and think about cancer cells—not about what kills the cells, but on the contrary about their sophistication and how they have been able to maneuver around so many attempts to eradicate them. Or a person might think about the rocks on the moon with a sense of wonder, or about the Pythagorean Theorem with a sense of order and admiration.

38

Hume thinks that morality is grounded in our sentiments of sympathy and benevolence, but he realizes that when we try to determine what is the right thing to do, we do not simply consult the sentiments that we have at the moment. If we were feeling very little sympathy on a given day, the right thing to do on that day would be different from the right thing on a day when we were feeling more kind. Hume thinks that the conclusions that we draw in morality instead have to do with the aggregated and average amount of sentiment that the members of our community tend to feel in response to a situation. He writes,

> The more we converse with mankind, and the greater social intercourse we maintain, the more shall we be familiarized to these general preferences and distinctions, without which our conversation and discourse could scarcely be rendered intelligible to each other. Every man's interest is peculiar to himself, and the aversions and desires, which result from it, cannot be supposed to affect others in a like degree. General language, therefore, being formed for general use, must be moulded on some more general views, and must affix the epithets of praise or blame, in conformity to sentiments, which arise from the general interests of the community. . . . Sympathy, we shall allow, is much fainter than our concern for ourselves, and sympathy with persons remote from us, much fainter than that with persons near and contiguous; but for this very reason, it is necessary for us, in our calm judgments and discourse concerning the characters of men, to neglect all these differences, and render our sentiments more public and social.[29]

One of the benefits of this qualification to Hume's view is that he can make sense of how we sometimes use reason (and not just sentiment) to determine what is right or wrong on a given occasion. We use reason to try to piece together the different amounts of information that are relevant in the situation and to calibrate the level of feeling that one normally has in it.

39

A problem that arises for Hume is that it becomes hard to see how anyone would be obliged to act morally if they did not have the same sentiments as the rest of humanity. Hume appears to recognize the problem, but he does not think it is very serious:

> And though the heart takes part not entirely with those general notions, nor regulates all its love and hatred, by the universal, abstract differences of vice and virtue, without regard to self, or the persons with whom we are more intimately connected; yet have these moral differences a considerable influence, and being sufficient, at least, for discourse, serve all our purposes in company, in the pulpit, on the theatre, and in the schools.[30]

Hume is saying that even if we did not have all the sentiments that give rise to the prescriptions of morality, we could still figure out what those prescriptions are. We could discuss them in company with others, and we could agree on what morality tells us we should do. A problem though is that it is difficult to see how any such prescriptions would be binding on a person who happens to lack the sentiments in question. Given Hume's understanding of the origins of morality, all that it would mean for an individual to refuse to act morally is that they refuse to act in the light of some sentiments that are had by others. If we then said—but it is immoral to not have those sentiments, or that it is immoral to not try to develop them— all that we would be saying is that some other people have negative feelings about our lack of interest in having certain sentiments.

40

Hume has the resources to argue that societies are making an error when they have as a moral code that (for example) it is good to kill an innocent. He can say that although there are no ethical qualities that exist out in the world, morality is a matter of the sentiments that are had by the vast majority of human beings, and in the presence of complete information. If a society happens to have butchered sentiments, or if these sentiments are in reaction to a butchered understanding of the facts on the ground, the society would draw its own conclusions about what is moral, but it would be wrong. For example, US slave-owners were capable of many of the sentiments that undergird morality, but they had a confused understanding of what it is to be a person.

41

Hume also has the resources to say that if there are beings that develop a code of behavior that is not based on the sentiments of sympathy and benevolence, their code of behavior is not a *moral* code, but a code of some other kind. The idea here is that the term "morality" is a word that we invented to refer to a specific kind of phenomenon—one that has to do with certain sentiments and inclinations had by humans—and so that is just what the word picks out. Similarly, the word "haircut" refers to an activity in which a person with hair has their hair shortened. If there are beings somewhere in the universe that do not have hair, and where "hair" is not even a category, we would be in error to call any of the treatments that they receive a "haircut." We can then say that certain codes of behavior have nothing to do with morality.

42

A couple of problems seem to emerge for Hume right way. One is that it is not clear that everyone (or most people) would have the same sentiments if they had all the same information. Another is (again) that it would not mean very much if we ever said that another culture is in error about a moral code, and it is not clear how or why this culture would be motivated to take heed. Perhaps Hume could say this in response: all human beings are similar enough that over time they could come to have the same sentiments to (roughly) the same degree, so there is at least a chance that the morally oblivious will change their behavior. But we might worry in that case that morality does not have the kind of ground or legitimacy that we want for it.

Possible discussion exercises

1   Is God so powerful that He could have made it the case that murder is good? Why or why not?

2   If there is objective morality that exists independently of God, and God does not exist, who if anyone should enforce morality?

3   Is there really as much cultural disagreement about morality and value as Mackie suggests?

4   Consider the following: mind, numbers, space, time, laws of nature, context, and free will. Are they weird? Are they too weird to exist?

5   Are there disagreements in science that suggest that science and morality might both be relativistic?

6   Imagine that Germany won World War II and the world developed in a very different direction. Would it still be correct to say in 2012 that Hitler was bad?

7   Are you able to take the same perspective on human misfortune that a human being is able to take toward the destruction of an anthill?

8   If objective value exists, are we under any obligation to take it into account when we decide how to act? Why or why not?

9   Imagine that the Wicked Witch of the North (from *The Wizard of Oz*) finds beautiful objects to be repugnant. Does she still have reason to incorporate beauty into her world?

10   Is there an important difference between saying that God prescribes certain moral rules, and saying that moral rules are facts that have no further explanation or reason?

11   Are there any important connections between morality and free will?

12   Assume for the moment that morality is relative to the concerns and traditions of the particular society in which it develops. If so, can there be such a thing as moral disagreement?

13   Do you agree that there are things that have nonmoral value—like winning a chess championship, or breaking a world record in track and field, or learning a new language? Are connections between friends valuable, or connections between parents and children? What are some other examples? How do we encounter such value or know about it?

14   Hume argues that the reason that morality has some pull on us is that it is grounded in our own sentiments. Do you think that morality would have any pull on us if it was not grounded in our sentiments?

15   People seem to be able to recognize all of the same facts about a situation, but still have different sentiments in response, and make different moral assessments. What is an example? What might Hume say here about the reason for the difference in assessment?

16   Socrates would remark that we say things all the time like—"I should not have done that; it was wrong." If there is no objective morality, can we still go on taking claims like this seriously?

17   Come up with your own everyday example for one of the views or arguments or objections presented in the chapter.

Notes

1   The distinction between moral value and nonmoral value is difficult to make with exact precision, but philosophers have attempted to offer examples. Things that have moral value presumably include helping a person who suffers, being honest, and not killing or torturing the innocent. Things that have nonmoral value presumably include achievements in music or poetry or sports, inventions

and products that are clever and sophisticated, and historic pieces of art. The distinction is tricky, but see, for example, the discussion in Susan Wolf, "The Meanings of Lives," in John Perry, Michael Bratman, and John Martin Fischer (eds), *Introduction to Philosophy: Classical and Contemporary Readings*, Fifth Edition, Oxford and New York: Oxford University Press (2010), 798.

2 For a transcript of Socrates' trial, see Plato, *Apology*, in G. M. A. Grube (trans. and ed.), *Five Dialogues*, Indianapolis and Cambridge: Hackett (1981), 17a–42a. Socrates (469–399 BC) was an ancient Greek philosopher who was known for wandering the Athenian marketplace and posing philosophical questions to anyone who would engage him. Plato was his younger contemporary and also transcribed many of Socrates' views. It is difficult to overestimate the importance of Socrates and Plato in the history of philosophy.

3 Plato, *Euthyphro*, 10a. Note that Socrates actually puts the question in terms of what is "pious"—whether God loves things because they are pious or whether things are pious because God loves them. Historically the debate that has been passed down is in the more familiar terms of whether God loves things because they are good or whether things are good because He loves them.

4 Ibid., 10a–b.

5 See, for example, *Apology*, 27c–d.

6 This has come to be known as the "Euthyphro Dilemma," from the name of the dialogue in which it appears.

7 I owe this example to Diane Jeske.

8 Phillipa Foot, "Morality as a System of Hypothetical Imperatives," *The Philosophical Review* 81 (1972), 305–16. Phillipa Foot specialized in moral philosophy and was Professor of Philosophy at the University of California, Los Angeles. She also taught at Oxford University. She is the author of a number of highly influential books and articles. One of her famous examples involves a trolley car driver who is trying to avoid five people on the track ahead, but who can only refrain from running them over if he changes to a track in which he would run over one person. The thought experiment then extends to a case in which a healthy person enters a hospital, and a doctor realizes that he can save five of his dying patients if he kills the person and uses their organs.

9 Linda Zagzebski, "An Agent-Based Approach to the Problem of Evil," *International Journal for Philosophy of Religion* 39 (1996), 132. Linda Zagzebski is George Lynn Cross Professor of Philosophy at the University of Oklahoma. In addition to numerous articles, she has authored five books, and she has edited or coedited four

volumes of philosophical papers. She has focused primarily on issues in epistemology, ethics, and philosophy of religion. She is a past president of the Society of Christian Philosophers.

10 Friedrich Nietzsche, *The Will to Power*, trans. Walter Kaufman and R. J. Hollingdale, New York: Vintage (1968), 16. Nietzsche was a German philosopher who wrote in the latter half of the nineteenth century. He had a position at the University of Basel for ten years, but he resigned for health reasons and lived in relative poverty after that. He is most famous for claiming that "God is dead" and for arguing that Christianity has led us to value the repression of impulses.

11 Ibid., 35.

12 Bertrand Russell, "The Faith of a Rationalist," in Al Seckel (ed.), *Bertrand Russell on God and Religion*, Amherst, NY: Prometheus Books (1947/1986), 91. Russell was an English philosopher and logician who worked for the first three-quarters of the twentieth century. He was also a political activist and was heavily involved in debates about the use of atomic weapons.

13 Sarah McGrath, "Moral Disagreement and Moral Expertise," *Oxford Studies in MetaEthics* 3 (2008), 98, and also 99–107. Sarah McGrath is Assistant Professor of Philosophy at Princeton University. She specializes in moral epistemology, metaethics, and normative ethics.

14 John Mackie, *Ethics: Inventing Right and Wrong*, London: Penguin Books (1977), 36–8. Professor Mackie was a philosopher who taught at a number of universities in Australia and England. He is perhaps most famous for his view that ethics is not discovered, but is invented.

15 There are different variants of the doctrine of moral relativism; here I am trying to capture the features that they tend to have in common. For a good discussion see Chris Gowans, "Moral Relativism."

16 Thomas Nagel, "The Absurd," *The Journal of Philosophy* 68 (1971), 720.

17 Hannah Arendt, *Eichmann in Jerusalem: A Report on the Banality of Evil*, New York: Penguin Books (1963), 21. Professor Arendt focused on issues in political philosophy and was University Professor of Political Philosophy at the New School for Social Research. She also taught at the University of Chicago, Columbia, Northwestern, and Cornell. She authored numerous works, including *Origins of Totalitarianism* (1955).

18 Mackie, *Ethics*, 38–42.

19 Diane Jeske, *Rationality and Moral Theory: How Intimacy Generates Reasons*, New York: Routledge (2008), ch. 1.

20 Penelope Maddy, *Realism in Mathematics*, New York: Oxford University Press (1992), 88. Penelope Maddy is Distinguished Professor of Logic and Philosophy of Science at the University of California, Irvine. She focuses on philosophy of mathematics and philosophy of logic, and metaphilosophy.

21 Mackie actually anticipates the "companions in guilt" response to his view (*Ethics*, 38–9).

22 Again, the distinction between moral and nonmoral value is difficult to make very precise, and there might be some interconnection and overlap.

23 This view has been defended recently by the philosopher David Brink in "Rational Egoism, Self, and Others," in O. Flanagan and A. Rorty (eds), *Identity, Character, and Morality*, Cambridge, MA: MIT Press (1990). Professor Brink is a philosopher at the University of California, San Diego. The view that reasons of self-interest are the only reasons that motivate us to act is associated historically with the ancient Greek philosopher Epicurus (342–270 BC).

24 See, for example, David Hume, *An Enquiry Concerning Human Understanding*, ed. Tom L. Beauchamp, Oxford: Oxford University Press (1748/1999), section 2, "Of the Origin of Ideas." David Hume was a philosopher and historian in eighteenth-century England. He is best known for his empiricist view that all knowledge is acquired through experience. He argued that all ideas are formed either through sensory perception or through observation of our own inner states. We cannot know, and we cannot even think, what we do not experience.

25 David Hume, *An Enquiry Concerning the Principles of Morals*, ed. Tom L. Beauchamp, Oxford: Oxford University Press (1998), 109.

26 Ibid., 113.

27 Ibid., 82, 120.

28 David Hume, *A Treatise of Human Nature*, ed. David Fate Norton and Mary J. Norton, Oxford: Oxford University Press (1739/2011), II.i.1, 457.

29 Hume, *An Enquiry Concerning the Principles of Morals*, 116.

30 Ibid., 119.

CHAPTER THREE

Material minds:
A no-brainer?

Abstract

This chapter considers the following: whether or not brain injuries and diseases (and their impact on our thinking) are evidence that thinking is a property or feature of the brain; whether or not we can explain how brains think or if it would just be a brute inexplicable fact; whether machines, especially computers, can think; and whether or not the freedom and autonomy and dignity of thinking are evidence that thinking is not a property of the brain after all.

Is thought a product of the brain?

1

One argument for the view that physical matter can think is that everything in the universe is ultimately composed of the elements of the periodic table—things like H and C and O and Cl. If everything in the universe is ultimately composed of physical elements or is a product of physical elements, thinking must be composed of physical elements or be the product of such elements. Thinking is clearly the result of some physical process or other, and the most obvious candidate for human thinking is the brain.[1]

2

This is a problematic argument as it stands. It supposes from the get-go that everything in the universe is composed of the elements on the periodic table, and so it is not so much arguing that thinking is physical as it is assuming that thinking is physical right from the start.

3

Another argument (for the view that thinking is physical) begins with the assumption that our minds accompany us when we travel and hence that they move along with us from place to place. The argument then assumes that things can only move from place to place or have a location if they are physical. We find a statement of this argument in the work of the seventeenth-century philosopher and scientist Margaret Cavendish:

> Though Matter might be without Motion, yet Motion cannot be without matter; for it is impossible (in my opinion) that there should be an Immaterial Motion in Nature.[2]

> I cannot conceive how it is possible, that . . . the Soul, being incorporeal, can walk in the air, like a body; for incorporeal beings cannot have corporeal actions, no more then corporeal beings can have the actions of incorporeals.[3]

> I am not able to comprehend how Motion can be attributed to a Spirit; I mean, natural motion, which is onely a propriety of a body, or of a corporeal Being.[4]

Here Cavendish is asserting that our minds admit of motion but that the only things that are capable of motion are material things. What it is for a thing to move is for it to change locations, but "place [is] an attribute that belongs onely to a Body."[5] We take a carriage from Oxford to London, she might say in her own time, and we are thinking all the way. We fly in an airplane from California to Iowa, we might say in our time, and as we think about our loved ones or return the tray-table to its upright position, we are thinking through and through. The friend who meets us at the airport announces that the first stop is the bookstore Prairie Lights in Iowa City, and we exclaim that we were just thinking about Prairie Lights on the plane. Cavendish argues that travel or movement is a matter of changing location and that strictly speaking only bodies move. If we were thinking on the plane and are now thinking on the ground, matter thinks.

4

Cavendish is supposing that we do not leave our thinking behind when we travel from place to place. But that supposition might be a bit loaded. To say that our minds are left behind is to assume that they always have some location—that either they move or they *stay where they are*—but a person who thinks that minds are immaterial would probably want to say that minds are not anywhere. Cavendish assumes that our minds are in some literal sense attached to our bodies and that they are located in the brain:

> I would ask those, that say the Brain has neither sense, reason, nor self-motion, and therefore no Perception; but that all proceeds from an Immaterial Principle, and an Incorporeal Spirit, distinct from the body, which moveth and actuates corporeal matter; I would fain ask them, I say, where their Immaterial Ideas reside, in what part or place of the Body? . . . [I]f it [the spirit] have no dimension, how can it be confined in a material body.[6]

We say this sort of thing: that a smart person is a braniac, or that there is not a lot going on upstairs in the case of a person who is dim. Cavendish takes these locutions literally and argues that ideas and other mental items are features or properties of the brain. The question that she wants to press is what the alternative view would be if the locutions were metaphorical: that particular minds are not anywhere in the physical domain, but are still connected to particular bodies, and they move along with these bodies but without being physical. We might want to oppose Cavendish and argue that our minds move, but without being physical, or we might want to argue that our minds do not move at all. Perhaps all that moves is the body to which the mind is attached, or perhaps minds are not attached to bodies but are in a different domain altogether.

5

Another argument for the view that thinking is physical is that minds and bodies interact. The early Roman poet and philosopher Lucretius argued that the only sort of thing that could come into contact with a body was another body, and that if minds and bodies interact—and they sure seem to interact—then minds and bodies are ultimately composed of the same stuff.[7] He writes:

> This reasoning also shows that mind and spirit
> Are corporeal. When they can move the limbs,
> Snatching the sleeping body and discomposing
> The features, wheeling and steering the whole person
> (None of which, we see, can come to pass without
> Touch, and all touch implies a body), must
> You not confess, the soul's corporeal?[8]

A similar argument appears in the writing of the seventeenth-century philosopher, Princess Elisabeth of Bohemia. Princess Elisabeth was worried in particular about Descartes' view that minds and bodies are united and come into contact even though minds are not physical:

> How can the soul of a man determine the spirits of his body so as to produce voluntary actions (given that the soul is only a thinking substance)? For it seems that all determination of movement is made by the pushing of a thing moved, either that it is pushed by the thing that moves it or it is affected by the quality or shape of the surface of that thing. For the first two conditions, touching is necessary, for the third extension. For touching, you exclude entirely the notion that you have of the soul; extension seems to me incompatible with an immaterial thing.[9]

Cavendish offered an argument along the same lines as well.[10]

6

Some seventeenth-century philosophers were happy to agree that mind-body interaction is impossible if minds and bodies are not made of the same stuff. However, they drew the opposite conclusion: that minds and bodies do not really interact. For example, Nicholas Malebranche and G. W. Leibniz argued that minds and bodies only *appear* to interact. When we decide to raise our arm, it goes up, but only because God has made arrangements so that decisions and bodily movements occur in a parallel order.[11] Lucretius and Cavendish and Princess Elizabeth are supposing that minds and bodies do interact and that this is only possible if minds are physical. If they are right, our minds are able to move our bodies and apply energy and force to them, and they can only do this if they have energy and force themselves. An opponent of Lucretius and company might concede that the position of Malebranche and Leibniz is too extreme, but note that according to contemporary physics there is such a thing as action at a distance—where entities interact without touching. If so, then perhaps a mind directs its body without being attached to it and without touching it in any way. The mind would not be a physical force acting at a distance, but a mental one.

7

Other thinkers (aside from philosophers) are struck by the appearance of mind-body interaction. The eighteenth-century French medical doctor Julien Offray de la Mettrie noticed the ways in which the mental capacities of his patients would be influenced by changes in their bodily states.[12] His aging patients would exhibit dementia, and patients with various kinds of brain injury would remember some things but not others. Other cases were more mundane. A person ingests a narcotic like opium, and their thinking is altered: what seemed like a really bad idea before is all of a sudden genius. Mettrie also noticed that climate appears to have an effect on our mood. Or, if we have not slept, we might not be able to think very clearly, and if we do not eat we become grumpy. Mettrie writes,

> Opium is so closely related to the sleep it brings that we cannot ignore it here. This remedy inebriates, as do wine or coffee, etc., each in its own way, according to the dose. . . . Opium even changes the will; it forces the soul, which wanted to stay awake and enjoy itself, to go to bed despite itself.[13]

We need only to have eyes to see the necessary influence of age on reason. . . . Such [also] is the power of climate that a man who changes climates feels the effects despite himself.[14]

There appears to be a strong dependence relation of thinking on the brain. If a certain part of the brain is removed, certain kinds of thinking just disappear. If the brain is severely injured, or if we are administered anesthesia, thinking appears to turn off completely.

8

One objection to dull the force of some of Mettrie's examples is that not all people who suffer from a given brain condition also suffer from the corresponding mental condition that Mettrie specifies. For example, not all people with aged brains have dementia. If old age was really the cause of dementia, then all people with aged brains would suffer from it, but clearly they don't. Here Mettrie would probably argue that the brains of some are differently configured than the brains of others and that it is not old age per se that is the cause of dementia, but certain very specific developments in the nervous system that tend to come with old age. Mettrie could make this argumentative move, but he would then need to point to empirical evidence that there is a brain configuration that elderly people have in common and that always produces dementia. He did not have that evidence, and so perhaps he was thinking that dementia *has* to be due to such a cause; otherwise people would not develop it. But then Mettrie would just be assuming his position and not arguing for it. Perhaps nowadays we can do a better job of isolating what is common in the cases in which people suffer from dementia, old or young. If so, Mettrie would have a stronger case.

9

Mettrie was familiar with instances of brain trauma, and we can come up with examples of our own. Currently (in 2014) there is a debate about whether or not football players are affected in later life as a result of the repeated hits that they take to the head. Former NFL-star Dave Duerson started to notice, and everyone around him started to notice, that he was having trouble forming coherent sentences. He reported that as the years went by he was not able think in the way that he did before.* On many occasions his thoughts would just fail to come together, or (perhaps to say the same thing) the thoughts that would come together did not strike him as making a whole lot of sense. A few hours before he killed himself at age 50, he texted his family and friends to ask that his brain be donated to science for further study on the effects of traumatic brain injury. Many other retired players—for example, Tony Dorsett and Jim McMahon—have testified that, as a result of concussions and related brain impairments, their psychological and emotional lives ended up taking a dramatic turn.[15]

10

But it is possible to argue that the repeated blows to Duerson's head did not cause the degeneration of his mental capacities. Indeed, an objection to the many cases that Mettrie presents is that perhaps there is a correlation between our bodily states and our mental states, but that does not mean that there is any causation. A worry for this objection is that if we say that brain injury and anesthesia and other such cases are just instances of correlation, it is going to be hard to say when *anything* is a case of causation. We say that eating certain kinds of food is a cause of health, for example, and that gasoline is one of the causes of the acceleration of a car. We do not pull punches and say that there is no causation in these instances, and the correlations in the case of the mind and the nervous system would appear to be just as tight. As the twentieth-century philosopher Bertrand Russell writes,

> All the evidence goes to show that what we regard as our mental life is bound up with brain structure and organized bodily energy. Therefore it is rational to suppose that mental life ceases when bodily life ceases. The argument is only one of probability, but it is as strong as those upon which most scientific conclusions are based.[16]

If we say that there is only a correlation between our mental states and our physical states, in such a way that our minds are not dependent on our nervous system and can continue to exist after the death of our body, we would have to say that similar correlations do not involve causation. But that seems a little strong.

11

In Mettrie's time there was no such thing as anesthesia, and there was not the formal condition identified as Alzheimer's disease. He would just have patients who started to notice that they were not remembering things. Eventually they would fail to recognize their loved ones, and they would no longer be able to recall the significant elements, or even any elements, of their past. The person's bare consciousness might be present—what Descartes would call the thinking I[17]—but it is no longer attached to the qualities and features and memories that make the person the person that they are (or were) and that make the person markedly distinguishable or different from the bare I of anybody else. Mettrie would insist that the best explanation for the symptoms of Alzheimer's disease is that thinking is produced by neuronal activity and that, when the cause of thinking is shut down, the effect is shut down as well.

12

Some philosophers have argued that because our mental states depend on the physiology of our brain, our decisions and ideas never actually cause anything to happen—and all the causal work is done at the level of the brain. Jaegwon Kim has defended this view, illustrating it with the following analogy. The image of an object in a mirror is produced by the original object and light, and if two images in a mirror appear to stand in causal relations with each other, they do not: the causal relation is between the original objects that are producing the reflection. Kim thinks that our decisions and ideas cause neither our bodily movements nor any aspects of our mental life: what does the causing is the brain activity that brings about our ideas and decisions in the first place.[18] We might make a decision to affect our psychology, or to affect the brain itself, but that decision only happens because of the prior brain state that brings it about.

13

A potential objection to Kim's view is that he is assuming that mental states and brain states are not both *together* the cause of the effects that come after them. If a given state of the brain always results in a given mental state, then that brain state would always be accompanied by the mental state, and there would never be an instance in which we could be sure that only the brain state was doing causal work. Perhaps Kim could argue that brain states and mental states are not necessarily tied together in this way, and that if we created an artificial person with an exact copy of someone's brain—down to the last subatomic particle—the two beings would not necessarily have all of the same thoughts. But in that case we would be allowing that the same cause does not always lead to the same effect.

Artificial intelligence

14

A final question to consider in the context of exploring the view that minds are physical is the question of whether or not machines can think. There are a number of movies and television shows that are dedicated to this issue—for example, *Blade Runner* (1982), *Bicentennial Man* (1999), *Battlestar Galactica* (2004–9), and *Her* (2013). A running theme in each is whether or not a machine can be said to think if it engages in all of the same kinds of behavior as human beings—responding to questions, laughing, crying, and doing things that are spontaneous and unexpected. In 1950, the mathematician Alan Turing proposed a test in which a human interrogator attempts to figure out whether she is interacting with another person or with a machine. The interrogator is cordoned off in a room posing questions to both, not knowing which is which. Turing's prediction was that computers would be so sophisticated by the year 2000 that an interrogator would have a lot of difficulty telling the person apart from the computer and that talk of thinking machines would be par for the course.[19]

15

Turing's experiment—known as the Turing Test—raises a lot of interesting questions. We might object that the experiment has nothing to do with the question of whether or not machines can think because there is an important difference between the behavioral *expression* of thinking and intelligence, on the one hand, and actual thinking and intelligence, on the other. Turing considers this objection in his paper; his reply is that the only way that we tell that other human beings have minds is by observing their behavior also. But we do not want to retreat to the solipsistic position—only *I* have a mind. If it is just on the basis of our observations of human behavior that we conclude that other humans have minds, then we should proceed in the same way in the case of a machine. Perhaps we would be more inclined to agree with Turing if the machine in question looked exactly like a human being (as we find in *Battlestar Galactica*). Indeed, cylons are made of flesh and blood. Or we might dig our heels in further and insist that a robot made of flesh and blood is still just a robot.

16

The philosopher John Searle has offered a famous argument for the view that computers—and machines more generally—cannot think.[20] Searle asks us to imagine that we are outside of a room that has an input slot and an output slot, where we are Chinese speakers who input questions in Chinese and then get answers. If we insert a piece of paper that asks "What day is it?" in Chinese, the response (also in Chinese) is "It is Tuesday." (And let's say that in fact it is Tuesday.) We insert Chinese symbols that ask, "Do you feel lonely?," and the response (again always in Chinese) is "Yes, and that makes me sad." Or we insert symbols that ask, "How are you doing this afternoon?," and the response is "Thank you, I am well." Some further information about the thought experiment is that there is a person inside the room who does not know any Chinese, but who has a rule book (in English) that specifies which input symbols are paired with which output symbols. The person in the room does not realize that the question that is being asked is "How are you doing this afternoon?" The person simply takes the input symbol, looks it up in the rulebook, and then sends out the symbol that the rulebook tells him to. Searle wants to argue that the person in the room does not understand Chinese and that *understanding* is more than just the manipulation of symbols. No matter how fast the person in the room is able to shuffle the symbols, and—by extension—no matter how fast a computer is able to process inputs and outputs, all that we have is symbol manipulation and not understanding or intelligence.[21]

17

Searle has to be very careful in addressing the more general question of whether or not there are any machines that are able to think. He subscribes also to the view that human beings are purely physical organisms and that all of our thinking is the product of the activity of our nervous system and brain. He is therefore happy to say that there are machines that think if human beings are categorized as machines as well.[22] But Searle is insisting that not just any machine can think. Thinking involves the manipulation of symbols or syntax, but thinking also involves *semantics*. That is, a machine only thinks if it also understands the meaning of the symbols that it manipulates, and the person in the Chinese Room is absolutely oblivious to the meaning of the Chinese symbols that he is handling.

18

People can have very different reactions to the Chinese Room Argument. Some might argue that Searle is absolutely right and that whatever a computer is doing, it is not thinking. Some might join Turing and argue that since our assessment that other human beings think is based just on our observation of their behavior, that is a good enough basis on which to make an assessment in the computer case as well. Some might argue alternately that since behavior is the only thing that we take into account when we judge that another person has a mind, thinking just *is* complex patterns of behavior. Or some might allow that thinking is different from observable behavior but argue that Searle is mistaken to hold that thinking has to involve conscious understanding. Searle is presumably right that the person in the Chinese Room is oblivious to the meaning of the Chinese symbols and does not understand what they mean, but it may be that fluent speakers of Chinese are so well versed in their language that they understand how to use it without paying attention to what they are saying. Searle might say that this is a misdescription of language use or that if there are such people, then whatever it is that they are doing, it is not *understanding.*[23]

19

Indeed, Searle accepts a version of the Cartesian view that thinking and understanding always involve some level of conscious awareness. As we saw in Chapter One, Descartes holds that although we can doubt the existence of external bodies, we can never doubt the existence of our own minds. If we *attempt* to doubt the existence of our minds, we have to conclude that they are there doing the doubting. For Descartes that means that our minds are to be equated with conscious awareness. First, he writes,

> I have convinced myself that there is absolutely nothing in the world, no sky, no earth, no minds, no bodies. Does it not follow that I too do not exist? No: if I convinced myself of something then I certainly existed. . . . So after considering everything very thoroughly, I must finally conclude that this proposition, *I am, I exist*, is necessarily true whenever it is put forward by me or conceived in my mind.[24]

This result may not seem especially substantive or surprising—that we cannot doubt the existence of our minds. Descartes is being a little bit sneaky, however, as perhaps is Searle. Both are right to hold that we cannot doubt the existence of the highly conscious and highly reflective activity of attempting to doubt our beliefs, but that does not mean that our minds are to be equated with consciousness. There might be other parts of a person's mind that she does not know as well, and whose existence is not so indubitable, but that again are still components of her mind. Descartes does not agree:

> At last I have discovered it—thought; this alone is inseparable from me. I am, I exist, that is certain. But for how long? For as long as I am thinking. . . . At present I am not admitting anything but what is necessarily true. I am, then, in the strict sense only a thing that thinks; that is, I am a mind, or intelligence, or intellect, or reason. . . .[25]

> As to the fact that there can be nothing in the mind, in so far as it is a thinking thing, of which it is not aware, this seems to me to be self-evident. . . . [W]e cannot have any thought of which we are not aware at the very moment when it is in us.[26]

Descartes is correct that the existence of highly conscious thinking is indubitable while we are engaging in it, but that does not mean that there are not other elements of the mind whose existence is less well known, and it does not mean that the mind is to be identified with those of its elements that *are* well known.

Are thoughts immaterial?

20

Thus far we have considered some arguments for the view that thinking is material, along with some of the possible extensions and implications of that view. There are also a number of compelling arguments for the view that minds are immaterial. One is that bodies are always composite and divisible into parts, but minds are simple and indivisible. Minds and bodies are therefore different kinds of things. Socrates puts forward a version of this argument:

> Is not anything that is composite and a compound by nature liable to be split up into its component parts, and only that which is noncomposite, if anything, is not likely to be split up? . . . The soul is most like the divine, deathless, intelligible, uniform, indissoluble, always the same as itself, whereas the body is most like that which is human, mortal, multiform, unintelligible, soluble, and never consistently the same.[27]

We find the same argument later in Descartes:

> [T]he body is by its very nature always divisible, while the mind is utterly indivisible. For when I consider the mind, . . . I am unable to distinguish any parts within myself. I understand myself to be quite single and complete. Although the whole mind seems to be united to the whole body, I recognize that if a foot or arm or any other part of the body is cut off, nothing has thereby been taken away from the mind.[28]

The two philosophers are defending the doctrine of substance dualism—the view that there are two kinds of things or substances in the universe. According to this view, there exist mental substances that are intangible and indivisible, and also physical substances that have dimension and are divisible. Minds are things that think and have ideas, and because they do not have dimension they cannot be decomposed into parts. Socrates adds that minds are different from bodies in that they are invisible.[29] So minds appear to be very different from bodies: they are invisible and indivisible, and hence indestructible and deathless, or at the very least they do not perish as a result of the death of the body.

21

A potential problem for this argument is that there appears to be evidence that if some parts of the body are cut off or damaged, then—to use Descartes' language—something *is* taken away from the mind. Socrates and Descartes may be correct that minds are not decomposable into parts, but when our brains shut down it appears that thinking shuts down as well. Socrates and Descartes would say that thinking may seem to shut down from an outsider's perspective, but in fact it does not.[30]

22

Another argument for the view that minds are immaterial substances is that minds are free and independent in a way that they would not be if thinking was material. We make choices and are (at least in part) the author of our own trajectory. If our thinking was due entirely to the cells of our nervous system, we would have no more independence or autonomy than anything else in nature.

23

A variant of this argument appears in Socrates. In *Phaedo*, there is a discussion of the relationship between harp strings and the music that they produce. The discussion begins when Socrates' interlocutor insists that just because a thing is invisible, that does not mean that it is immaterial:

> One might make the same argument about harmony, lyre and strings, that a harmony is something invisible, without body, beautiful and divine in the attuned lyre, whereas the lyre itself and its strings are physical, bodily, composite, earthly, and akin to what is mortal. . . . If then the soul is a kind of harmony or attunement, clearly, when our body is relaxed or stretched without due measure by diseases and other evils, the soul must be immediately destroyed, even if it be most divine, as are the other harmonies found in music and all the works of artists.[31]

Socrates responds with the claim that a harmony is very different from a mind. A harmony depends for its existence on the instrument that produces it; a harmony cannot go off in its own direction, independent of the strings, and if it did we would look for another musician hiding in the bushes. Nor can a harmony have an impact on the strings that produce it and make the strings proceed in a different order. Or perhaps a harmony can affect the strings, but only if it was produced and then guided by the vibrations of the strings to begin with. A mind is different: it is able to direct its body independently of the way that the body (or the brain) is behaving. Socrates writes,

> Do you think it natural for a harmony, or any other composite, to be in a different state from that of the elements of which it is composed? . . . Nor, as I think, can it act or be acted upon in a different way than its elements? . . . One must therefore suppose

that a harmony does not direct its components, but is directed by them.[32]

Socrates has put his finger exactly on the problem. He is assuming that the dependence relation between thinking and the brain is very different from the dependence relation between music and an instrument. It sure seems to be different—if we are autonomous agents—and it seems outrageous to deny that we are autonomous at least to some degree.

24

We are at a critical juncture in the debate about whether or not thinking is material. One view is that all of our mental life is dependent on the brain and that if our ideas and decisions are able to guide our bodies, it is because our brains produced those states to begin with. Another view is that we have a kind of control and autonomy that would not be possible if the entirety of our mental life depended on the underlying cellular activity of the nervous system, and so it doesn't.

25

Things come to a head in cases like that of the impressive politician and actor, Ronald Reagan. The reason why the case of President Reagan is so central is that a pillar of his political platform was to argue that individuals should exercise mind over matter and use willpower to pull themselves up from difficult circumstances. Reagan was a remarkable human being. His energy and charisma, the thoughts that came to him at just the right time, and his charm and poise—on the view that thinking is physical, every aspect of his mental life depended entirely on the underlying neuronal activity in his brain. On that view, Mr Reagan could not have summoned up willpower to neutralize the symptoms of his Alzheimer's disease; the very faculty that he would need to employ to do that—his will—was among the things that the disease was holding hostage. On the view of Socrates and

Descartes, minds are *not* the product of the nervous system. The original self and mind of an Alzheimer's victim is still present somewhere, even if it appears to an outside observer that it has disappeared. The decisions of a person are not produced by the antecedent states of their brain, and no matter the configuration of their brain at any given moment, a lot of different decisions are possible for them. On this second view, our ideas and decisions are not like the music of a harp but are autonomous and have a life of their own.

26

We have to be very careful here. If we accept the first view (that thinking is produced in the brain), we might feel inclined to criticize our opponent. We might suggest that our opponent is wrong and that they should be held accountable for their blunder. But in that case we would be supposing that human beings do have control over their mental lives. They *should* believe differently, and hence they *could* believe differently.

27

Another argument for the view that minds are immaterial substances is that bodies are low-grade entities and cannot have impressive features like thinking. A number of philosophers since antiquity have defended the view that bodies are relatively speaking degenerate. Socrates equated them with death.[33] The early Roman philosopher St Augustine took bodies to be vile and worthless and argued that sin itself was to be identified with turning our attention toward sensible bodies and away from ideas and the affairs of the soul.[34] His follower Plotinus wrote of the "the darkness inherent in matter," and warned against the pursuit of physical objects.[35] He speaks favorably of (sensible) fire, but only because it is relatively intangible, and somewhat mind-like:

> This is why fire glows with a beauty beyond all other bodies, for fire holds the rank of idea in this regard. Always struggling aloft,

this subtlest of elements is at the last limits of the bodily. . . . It sparkles and glows like an idea.[36]

Fire is still material, of course, and material things are no substitute for things that are immaterial and hence divine.[37] Plotinus continues,

> [A]n ugly soul . . . is friend to filthy pleasures, it lives a life abandoned to bodily sensation and enjoys its depravity. . . . If someone is immersed in mire or daubed with mud, his native comeliness disappears; all one sees is the mire and mud with which he is covered. Ugliness is due to the alien matter that encrusts him. If he would be attractive once more, he has to wash himself, get clean again, make himself what he was before. Thus we would be right in saying that ugliness of soul comes from its mingling with, fusion with, collapse into the bodily and material.[38]

This is a view that is common in the work of a lot of figures in the history of philosophy, and it is a component of religious traditions that emphasize the priority of the soul over the body. The seventeenth-century philosopher and clergyman Ralph Cudworth put it this way:

> There is unquestionably, a *Scale* or *Ladder* of *Nature*, and Degrees of *Perfection* and *Entity*, one above another, as of *Life*, *Sense*, and *Cogitation*, above Dead, Sensless and *Unthinking Matter*; or *Reason* and *Understanding* above *Sense*, *&c.*[39]

If bodies are low-grade beings, then they have very limited capacities, and they would not be able to bring about something so exalted as thought.

28

An objection to the view that bodies are low-grade entities is that, if we take the time to pay attention, we will notice that bodies are quite sophisticated. We consider the orderly behavior of bodies in nature, for example, and the way that very simple organisms are able to respond skillfully to their environments, and we might conclude that bodies are remarkable. That is, we might conclude that they are not unimpressive at all and that they even have the wherewithal to think.

29

A response to this objection is that bodies *are* low-grade entities and that when they do behave in sophisticated ways, they are being assisted by a mind. Cudworth offers a response along these lines. In his ambitious book, *The True and Immutable System of the Universe*, he addresses the question of whether or not bodies ever behave in a sophisticated manner. He thinks that they do. He focuses on examples like the fingers of the "Exercised Lutonist," and the movements of the expert dancer.[40] According to Cudworth, the expert lutonist (or guitar-player) performs so gracefully, and so expertly, that her fingers *have* to be guided by intelligence. She is not consciously moving each finger, and her fingers are not conscious themselves, but still there must be some intelligence that is guiding them along. But Cudworth also thought that intelligence was only had by immaterial minds. It follows quite logically (if we grant Cudworth's assumptions) that any time bodies appear to be behaving in a sophisticated or intelligent way, there is unconscious and immaterial mentality present that is running the show. An explanation that Cudworth (and Cavendish) wanted to avoid is that the orderly behavior of bodies is due to the existence of laws of nature. The worry (prominent in the seventeenth century) was that it is unclear what kind of entity a law of nature would be, or how laws would be able to do anything, and in particular how they would work to keep bodies in line. Instead, when a body follows a law of nature, Cudworth and Cavendish thought, it is guided by unconscious thinking. When cells seem to know where to go in the human body, they are guided by unconscious thinking. When a spider builds an intricate web, or when the heart pumps blood at an accelerated rate to energize the body in reaction to a threat, there is an unconscious mind that is holding the reins. Cudworth concludes that in addition to material objects, the natural world contains immaterial "plastic natures" that work to move things around in an orderly fashion.[41] If someone like Cavendish points to examples in which a material object is sophisticated and impressive,[42] and concludes that matter has the wherewithal to think, Cudworth responds that the body itself is unimpressive but is accompanied by an immaterial mind.

30

Another argument for the view that minds are immaterial substances is that human beings are made in the image of God and that since God is an immaterial substance, there must be an immaterial component to us as well. There is no question that our bodies are material, but we have a second component—the mind. A potential worry for this argument is that if bodies are the product of God, then presumably they would be high-grade entities, and if they are high-grade entities we would have little reason to deny that they have the ability to think. If bodies are sufficiently sophisticated to be able to think, we could be created in God's image and be thinkers, with minds that are wholly physical.

31

Another argument for the view that minds are immaterial substances is that there is no way to explain or make sense of how thinking could arise from physical elements, and so it does not. Leibniz offered this argument, and it was very popular in the early modern period. He writes,

> [W]e must confess that the perception, and what depends on it, is inexplicable in terms of mechanical reasons, that is, through shapes and motions. If we imagine that there is a machine whose structure makes it think, sense, and have perceptions, we could conceive it enlarged, keeping the same proportions, so that we could enter into it, as one enters into a mill. Assuming that, when inspecting its interior, we will find only parts that push one another, and we will never find anything to explain a perception.[43]

There is no way to make sense of how a bunch of unthinking bodies can combine together and form a composite that thinks and perceives. We could understand how the composite would come to have a new size and weight, for example—as a function of the size and weight of the added parts—but we would not understand how or why it would all of a sudden think.

32

A response to this argument is that we should not expect to understand everything that happens, and that reality is under no obligation to exist in ways that are intelligible to us. Cavendish offers this response—not surprisingly, given that she holds that matter thinks, but she does not pretend to have an explanation of *how* it thinks. She argues however that there is a lot that we do not understand in nature: magnetic attraction, fire, or even why food that is poisonous to some is healthy to others. She writes,

> [W]e have only found that Effect of the Load-stone [or magnet], as to draw Iron to it, but the Attracting motion is in obscurity, being Invisible to the Sense of Man, so that his reason can only Discourse, and bring Probabilities to Strengthen his Arguments, having no Perfect Knowledge in that, nor in any thing else; besides, that Knowledge we have of several things, comes as it were by Chance, or by Experience, for certainly, all the Reason man hath, would never have found out that one Effect of the Load-stone, as to draw Iron, had not Experience or chance presented it to us, nor the Effect of the Needle.[44]

Cavendish thinks that magnetic attraction is a mystery. Attraction is a matter of two things being apart from each other, and not touching, but still having an influence on one another. And attraction, she thinks, is not alone. There are many things that we say we understand, which we explain by appeal to general principles that we have noticed to obtain in nature, but where we do not understand why it is that those principles obtain and not some others. For example, the reason why a certain food is good for us, but not for some other organism, is that we have a different constitution, but we do not understand why our constitution reacts as it does. If we attempt to explain the reaction of our constitution by appeal to the behavior of the elements that make it up, Cavendish would point out that in the final analysis we do not understand why the elements behave like that—it is just a brute fact that they do. The same applies in other situations—we might try to explain the structural integrity of a table or chair in terms of the bonds that obtain between the molecules that compose the chair, or in terms of the bonds that obtain between the elements that compose the molecules, but in the end we have to say that these bonds are just there and that things exist that have basic features and capacities.[45] We say that we *understand* these things, Cavendish thinks, because they are familiar. She writes,

> [T]he Load-stone may work as various effects upon several Subjects as Fire, but by reason we have not so much Experience of one as the other, the Strangeness creates a Wonder, for the Old saying is, that Ignorance is the Mother of Admiration, but Fire, which produces greater Effects by Invisible motions, yet we stand not at such Amaze, as at the Load-stone, because these Effects are Familiar unto us.[46]

If Cavendish is right, there is "Natural Magick" all around us.[47] There are a lot of things that we do not understand, but we do not conclude on the basis of the fact that we do not understand them that they do not happen or do not exist. If so, it is no problem that we do not understand how or why matter thinks. Cavendish would argue that it is enough that we understand *that* it thinks.

33

This response gets problematic rather quickly. The response takes the form of insisting that there is no reason to suppose that reality is fully intelligible to us. Reality is as it is, and if there is an account of reality that makes the most sense to the human mind—even if it is one on which we could all agree—that just tells us which account makes the most sense to the human mind. It does not tell us what reality is like in its own right, and for all we know an accurate picture of reality is a picture that we cannot even fathom. A worry is that the more that we press this line of thought, the harder it is to see how we could ever settle on a picture of what reality is like. Presumably, we do not want to piece together a view that is *not* intelligible to us. That would be silly. We want a view that makes sense of reality, and that makes it make sense to us. When

Cavendish comes up with her own picture of reality, for example, she makes assumptions about the kinds of things that can partake of motion, and about the kinds of things with which bodies can interact. These are assumptions that make reality intelligible to her. But perhaps it is a brute inexplicable fact that immaterial minds can move or that minds and bodies can interact even if they have nothing in common.

34

Another argument for the view that minds are immaterial is similar to the argument from Leibniz, and it has been offered more recently by the philosophers Thomas Nagel and Frank Jackson. Nagel asks us to consider a situation in which we know all of the physiological facts about an organism that is significantly different from us—a bat. He argues that even if we uncovered all of these facts in the course of doing science, there would still be something that we did not know—what it is like to be a bat, or what it is like to have experiences from a bat's point of view. A bat navigates the world by sonar, and presumably its experiences are almost nothing like our own. So it appears that there is something that we would not know even if we knew all of the physiological facts about a bat, and even if we knew all of the physical facts about the universe. Nagel writes,

> If we acknowledge that a physical theory of mind must account for the subjective character of experience, we must admit that no presently available conception gives us a clue how this could be done. The problem is unique. If mental processes are indeed physical processes, then there is something it is like, intrinsically, to undergo certain processes. What it is for such a thing to be the case remains a mystery.[48]

Nagel says that strictly speaking we are not required to conclude that minds are not material. We can draw the weaker conclusion: at present, there is no conception of materialism that makes room for minds to be material, but we might converge on a more expansive conception later on.[49] But a question for Nagel is why that would still count as a version of materialism or physicalism if it is so differently conceived.

35

Jackson's argumentation is similar. He asks us to consider a hypothetical scenario in which a scientist (Mary) has been confined to a black-and-white laboratory all her life, and where she comes to learn all of the physical facts about reality. In a surprise moment she is allowed to go outside, and she sees red. She knows all of the physical facts about reality, but she learns something new (upon seeing red). Jackson writes,

> If physicalism is true, she [Mary] knows all that there is to know. For to suppose otherwise is to suppose that there is more to know than every physical fact, and that is just what physicalism denies. . . . When she is let out of the black-and-white room or given a color television, she will learn what it is like to see something red, say. This is rightly described as *learning*—she will not say "ho, hum." Hence, physicalism is false.[50]

Physical facts are not all that there is.[51]

36

Nagel and Jackson do not conclude that the universe contains immaterial substances. They just conclude that a complete physical description of the universe does not capture all that there is in the universe. At the very least, the universe contains features or properties that are not physical—things that a complete physical description leaves out. These might still be properties of the brain, and physical substances might be the only substances that exist, but in that case there would also exist nonphysical properties in addition to physical properties and physical substances.

37

There are a number of responses to the (very similar) reasoning set forward by Nagel and Jackson. One is that they are being presumptuous about what counts as physical. Perhaps there is a biological fact about certain bodies that when they interact in certain ways, they come to have qualities like mentality and awareness. If so, we might be inclined to say that Mary does *not* know all of the physical facts about the universe when she is in her black-and-white lab, and that we do not know all of the physiological facts about a bat unless we know what it is like to be a bat. Nagel or Jackson might respond that mental properties should be treated as a new kind of (immaterial) property because they are not reducible to or explicable in terms of the properties that are posited by the ideal scientist. The interesting question for this sort of response is about the criteria for deciding when properties are of a different kind. For example, one might argue that if mental properties are wholly dependent on the brain and nervous system—as in the case of Alzheimer's disease and anesthesia presumably—then mental properties should be classified as physical properties, even if they are very different from properties like size and shape and charge. Alternately, one might argue that because mental properties are very different from properties like size and shape and charge, and cannot be described in terms of them, mental properties are *not* physical. There is also a question of whether the various sides of the debate might be mostly in agreement. They might agree that mental properties are dependent on the brain and that they are not explicable in terms of qualities like size and shape and charge. Perhaps they just disagree about how mental states ought to be labeled.

Maybe thought just doesn't exist?

38

Some philosophers have insisted that we should stop using the language of "mind" altogether. The philosopher Paul Churchland has argued that we are radically misconceiving our mental life when we spell it out in terms of states like belief, desire, intention, and decision. To talk in such terms is messy and imprecise; we would have a more accurate understanding of our mental lives if we talked in terms of different categories instead. Churchland writes,

> Our common-sense psychological framework [according to which there are beliefs, desires, decisions, etc.] is a false and radically misleading conception of the causes of human behavior and the

nature of cognitive activity. On this view [*eliminative materialism*], folk psychology is not just an incomplete representation of our inner natures; it is an outright misrepresentation of our internal states and activities.[52]

Churchland thinks that we should eliminate our use of mental categories like belief and desire because they are misleading and because strictly speaking nothing answers to them. To make his point, he offers an analogy that compares nonexistent beliefs and desires to nonexistent witches:

> Psychosis is a fairly common affliction among humans, and in earlier centuries its victims were standardly seen as cases of demonic possession, as instances of Satan's spirit itself, glaring malevolently out at us from behind the victims' eyes. That witches exist was not a matter of any controversy. One would occasionally see them, in any city or hamlet, engage in incoherent, paranoid, or even murderous behavior. But observable or not, we eventually decided that witches do not exist. We concluded that the concept of a witch is an element in a conceptual framework that misrepresents so badly the phenomena to which it was standardly applied that literal application of the notion should be permanently withdrawn. Modern theories of mental dysfunction led to the elimination of witches from our serious ontology. . . . The concepts of folk psychology—belief, desire, fear, sensation, pain, joy, and so on—await a similar fate.[53]

Churchland is not denying that there have existed people who were called "witches." Those exist, but what does not exist is anything that corresponds to our idea of witch. We get a better and more accurate understanding of the phenomena in question if we just retire that notion. By the same token, we would get a better understanding of human behavior if we abandoned the notion of belief and desire. For example, it is hard to say for sure when someone has a particular belief or desire: we might ask the person himself what he believes or desires, but a person can be deluded about such things, and it is not clear that things get a lot more precise and accurate if we rely on the verdict of an outside observer. There seems to be a heavy amount of interpretation and filter in any such assessment. There is a lot at stake in making sense of our mental life, and the terms that we use to nail it down should not be a moving target.

39

An initial objection to the doctrine of eliminative materialism is that it is self-refuting. Presumably, Professor Churchland *believes* that the doctrine is true, in which case it would seem that it is false. Another way to put the objection would be to ask Professor Churchland if he can really deny the existence of such things as horrible pain. Or perhaps he has just been very lucky in life, but if so he would not be offering a theory that makes sense of the mental experience had by a regular human being. Churchland has a response to these sorts of objection. First, he would say that he does not believe that eliminative materialism is true. That does not mean that he thinks it is false, but just that he does not have beliefs about it because he holds that strictly speaking beliefs do not exist. Something exists that we have used the word "belief" to describe, and we just need to come up with a new and less sloppy way to talk about it. Churchland would say the same thing about the state that we call "pain." If he was wounded, he might scream out, but he would deny that he was screaming out *in pain*.

40

Another problem for eliminative materialism is that even if terms like "belief" and "desire" and "decision" are imprecise, the things that we use those words to describe would appear to be subjective and slippery and private, and so it is not clear that a new terminology would do much better. We do not want to impose a language on our mental life in order to make it neat and explicable if the neatness is not there to begin with. Professor Churchland might respond here that once we switch over to the new language, we will see the lay of the land very differently, and that what we thought was ineliminable messiness and subjectivity was never present at all. That would be to suppose that our use of language actually shapes the way that we take things in and that, if our language changed, our experience of the world and our own inner life would change with it.

Possible discussion exercises

1   What do you think is the best argument for the view that minds are physical? Why? What is the worst argument? Why?

2   What do you think is the best argument for the view that minds are not physical? Why? What is the worst argument? Why?

3   Do you think that it is correct to say that a mind moves along with the body to which it is connected?

4   Do you think that willpower is dependent on our brain physiology, the outside world, and on the food that becomes our body?

5   Is a mental illness or injury especially different from a physical illness or injury? Why or why not?

6   If mental states are wholly dependent on the brain, is it reasonable or fair to punish or reward people? What would a society look like that embraced the view that mental states are wholly dependent on the brain?

7   Do you think that the same exact cause can lead to different effects? Illustrate your response with an example. How is the question relevant to the relation between the brain and thinking?

8   It is a common presupposition among the historical philosophers that bodies are low-grade beings. Are there ways in which the presupposition is at work in popular culture? Are there ways in which the opposite presupposition is at work?

9   Do you think that bodies are impressive and sophisticated? Do you think that they are sophisticated enough that they can think?

10   It is a common presupposition among the historical philosophers that minds and mental activity are exalted. Are there ways in which the presupposition is at work in popular culture? Are there ways in which the opposite presupposition is at work?

11   What is an *explanation* for why one thing brings about another? Do you think there is an explanation for how brains could come to think?

12   Do computers *understand* anything? Do they think?

13   Do you think that thinking is ever unconscious? Do you think that a being could have no conscious states whatsoever but still be intelligent?

14   Are human beings autonomous and free in ways that the rest of the beings in nature are not?

15   Does it make a difference to say that minds are material rather than immaterial?

16   Are there any examples from science in which we had a term that we thought referred to something, but the thing turned out not to exist? Do such examples lend support to eliminative materialism?

17   Can you think of an example in which a person reports that they have a certain belief, but it turns out that they are mistaken? How about a desire?

18   Could we retain the word "witch" but just remember to detach all of its problematic connotations?

19   Come up with your own everyday example for one of the views or arguments or objections presented in this chapter.

Notes

1   This is an argument that might be offered by any philosopher attempting to square what we might call the "scientific conception of the universe" with the existence of minds. See, for example, John Searle, *Minds, Brains and Science*, Cambridge, MA: Harvard University Press (1984), ch. 1, and J. J. C. Smart, "Sensations and Brain Processes," *The Philosophical Review* 68 (1959), 141–56.

2   Margaret Cavendish, *Grounds of Natural Philosophy*, ed. Collette V. Michael, West Cornwall, CT: Locust Hill Press (1668/1996), 2. Cavendish was an English philosopher, novelist, playwright, and would-be scientist who wrote in the mid-seventeenth century. She

was not read very widely in her own time, and she was refused memberships in research groups like the Royal Society of London, but much of her work is studied today.

3 Cavendish, "Observations Upon the Opinions of Some the Ancient Philosophers," in *Observations Upon Experimental Philosophy*, 20.

4 Cavendish, *Observations Upon Experimental Philosophy*, 113. Note that in some cases the original Cavendish passages include spellings that are not used today.

5 Cavendish, *Philosophical Letters*, London (1664), 8.

6 Cavendish, *Philosophical Letters*, 185–6.

7 Lucretius, *On the Nature of Things*, trans. and ed. Anthony M. Esolen, Baltimore: Johns Hopkins University Press (1999), 33, 37, 95–6. Lucretius (approximately 99–50 BC) was a philosopher of Ancient Rome who argued that everything that exists is either matter or void.

8 Ibid., 95. There is a scene from the movie *Ghost* (1990) that attempts to illustrate this view.*

9 "Princess Elisabeth of Bohemia to René Descartes, 16 May 1643," in Andrea Nye, *The Princess and the Philosopher*, New York: Roman and Littlefield (1999), 9–10. Princess Elisabeth did not have much opportunity to be a recognized philosopher in the seventeenth century; her most well-known contributions appeared in her exchange of letters with Descartes. She was one of his most valuable correspondents, however. Descartes' *Passions of the Soul* is thought to be based on his exchanges with Elisabeth, and Descartes' masterpiece work *Principles of Philosophy* (CSM 1:179–291) is dedicated to her.

10 Cavendish, *Philosophical Letters*, 197, 207.

11 G. W. Leibniz, *Discourse on Metaphysics*, in Roger Ariew and Daniel Garber (trans. and eds), *G. W. Leibniz: Philosophical Essays*, Indianapolis: Hackett (1984), 46–7; Nicholas Malebranche, *The Search After Truth*, trans. and ed. Thomas Lennon and Paul Oscamp, Cambridge: Cambridge University Press (1674–5/1997), 446–52. Leibniz (1646–1716) was a German philosopher and mathematician. He is famous for inventing the calculus (contemporaneously with Isaac Newton) and for his long-standing debate with Newtonians about whether there is such a thing as absolute space. Malebranche was a French philosopher and priest who wrote in the second half of the seventeenth century. He is famous for the view that when we reflect upon ideas that are infinitely complex—for example, the idea of a mathematical or

geometrical infinite, or the idea of God—we are directly interfaced with the mind of God. That is the only mind that could house an infinity.

12 Julien Offray de la Mettrie, *Man Machine*, in Ann Thomson (trans. and ed.), *Man Machine and other Writings*, Cambridge: Cambridge University Press (1748/1996), 6–10. Mettrie (1709–51) was a French physician and sometime philosopher. He was especially interested in the study of apes and similarities between human behavior and sophisticated ape behavior.*

13 Ibid., 6–7.

14 Ibid., 8–9.

15 Another prominent (and tragic) case is that of Junior Seau.*

16 Bertrand Russell, *What I Believe*, New York: E. P. Dutton and Company (1925), 7.

17 Descartes, The Second Meditation, 16–18.

18 Jaegwon Kim, "Epiphenomenal and Supervenient Causation," *Midwest Studies in Philosophy* 9 (1984), 257–81. Jaegwon Kim is William Herbert Perry Faunce Professor of Philosophy at Brown University. He has written numerous books and articles on issues in the philosophy of mind, metaphysics, action theory, epistemology, and philosophy of science.

19 Alan Turing, "Computing Machinery and Intelligence," *Mind* 59 (1950), 433–60. Alan Turing was a British mathematician, computer scientist, and philosopher in the early twentieth century. He is often regarded as the founder of the fields of computer science and artificial intelligence. During World War II, he was very successful at decrypting the codes of the German military. In 1952 he was convicted of homosexuality (when it was still against the law in England). He died at age 41 of an apparent suicide.

20 John Searle is Slusser Professor of Philosophy at UC Berkeley. He has written 17 books and over 200 articles on issues in philosophy of language and philosophy of mind.

21 Searle, *Minds, Brains and Science*, ch. 2.

22 Ibid., 36. Note that the details of Searle's view on mind-brain relations are treated in the Chapter Six discussion of free will.

23 There is a terrific book that is dedicated to responses to the Chinese Room Argument. See John Preston and Mark Bishop (eds), *Views into the Chinese Room: New Essays on Searle and Artificial Intelligence*, Oxford: Clarendon Press (2002).

24 The Second Meditation, CSM 2:16–17.

25   Ibid., CSM 2:18.

26   *Fourth Replies*, CSM 2:171.

27   *Phaedo*, 78c–80b.

28   Descartes, The Sixth Meditation, 59.

29   *Phaedo*, 79a–b.

30   Descartes develops this view in *Fourth Replies*, CSM 2:171–2.

31   *Phaedo*, 85e–86c.

32   Ibid., 92d–93a.

33   *Phaedo*, 142, 101–3.

34   St Augustine, *On Free Choice of the Will*, trans. Thomas Williams, Indianapolis: Hackett (395/1993), 19, 27. St Augustine (354–430) was a philosopher in the Socratic-Platonic tradition and was Bishop of Hippo (which is present-day Annaba, Algeria). He is famous for his attempts to reconcile freedom with divine preordination, and is perhaps most famous for his proclamation—"Grant me chastity and continence, but not yet." This is in his *Confessions*, 8.7.17.

35   Plotinus, "On Beauty," in Elmer O'Brien (trans. and ed.), *Essential Plotinus: Representative Treatises from the Enneads*, Indianapolis: Hackett (1975), I.6, 37. Plotinus (204–70) was a philosopher in the Socratic-Platonic tradition and had a tremendous influence on St Augustine and on the development of Christian theology more generally.

36   Ibid., 37.

37   Ibid., 40.

38   Ibid., 39.

39   Ralph Cudworth, *The True Intellectual System of the Universe*, Stuttgard-Bad Cannstatt: F. Fromann Verlag (1678/1964), 858.

40   Ibid., 157–9.

41   Ibid., 155.

42   And of course she does. See, for example, "Observations Upon the Opinions of Some the Ancient Philosophers," in *Observations Upon Experimental Philosophy*, 16.

43   G. W. Leibniz, *Monadology*, in Roger Ariew and Daniel Garber (trans. and eds), *G. W. Leibniz: Philosophical Essays*, section 17. For similar reasoning, See Descartes, *Principles of Philosophy*, part I, section 53, and Nicolas Malebranche, *Dialogues on Metaphysics and on Religion*, trans. and ed. Nicholas Jolley and David Scott, Cambridge: Cambridge University Press (1997), 6.

44 Margaret Cavendish, *Philosophical and Physical Opinions*, London: Printed for William Wilson (1663), 191.

45 Ibid., 191–4.

46 Ibid., 194.

47 Cavendish, *Philosophical Letters*, 299.

48 Thomas Nagel, "What's it like to be a bat?," *The Philosophical Review* 83 (1974), 445–6. Professor Nagel is a philosopher at Princeton University. His arguments concerning subjectivity and consciousness have had a tremendous influence on philosophers who seek to use physics and other natural sciences to offer a complete description of reality.

49 Ibid., 446–7.

50 Frank Jackson, "What Mary Didn't Know," *The Journal of Philosophy* 83 (1986), 291. Professor Jackson is a philosopher at Australian National University and Princeton University. Jackson has changed his view actually, and now argues that the Mary thought experiment is not evidence that minds are immaterial. In part, he thinks that the evidence for the physicalistic scientific worldview is overwhelming and that our philosophical intuitions do not have the credentials to counter it. See Frank Jackson, "Mind and Illusion," in Anthony O'Hear (ed.), *Minds and Persons*, Cambridge: Cambridge University Press (2003), 251–71.

51 Another nice way to illustrate the Jackson thought experiment is through the 1998 movie *Pleasantville*, in which a town gradually changes from black-and-white to color.*

52 Paul Churchland, *Matter and Consciousness*, Cambridge, MA: MIT Press (1984), 43. Paul Churchland is Emeritus Professor of Philosophy at the University of California, San Diego. His research and teaching has focused on issues in philosophy of science, philosophy of mind, epistemology, philosophy of language, and the history of philosophy.

53 Ibid., 44.

CHAPTER FOUR

The meaning of life

Abstract

This chapter considers the following: whether a life dedicated to pleasure is the most fulfilling life possible, or if we also require meaning and significance; whether life can be meaningful if there are no objective values; whether life can be meaningful if God does not exist; and whether there would be meaning or significance in an immaterial afterlife or whether the afterlife would only be meaningful if it was pretty much like the life that we are living now.

Hedonism—the maximization of pleasure and the avoidance of pain

1

There are a number of different approaches to the question, "What is the meaning of life?" One is to treat the question as concerned to ask what is the most fulfilling sort of life an individual can lead. Another is to treat the question as asking what is the most valuable or significant life an individual can lead.

2

The ancient Greek philosopher Epicurus held that the most fulfilling life for an individual is to experience as much pleasure as possible and as little discomfort or pain. He writes,

> For it is to obtain this end that we always act, namely, to avoid pain and fear. . . . [W]e recognize pleasure as the first good innate in us, and from pleasure we begin every act of choice and avoidance, and to pleasure we return again, using the feeling by which we judge every good.[1]

Epicurus thinks that we should embrace the joint goal of pursuing pleasure and avoiding pain. We should not attempt to pursue every desire we have, as that would lead unfulfilled desires (and pain and frustration), but nor should we go to the extreme of avoiding all pleasure and subsisting in a neutral (but pain free!) state. A compromise position would be to locate desires that are extremely pleasurable to fulfill, but that are also easy to fulfill, so that we are constantly satisfied. For example, a person might have 50 desires that they can fulfill easily and to great pleasure, but they might have 50 other desires that are extremely difficult to fulfill. This person would have a desire satisfaction ratio of approximately 50/100, or perhaps 55/100, and they would also experience a good deal of pain. The person might try to improve the ratio by working harder to fulfill all one hundred of their desires, but if Epicurus is right, that would not be energy well spent. The person might instead attempt to disassociate from the 50 desires that cause them so much grief, and get to the point where their desire satisfaction ratio is 1:1. Epicurus writes,

> The wealth demanded by nature is both limited and easily procured; that demanded by idle imaginings stretches on to infinity.[2]

> To grow accustomed therefore to a simple and not luxurious diet gives us health to the full, and makes a man alert for the needful employments of life, and when after long intervals we approach luxuries disposes us better towards them, and fits us to be fearless of fortune.[3]

There might be simple pleasures that we do not give a chance because, being simple, we think they will not lead to a high level of satisfaction. Epicurus is worried that that judgment is hasty and that our expectations with respect to hard-to-fulfill desires are overblown. He offers an example of a good that we can easily overlook for the sake of goods that in reality do not compete:

> Of all the things which wisdom acquires to produce the blessedness of the complete life, far greatest is the possession of friendship.[4]

According to Epicurus the best life is one in which we experience sustained pleasure. Not all of our desires tend toward sustained pleasure, and so we have to be selective.

3

Some potential problems arise for Epicurus. One is that it is not clear that we have the sort of control over our desires that he is suggesting we have. If we have a strong desire, we can try to will the desire to go away, but that does not mean that it will happen. Perhaps Epicurus has in mind a process that is more gradual. Another potential objection is that even if he is right about the steps that a person should take to maximize pleasure and minimize pain, there might be more that we are seeking in the quest for a fulfilling life. That is, we might want our lives to have *value*, and to amount to something. However enjoyable an Epicurean life would be, it might also seem frivolous.

Stoicism—the benefits of going with the grain

4

A similar view of the most fulfilling life for human beings is in the work of the ancient Roman philosopher Epictetus. Epictetus agrees with Epicurus that we are going against the grain when we try so hard to fulfill all of our desires. Often, the world just does not cooperate. Instead of trying to change the world to be as we want it to be, we should try to like the world as it is:

> Do not seek to have events happen as you want them to, but instead want them to happen as they do happen, and your life will go well.[5]

If we do like the world just as it is—and if whatever happens is what we want to happen—then it is hard to see how we would ever be displeased. We would root for things to happen exactly as they do, and we would always get our way.

5

Epictetus offers a number of examples of ways in which our hopes and expectations about objects and situations and people lead us to disappointment and frustration. His central text, at least insofar as the material has survived through the ages, is *Encheiridion*, which translates to *handbook*. A follower of Epictetus might carry around the handbook and look to it for instruction when a difficult situation would arise. For example, the person might go to the public bathhouse and get frustrated at all the splashing. The handbook then serves a reminder:

> When you are about to undertake some action, remind yourself what sort of action it is. If you are going out for a bath, put before your mind what happens at baths—there are people who splash, people who jostle, people who are insulting, people who steal. And you will undertake the action more securely if from the start you say of it, "I want to take a bath and to keep my choices in accord with nature"; and likewise for each action.[6]

Epictetus says that we should have beliefs that are in accord with nature, or in accord with how things actually are. If our belief about a public bathhouse includes that it is the sort of place where everything is calm and quiet, then our belief is fictional. The desire to go to a bathhouse that is calm and quiet is like a desire to adopt a unicorn. If what we want is to go to a *bathhouse*, then we should temper our expectations accordingly. Epictetus offers other examples as well:

> In the case of everything attractive or useful or that you are fond of, remember to say just what sort of thing it is, beginning with the least little things. If you are fond of a jug, say "I am fond of a jug!" For then when it is broken you will not be upset.[7]

Epictetus thinks that if we get very upset at the destruction of an entity to which we are attached, we must have been supposing that the object was not fragile or that it was the sort of thing that could not be lost. But the things to which we tend to be attached— especially material objects—are not of that sort, and if we think that they are then our conceptions of such objects are fictional. Epictetus thinks that we would be best off if our expectations could be stoic and measured even with respect to the loss of loved ones.[8]

6

Epictetus is emphasizing that one of the main causes of frustration and unhappiness in a human life is our judgments and expectations. He says that if we bracket these judgments, we can handle anything that comes our way—with a sort of cognitive armor. Even the insults and cruelty of other people can be embraced with a kind of joy:

> Remember that what is insulting is not the person who abuses you or hits you, but the judgment about them that they are insulting. So when someone irritates you be aware that what irritates you is your own belief. Most importantly, therefore, try not to be carried away by appearance.[9]

> When someone acts badly toward you or speaks badly of you, remember that he does or says it in the belief that it is appropriate for him to do so. Accordingly he cannot follow what appears to you but only what appears to him, he is harmed as much as he has been deceived. . . . Starting from these considerations you will be gentle with the person who abuses you. For you must say on each occasion, "That's how it seemed to him."[10]

Here Epictetus is arguing that the behavior of other people is guided by how they see their situation, the information that they have available, their prior beliefs, etc. People see things as they see them, and to see things differently they would have to have different information or different prior beliefs, but in that case they would also be seeing things as they see them, just differently. In dealing with others, we should not take insults personally, but take a more informed perspective in which we have command of the larger story. If Epictetus is right, we can get to the point where we never feel hatred, disappointment, sadness, or frustration.

7

Epictetus also offers some very useful advice for dealing with relatives. We all know the sort of conflict that can ensue at a reunion or over the course of a holiday like Thanksgiving. Appealing to his stoicism, Epictetus thinks that if we fight and argue with people who are unlikely to change, we will just get more frustrated. Indeed, to the extent that there *is* any chance that a person might change, we would need to be more pliable. Epictetus writes,

> Everything has two handles, one by which it may be carried and the other not. If your brother acts unjustly toward you, do not take hold of it by this side, that he has acted unjustly (since this is the handle by which it may not be carried), but instead by this side, that he is your brother and was brought up with you, and you will be taking hold of it in the way that it can be carried.[11]

Here we might call to mind the example of the Chinese Finger Puzzle: we insert our fingers into opposite ends of the tube, and they get stuck; but if we try to pull our fingers out, they get stuck even more. The only way to remove our fingers is to push them in further.

8

We all have our own examples of relatives and friction. An example in my own case is when my dad once called me at 6.00 a.m. local time to inquire about the remodeling work that was underway at my house. A new bedroom (along with a bath) was to be built above our garage, and my dad had stayed up all night worrying about whether the contractors remembered to put enough supports on the garage ceiling to support the new weight. He said, "Make sure that they add a couple of very thick beams, because sometimes they don't do that, and the whole house comes crashing down." I had really two options on how two proceed. First, I could have taken issue with my dad and told him that I was a grown-up, and that it was really insulting that he thought that I would hire someone so foolish. I am also a little embarrassed to say that I had had the same thought at one point—after all, I am his son—and I had asked the contractor (but very diplomatically) what kind of support would need to be added to the ceiling when previously it had just supported a roof. So I could have had a big fight with my dad about how he was overbearing and about how he was also selling me short. The second option was to just accept that my dad is my dad. He called at 6.00 a.m. local time, which was 4.00 a.m. Las Vegas time, and he insisted that he waited to call until 6.00 because that was the earliest possible time that was still within the range of respectful. My dad is a person who is extremely accomplished and has a tremendous number of strengths, but he also struggles, and I think about what it must be like to be someone who gets so worried about things like garage ceilings. He sees disaster where there is none to be had, and that must be a burden. I could try to force him to not worry so much, but that would not be effective. Even if somehow it was effective, the new person would not be him any more, and I wanted to have a relationship with *my dad*. So I thanked him for calling and mentioned that I had thought of his concern also, and then we talked about our plans and goals for the rest of the day.

9

Epictetus thinks that there is a kind of harmony and joy that comes with filling in the complete story of how and why things unfold in the way that they do. Our fictional beliefs are neutralized, and it makes sense to us why things happen exactly as they do:

But what do I want? To learn and understand nature and follow it.[12]

Whoever has complied well with necessity
Is counted wise by us, and understands divine affairs.[13]

We can consider some examples. A person notices a parking spot
that is available on a busy street, but is momentarily disturbed
when she sees a sign on the meter that says "No Parking Today."
She yells—"This stinks! If the sign was not there, I could have
parked." Then she realizes that if the sign had not been there,
someone else would have already taken the spot—given that it is
such a busy street. Then she notices that the sign indicates that the
spot is saved for construction vehicles. She remembers that streets
and sidewalks are made of material that requires upkeep, and if
repairs are not done, streets and sidewalks will not be there for
us to use for our many goals and aims. In addition, if a spot was
not reserved for construction vehicles, the workers would have to
park far away, and the repairs would take much longer, interfering
with our goals yet again. The person who was initially upset at not
getting the spot now appreciates the larger causal story, and is very
happy that the spot is not available. She continues in the search for
a different spot, having a richer experience all the while.

10

Another example might be a person who is driving by the local
hospital at 5.00 p.m., stuck in traffic. The person becomes angry
at the holdup, and at the thought of all the hospital employees who
are leaving work at the same peak time. He wishes that the hospital
shifts could end at 3.00 p.m., so that his commute would be more
fluid. But then he thinks about how the workers would need to start
work at 6.00 a.m. if they were to get a full shift, or how they would
otherwise need to work reduced hours. If the hospital restricted its
employee pool to workers who were willing to start at 6.00 a.m. or
work a half-day, some of the best employees would take the option
of working at a different hospital. But it is important to have a
hospital that offers high-quality health care. The man stuck in
traffic rejoices, and his drive home is more rich and interesting. He
even understands why his initial reaction of anger and frustration
had to happen, given the combination of variables that were in play
at the moment that the reaction occurred.

11

Some potential problems emerge for Epictetus. One concerns his view that other people can only act in the light of how things appear to them. Each of us is the "other person" in the eyes of someone else, and so the view would appear to apply to all of us and in particular to the ability that we have to adopt any of Epictetus' recommendations. If it appears to us that it is a good idea to take Epictetus seriously, then we will, but otherwise it just is not in the cards. There are also worries about Epictetus' view that we should minimize our attachments to the point that we can be okay with the loss of our loved ones. Perhaps he would say that this is just an ideal, and that human beings should be stoic with respect to their inability to achieve it. But it can be hard to see how an Epictetan life would be especially exciting or fulfilling. We would not have many lows, but at the same time there would not be a lot of passion.

12

There is a more moderate version of Epictetus' view that would seem more practical. Individuals in the business world have adopted stoicism as a tool for staying focused and calm when a plan comes undone or when a situation goes haywire. This idea is this: if we get very discombobulated, and we dwell on our prior expectations of what should have been or could have been, we can lose sight of what actually happened and why, and we can lose sight of how to fix it.* Epictetus would also say that stoicism is of use in maximizing our own individual potential. We all have different strengths and talents, but some of us wish that our strengths and talents were different from what they are. If we have a realistic sense of what we can and cannot do—and of the abilities in us that can be nurtured and the abilities that we will never have—we will be less frustrated, and we will not be neglecting our true potential.[14]

13

Another view of the most fulfilling life for human beings appears in the work of the philosopher Martin Heidegger. It is difficult to make Heidegger's view intelligible without a discussion of embodied intelligence—and the view that matter is extremely sophisticated when left to its own devices—so Heidegger's view will be considered at the end of Chapter Five.

Meaning and significance as essential components of a fulfilling life

14

Some philosophers have argued—contra Epicurus and Epictetus— that an important component of personal fulfillment is to be found in a life that exhibits meaning, value, and significance. The philosopher Susan Wolf has proposed a view along these lines.[15] Wolf does not necessarily have anything against a life that is focused on avoiding frustration or satisfying desires. She just thinks that one of the things that we also want in life is *meaning*. But she has to be careful not to be too specific about what will generate meaning—she does not want to just look at the lives that she herself would regard as meaningful and insist that they are supposed to be a model for everyone. And the world would presumably not be that interesting if we restricted ourselves to such a small number of activities only. Instead, Wolf wants to consider paradigm cases of lives that we would all tend to regard as meaningful, and then locate the kinds of features that those lives have in common. She uses some playful examples to illustrate her case.

15

One condition that Wolf thinks we have in mind when we identify a life as meaningful is that the person living it be excited about, and actively engaged in, some set of projects. To make her case, Wolf has us consider the extreme of a person who is not excited or actively engaged—a person who sits on the couch all day drinking beer and watching whatever it is that happens to come on the television.[16] Wolf has to set up the example very carefully, so that she is not making a reckless judgment about beer or TV. The person that she has in mind is somewhat drunk and in a daze, and they are not particularly invested in the shows that they watch. This person is dubbed "The Blob." We could imagine a very different sort of case, where a person would not be a Blob: the case of a person who is very excited to watch television, and who gets excited to watch some shows rather than others. This (very different) person keeps track of the particular aspects of the television world that concern him. He communicates about that world with people who are like-minded; he might even keep a journal or blog. The person might also be discriminating about which beer they drink. This is not Wolf's Blob, and we might call him instead "Blobe." An unfortunate feature of Wolf's own example is that because "The Blob" is a beer-drinking television-viewer, she might appear to be suggesting that any life along those lines is the life of a Blob. Wolf realizes this and remarks,

> Not that I have anything against television or beer. Still, the image [of the Blob], understood as an image of a person whose life is lived in hazy passivity, a life lived at a not unpleasant level of consciousness, but unconnected to anyone or anything, going nowhere, achieving nothing—is, I submit, as strong an image of meaninglessness as there can be.[17]

Wolf is using the example to emphasize that a life of passivity and disinterest is not one that we would typically identify as significant or fulfilling. She might have also used the example of the person who frequents an art museum, and who is not excited about or invested in the activity, but does it just because that is a thing that people do.

16

We might object that if a person likes sitting in front of the television all day, and watching whatever might happen to come on, then that person is living a life that is significant to them. The objection is fair enough, but Wolf is trying to manufacture the case in such a way that the Blob in question does not even find their life particularly significant, from their own point of view. If the person insists that they prefer such a life, that is fine, it just means that they are not especially concerned about meaning. The Blob might be doing what they prefer to do, and they might not want to do anything else, but as Wolf is setting up the case their projects do not matter much to them.

17

Another criterion that Wolf thinks we have in mind when we speak of a person as living a meaningful life is that the person have some goal or goals that they see as having long-term value, and that their everyday pursuits contribute to these. Wolf considers the case of a whimsical person who is active, but who does not regard their pursuits as especially sacred:

> In contrast to the Blob's passivity, for example, we may imagine a life that is full of activity, but silly or decadent or useless activity. (And again, I have nothing against silly activity, but only against a life that is wholly occupied with it.) We may imagine, for example, one of the idle rich, who flits about, fighting off boredom, moving from one amusement to the other. She shops, she travels, she eats at expensive restaurants, she works out with her personal trainer.[18]

This might be a person who goes on a shopping spree one day, and then gets on a plane to Europe the next, and who just jumps from activity to activity. This is a person who never regards her current activity as especially significant, but instead sees it as highly disposable. She does not regard it as sufficiently valuable to be worthy of commitment for the long haul.[19] As Wolf is crafting the case, the person does not take her activities to be important in their own right, nor does she have a larger goal that she takes to be sacred and which these activities are working in concert to achieve. Wolf dubs this extreme character "The Useless." This is a person who unlike the Blob is excited about their pursuits and projects. The person likes to shop on the day that she does it, and she is excited as she lands at the airport as well.

18

As we did in the case of the Blob, we could conjure an alternative version of the person who shops or travels. This person ("Yoseless") might be very passionate about the aesthetics of clothes and the latest developments in fashion. They might read magazines about the world of clothes and accessories, and the different personalities that inhabit it. If for some reason the person is no longer able to shop, or to read about fashion, they experience a real sense of loss. The person (as an analogue of the Useless) might incorporate travel into their life as well. Perhaps they go once or twice a year to a place that is connected to some of their interests; perhaps they travel to Italy to see a fashion show or to do a workshop with a groundbreaking designer. So described, the person's activities would matter to her, and they would matter enough that the person would not cast them aside for other projects at whim. She would be involved in the finite number of projects that are extremely important to her and be able to give each of these projects its due.

19

A third criterion that Wolf thinks we have in mind when we identify a life as meaningful is that the person living it is to some degree successful at the pursuits to which they are committed. She offers the example of the scientist who works his whole life to find a cure for a disease, but ends up failing. She dubs this sort of case, "The Bankrupt." Another example might be a person who is very committed to becoming a professional figure skater, or artist, or comedian, or writer. If the person is not sufficiently talented to succeed at their chosen goal, or if circumstances otherwise get in the way, their life would not be nearly as meaningful as if they were successful. There might be exceptions—for example, the scientist who describes their project as getting closer to a cure for a disease, where they make progress, and where the next generation finishes the job. Wolf would presumably argue that to the extent that these lives are meaningful, they are not in fact bankrupt. Or a person might fail to achieve certain long-term goals, but as a result of their efforts they might be successful at related ventures.

20

Wolf is supposing that one of the things that comes with meeting the first three criteria for a meaningful life is an *experience* of meaning or value. A person who lives a meaningful life is actively immersed in their pursuits; they take them to have long-term value and not to be disposable; and the person is (at least somewhat) successful at them. Wolf thinks that there is also another criterion that we have in mind when we speak of a life as meaningful: the person engages in projects that actually have value.[20] One of the things that is common to the life of Blobe and Yoseless is that both have an experience of significance. But a person can have an experience of significance when their life is not significant at all. To delineate the distinction between the two, imagine (if we can return to some material from Chapter One) that Blobe and Yoseless have been hooked up to a Matrix machine for their entire lives. They have not been doing the things that they believe they have been doing, and their entire lives are a lie. But while they are in the machine, they certainly have an *experience* of their lives as meaningful and significant. There is then a separate question about whether or not a life in the machine is significant or meaningful in fact.

21

Or we might think of other (and less science-fictional) ways in which a person's life might be a lie but in which they still have an experience of meaning. We can imagine a person whose wife has been cheating on him for years, and everyone seems to know it, but he does not know it himself. He feels loved and happy and fulfilled, but there might be a separate question about whether the life that he is leading is actually meaningful or significant. Or we can imagine a mass-murderer who is fulfilled by torturing and killing the innocent. This person might have an experience of meaning and significance, as presumably did Hitler, but we are inclined to say that the life led by Hitler was not in fact meaningful. It is not the appropriate sort of life to select if what we are seeking is a life of meaning and value. Wolf wants to isolate the *experience* of significance as one feature of a meaningful life, in part to show that it is not all that we are after when we are after a life of meaning.

22

Wolf is proposing that part of what we have in mind when we speak of a life as meaningful is that the life produces or exhibits actual value.[21] Her other criteria might seem uncontroversial in comparison. For example, she has not put a limit on which activities people can be actively engaged in, and she has not specified what activities people will find worthy of commitment for the long haul. Instead, she includes a broad range of activities that range from helping the poor and engaging in social activism to pursuits that appear to have nonmoral value, like painting, writing, becoming good at golf, and winning an Olympic medal.[22] Nor does Wolf suggest that any of these are more able than the others to deliver an experience of meaning. There will be constraints on how a person goes about meeting the three criteria, but these constraints will be set by the world and by a person's talents and abilities. A person who is very uncoordinated will probably not have a meaningful life as a dancer. They would not be able to perform their central activity very well, and they would probably not enjoy it very much and so not have an experience of meaning. They might be wise to commit to something else instead. Or a person might be really good at math, but hate every minute of it. In that case the person would be burdened with a tremendous amount of skill and talent at an activity that they despise, and it is likely that they would not have an experience of meaning in building a life around it. Instead, they might pursue something else that they are good at, but perhaps less good at, and that they to some degree enjoy. Or perhaps they would need to do what they hate in order to pay the bills, and attempt to leave space and time for other activities that are not on the clock. If we find ourselves in an environment in which there is no way for us to meet Wolf's first three criteria—perhaps we want to be a witch-doctor or sword-swallower or nudist—we would probably have to locate another environment instead.

23

Wolf wants her first three criteria to be broad enough to capture all the projects and pursuits that are able to provide human beings an experience of meaning and significance. She adds, however, that

> The exception I would make to this otherwise maximally tolerant interpretation of the idea of positive value is that we exclude merely subjective value as a suitable interpretation of the phrase.[23]

The fourth criterion that Wolf thinks we have in mind when we identify a life as meaningful is that the life actually be valuable or important. That is, it is not enough that a person just have an experience of meaning or significance. Here Wolf is attempting to make sense of a sort of epiphany that is possible—where we notice that even though our lives have seemed meaningful to us, they have been a lie, and they were not meaningful.[24] If we can make a distinction between a life that is experienced as meaningful and a life that is actually meaningful, then we can say that there is more to a life that has both of these than there is to a life that has just the one. The trick of course is how we tell that our lives actually have value, and not just that we experience them as having value. Presumably all that we have to go on is our experience. However, human beings can be very deluded. Plenty of people throughout history have been certain that they were doing something important and significant, where we would want to say that they were mistaken. Hitler is the obvious example that comes to mind, but in addition there have also been slave-owners who thought they were maximizing productivity in a way that would be pleasing to God, and (if this could make it any worse) slave-owners who would separate parents and children at the time of purchase, all in keeping with "the good." By extension of reasoning, there might be things that we think are virtuous today—at the moment when we are assessing whether or not a particular life is worth leading—but that later will be recognized to be beyond the pale. Wolf thinks that we have a pretty good ability to tell which pursuits are valuable and which are not, but we might be wrong, and so a worry (as in Chapter Two) is whether or not our faculty for detecting value and importance is significantly more fallible than the other faculties that we have. If anyone has any good ideas on how to resolve this worry, please let me know.

The desirability of our desires

24

Another issue that arises in addressing the criteria that Wolf proposes is that there can be a distinction between the desires and interests that we in fact have, and desires and interests that we do not have but that we would prefer to have or that it would be more satisfying for us to have. The philosopher Friedrich Nietzsche spends a lot of time thinking about this distinction. He recognizes that there are things that we pursue and care about, but he worries that there might be other things that it would be more valuable for us to care about, and whose pursuit would better fulfill our needs and our nature. He proposes that we engage a critique of our values:

> So let us give voice to this *new demand*: we need a critique of moral values, *the value of these values should itself, for once, be examined.* . . . People have taken the value of these "values" as given, as factual, as beyond all questioning. . . . What if a regressive trait lurked in the "good man," likewise a danger, an enticement, a poison, a narcotic, so that the present *lived at the expense of the future*? Perhaps in more comfort and less danger, but also in a smaller minded, meaner manner? . . . So that morality itself were to blame if man, as species, never reached his *highest potential power and splendor*?[25]

We can imagine some commonsensical cases in which a person has a value that it is not valuable for them to have. A person might place a lot of value on the practice of telling people exactly what is on their mind the moment that it occurs to them, but this practice could lead to trouble down the road, and interfere with the person's other goals and pursuits. Alternately, a person might be a control freak who refuses to enter into activities in which he cannot easily see what is coming next. This would preclude many kinds of social interaction, and also preclude attempts to dive into activities that are unfamiliar and new. If the person also wants company and companionship, he might feel very isolated. He would be like the person who has dropped his keys in the bushes but who looks for them under the streetlight: he is getting some of what he needs, but not really. Nietzsche is concerned to critique Western values more generally, in which (he thinks) there is an emphasis on the value of the mind and soul over the body, and a corresponding devaluation of impulse and passion.[26] He thinks that we all have passions and impulses, and that we recognize that we would be more fulfilled to act on these, but we repress them for the sake of safety, security, and convention. This sort of repression would presumably take a toll, where maybe 40 percent of our energy is repressed, another 40 percent is used to repress it, and the other 20 is a twisted and truncated remainder. Nietzsche thinks that our values are doing us a disservice and that they are not particularly valuable.

25

More recently, the philosopher Harry Frankfurt has worked to flesh out a closely related distinction—between desires that we in fact have and desires that we do not have but that we would like to have.[27] He notes that any given person will have a lot of desires and that these are a source of motivation and pull—for example, a desire to eat pizza, or to smoke, or to go to the gym. But sometimes we lack a desire that we wish we had, or we have a desire that we wish would go away. We might not have any desire to go to the gym, for example, but we realize that it would be good for us to be healthy and that it would be a lot easier to go the gym if we actually wanted to. We might hate to read or study, but we are students and we realize that we would be better off if we actually *liked* to study. Then we could study more efficiently, and without all of the frustrating distractions. Or we might want to stop smoking and wish that we did not have the desire for nicotine. Or perhaps we do not smoke, but every day at work we feel left out when the smokers go out for a break. If only I liked smoking, we might think to ourselves, and it did not make me cough or feel ill.[28]

26

Frankfurt calls a "first-order desire" any desire that we actually have and that provides us with some motivation to act. A "second-order desire" is a desire to have our desires be a certain way.[29] For example, it is a desire to have a desire that we do not already have, or a desire to have a stronger version of a desire that we do already have. It can also be a desire to extinguish a desire that we have, or to take a desire that we already have and make it weaker.

27

With the recognition that (for example) we would like to have the desire to go to the gym, we might take steps to obtain that desire. Perhaps we ask a friend to accompany us to the gym for the first ten visits, so that the experience is less unpleasant, where we can talk with someone we know and feel assured that a person is there to block the door. By that point there might be things about the gym that we have come to enjoy, or perhaps we have more energy and feel more alive. If so, we have succeeded in developing a desire to go to the gym. Initially we had a "first-order" desire not to go to the gym, but then we had a "second-order" desire—a desire to have the desire to go to the gym. With effort and luck the second-order desire is successful and we have the desire that we wanted to have.

28

Frankfurt is worried primarily about an issue of integrity that arises if we take our first-order desires at face-value. The worry is that if we do not choose our first-order desires, but they are just a given, and we accept them uncritically, then we do not care what motivates us to act.[30] Frankfurt says of such a person that "he is not concerned with the desirability of his desires themselves."[31] If we had no say in our desires, we could still have what Frankfurt calls "freedom of action," or the ability to do what we want to do. That is, we might be free in the sense that we could do what we desire, without interference or obstruction, but that does not mean that we would have freedom over our will, or control over what we desire itself. In particular, it does not mean that we would have control over which of our (first-order) desires are strongest and characteristically guide our behavior. We need to have *some* desires if we are going to be motivated to do anything, but if we do not step back and take a stand on which desires these are, we are basically saying: give me a desire, any desire, and I will act on it. If we do not step back and evaluate our desires for their desirability, then our behavior and trajectory are being determined by forces over which we had no say.

29

Frankfurt uses the term "volition" (and sometimes the term "will") to refer to our strongest first-order desire. That is to say, a volition is our strongest first-order desire on any given occasion, the one that wins out. Volitions are an important component of our behavior, and so these should be important to us as well. It should matter to us which of our desires are strongest and tend to translate into action.

30

A nice example is from the movie *Defending Your Life* with Albert Brooks. The main character has a lifelong history of backing down in the face of confrontation. In the movie, he has just been offered a job, and he wants his annual salary to be $65,000. However, he knows that he will cave if his boss offers him something less, and so he practices the negotiation at home with his wife. If he is not in the heat of the moment, he can acquire discipline and practice, and he can take steps to overcome his weakness. He does well in "rehearsal," and he is finally ready for real life.* His boss sits across from him at work and says, "Daniel, I am prepared to offer you forty-nine thousand." Daniel immediately reaches his hand across the table and says, "I'll take it."

31

We might imagine a similar case in which a person has a habit of saying awkward things in social situations, but they practice at home to increase the odds that they get things right. In the heat of the moment, they say to the person in whom they are romantically interested, "I like your hat. I have seen it all over town. I think that everybody has one, and I think I even saw them at the store in a gigantic bin." Afterwards the person might beat himself up: "why do I keep doing that?" Presumably it is possible for a person to override their strongest desire on any occasion, but in the heat of the moment this can be very hard to do, and it would be nice if the desires and motivations that won out on each occasion were desires and motivations that we fully endorsed. Frankfurt would also allow that there are cases where we are in the heat of the moment and we are able to override a desire on which we are about to act, but he would say that that just means that the overriding desire was in fact the stronger.

32

A second-order desire is a desire to have a desire. We can have a desire to have a fairly weak desire—for example, I might be a better parent to my daughter if I could understand the politics of the princess game that she plays at school, and for that I might want to develop some amount of desire to play the princess game myself. I would not want that to be my strongest desire, however. To use an example that Frankfurt presents, a psychologist might be better able to help her drug-addicted patient if she had some sense of what it was like to feel the pull of a drug, but she would not want to become an addict herself. So we might call a *second-order inclination* a desire to have a desire that is not strong enough to lead to behavior. A second-order volition is a desire to have a desire that is so strong that it is effective and wins out.[32] Frankfurt thinks that it is important to have second-order volitions and also second-order inclinations so that we are taking a stand on what motivates us. The person who has these desires and is able to come to have the inclinations and volitions that they seek—they have control over their motivations.

33

Frankfurt thinks that we have more integrity—and that we retain our place above animals—if we are not just guided by whatever desires we happen to find ourselves with. But Frankfurt does not get into much detail about how an individual should go about updating their desires. He is not interested in how we step back and assess our desires; it just matters that we do it. Presumably, he wants to avoid the situation where he is telling people what desires they should have and what they should find fulfilling. But there are some fairly general things that we might try to say, in the spirit of Frankfurt's view.

34

One is that a person who steps back to assess their first-order desires might realize that there are other desires that they would find more fulfilling to satisfy. For example, a couple might never have had any interest in camping, opting to spend weekends at home. But their grandson provides the impetus to give camping a try. They do it, and it turns out that they enjoy it more than most of the things that they had been doing before. They might find themselves back at home a few weekends later, not able to work up the energy to go on another trip. But they remember how much they enjoyed it. They force themselves to take a few more trips, and in time they can barely get enough. Another example might be a male who has always thought that ballet is for sissies, and so has never tried it. He gives it a chance and finds that he is much better at dancing than at the other things he has been doing, and that he gets more mileage out of it as well. Still he might have some difficult negotiating to do in other parts of his life.

35

Another benefit of stepping back to take inventory of our desires is that we might come to have a tighter core of desires that are more integrated and that we can more wholly fulfill. Perhaps we have so many desires right now that we cannot fulfill them all, and we always feel a sense of loss and dissatisfaction. Or maybe we have to spread ourselves so thin that in order to attend to all of our desires we cannot spend a sufficient amount of time in pursuit of any of them. An analogy is the case of a child who has a bunch of posters up in their room, representing an extremely wide variety of interests and concerns. There might be featured a rock star, a basketball player, an actor, a destination like the grand canyon, a Disney character, some animals, and a host of other things. If there are too many of these, it is hard to see how the child could really be into all of them. The child would not be able to incorporate all of them into their life without giving some of them short shrift. So the child might do some pruning. Or perhaps this is a better proposal for a grown-up. If a person could cut back on their interests and have a collection of posters that is more finite, where some of the themes are more integrated and overlapping, they would be more immersed in all that they do. There may be a lot of unpleasantness in the world, but there is more than enough that is rosy and that could fill a life to the brim.

36

Wolf argues that part of what we have in mind when we identify a life as meaningful is a life in which a person is actively engaged in projects that they take to be of value for the long haul. A consideration of the Frankfurt material is relevant because we might attempt to meet Wolf's criteria by considering the desires and interests that we already have, but in fact we might be more fulfilled if we had second-order desires and were successful in our pursuit of them. Note that Wolf's view is put so generically that I have been assuming that some version of it must be pretty close to correct. She is saying that we would have an experience of meaning and significance in a life in which we are excited about our projects, we see them as having value for the long haul, and we are at least somewhat successful at them. She does not attempt to specify exactly what sorts of projects give us that sense of meaning, and she is aware that her fourth criterion (that our projects exhibit actual value) is controversial.

37

Another benefit of having second-order desires is that they can help us to bring our ethical principles into line with our first-order desires and first-order volitions. For example, perhaps there is a sort of charity work that we have always said is important to us, but we never made the time. Or a person might worry a lot about poverty, and wish that they had a stronger desire to help the less fortunate. Or a person might hold instead that the best thing to do for the impoverished is to leave them alone to help themselves. Still, this person might succumb to a sentimental feeling of sympathy in the face of a homeless family. The person might wish that they were not overwhelmed by their sympathy—they might wish that instead of giving in and offering money to the family, they could summon the composure to tell them very clearly and concisely why they should not be begging, or tell the family where they could go for help to get back on their feet. Generally speaking, we might feel more consistent and whole if we adjusted our first-order desires in line with our ethical principles. Alternately, we might retain our first-order desires and acknowledge that our ethical principles are different from what we thought. I used to think that I cared a lot about the environment, but I have come to recognize that I care a lot more about the convenience of driving a car to work. I do feel bad though about my colleague who rides his bike, even in winter, especially when he ends up behind me and has to breathe in my exhaust.

38

One of the ways in which Wolf's position is controversial is that it leaves open that a life can be fully meaningful even if God does not exist.[33] If God does exist, then presumably we are given a purpose, and we would locate that purpose by noticing some activity that we enjoy and are able to do well. We would take that to be our calling. If God does not exist, we would not have an explicit purpose, but as long as we had a skill or talent that we could exercise with intensity and joy, and our efforts promoted value, we would be in pretty much the same position. Wolf's view is controversial because, if she is right, our lives have just as much chance at being meaningful whether God exists or not. Or that is a little too strong. If God exists, there might be more of a guarantee that each of us would have a skill or talent that it would be fulfilling for us to exercise and whose exercise would bring about good. If God does not exist, our talents and skills would be due more to our physiology, and we would have to hope that there is at least one activity that is value-adding and that we could perform well and enjoy. We should recall at this point that Wolf's view depends on the assumption that there is such a thing as objective value and that human beings have the wherewithal to detect it.

The relative significance of mind versus matter

39

A very different view of the most fulfilling human life is advanced by Socrates. He argues that the best life is one that emphasizes spiritual and intellectual activity over embodiment. The basic idea is that intellectual activity is more exalted than embodied activity and hence that that is the sort of activity in which we ought to engage. We have already considered some of the arguments for the view that minds are higher grade beings than bodies. There are additional arguments that we might consider as well.

40

One is that there are perfect objects that we are able to conceive and that these are far superior to the physical things that surround us. We can think of idealizations, for example, and argue that actual bodies always fall short of them. Socrates focuses on our idea of equality. He notes that when we speak of the equality of two things, we are talking not just about the two things but also about a third thing—their *equality*. He writes,

> We say that there is something that is equal. I do not mean a stick equal to a stick or a stone to a stone, or anything of that kind, but something else beyond these, the Equal itself.

He then asks how we acquire this idea of equality. It is not by observing things that are equal, because no two things that we observe are exactly equal. Two sticks or stones might be very similar, but there will always be some slight difference between them, at least at some level of observation. Socrates continues,

> In the case of equal sticks and the other equal objects we just mentioned . . . . Do they seem to us to be equal in the same sense as what is Equal itself? Is there some deficiency in their being such as the Equal, or is there not?[34]

Perfect equality is something that we all know, and strictly speaking no physical objects are exactly equal. We can think of other perfections as well—for example, perfect beauty and perfect goodness. We can also think of perfect circles and squares, and perfect mathematical entities. These idealizations never change. Actual bodies always fall at least a little bit short of them, and actual bodies *do* change. Nor do bodies last forever. But two and two are equal to four at all times, whether there are minds there to think about it or not. Perfections are therefore not physical. As Socrates had said in arguing that minds are indivisible and eternal and divine, bodies are imperfect, finite, and multiform.[35] Immaterial things are the highest grade entity, and so the best life is one that attends to these as much as possible. We engage in intellectual activities that are spiritual and pure, in the company of other minds.[36]

41

A potential worry is whether the idealizations that Socrates is highlighting really are perfect, and whether physical things really pale in comparison to them. An alternative explanation to account for our ideas of idealizations is that we observe particular physical objects—sticks or stones—and then we imagine better and better versions of them.[37] That would be to say that we do not have the ideas that Socrates says that we do, and that (for example) our best idea of a triangle or equality is only as good as we can picture in our mind. If we have done a lot of geometry, though, it is easy to feel the pull of Socrates' position.

42

Another argument for the view that physical objects are low-grade entities is that they do not admit of much certainty or knowledge. Socrates writes,

> Then what about the actual acquiring of knowledge? Is the body an obstacle when one associates with it in the search for knowledge? I mean, for example, do men find any truth in sight or hearing, or are not even the poets forever telling us that we do not see or hear anything accurately, and surely if those two physical senses are not clear or precise, our other senses can hardly be accurate, as they are all inferior to these? Do you not think so?[38]

Socrates is not suggesting that the senses are useless for acquiring information. He is pointing out instead that that information is always imprecise. Our senses can mislead us, but even at their best the knowledge that they secure is never exact. Socrates wants to contrast this with the knowledge that we get in disciplines like mathematics and geometry, where our knowledge *is* exact. Knowledge itself is something very important, and knowledge of the highest and most perfect sorts of entity is not had through the senses but through "purely mental scrutiny."[39] As St Augustine puts it,

> knowledge is a higher and more genuine sort of life, a life that no one can know unless he understands. And to understand is simply to live a brighter and more perfect life by the light of the mind.[40]

At its upper limit, Augustine is describing the ideal of the afterlife.

43

Another argument (though in a way we have already considered it) is that our minds control our bodies, and rule our bodies, and hence are superior to them. Socrates writes,

> When the soul and the body are together, nature orders the one to be subject and to be ruled, and the other to rule and be

master. Then again, which do you think is like the divine and which is like the mortal? Do you not think that the nature of the divine is to rule and lead, whereas it is that of the mortal to be ruled and be subject?[41]

As we have seen, Socrates identifies the mind with the divine and the body with the mortal. A reason for prioritizing mental activity over embodied activity is that one of the most dignifying aspects of human existence is the exercise of our mental capacities and the exercise of our will. We are not like rocks or trees; we think and choose, and are not automata.

44

For Socrates, bodily things are imperfect and impure. They distract us from things that are more worthy of our attention. The best life (he argues) is the life of the philosopher—in which we detach from the senses, cleanse the mind of the body, and identify with the side of ourselves that is pure.[42] Socrates does not pull any punches. He says, for example, in *Phaedo* that "the aim of those who practice philosophy in the proper manner is to practice for dying and death."[43] The immaterial afterlife is better still, where we would engage in spiritual activity alone.

45

The mathematician and philosopher Blaise Pascal also thought that the afterlife (if it exists) is extremely fulfilling.[44] He proposed a wager: believe in the existence of God and be rewarded for eternity, or risk the (equally eternal) torment that is due the nonbeliever.[45] If God does not exist, Pascal assumed, embodied life would be short and relatively inconsequential: there is no significant gain if we embrace our embodiment and believe that all that we have is our 70–80 years, and there is no significant loss if we spend that time in faith. If God *does* exist, however, things are very different. The most rational choice is to believe:

> Which will you choose then? Let us see: since a choice must be made, let us see which offers you the least interest. You have

two things to lose: the true and the good; and two things to stake: your reason and your will, your knowledge and your happiness; and your nature has two things to avoid: error and wretchedness. . . . Let us weigh up the gain and the loss involved in calling heads that God exists. Let us assess the two cases: if you win you win everything, if you lose you lose nothing. Do not hesitate then; wager that he does exist.[46]

Pascal is supposing that the afterlife of a believer would be fulfilling. It would not be rational to have faith if faith guaranteed us an afterlife that was awful. For example, hell is clearly bad. An eternal experience of boredom might be torture as well, and also an eternal experience in which we are engaged in projects and pursuits that do not matter to us.[47] To piggyback on some of Wolf's terminology, the question arises about what an eternal afterlife would have to be like for it to be meaningful to us. In short, we would have to be able to actively participate in projects that we take to be of value for the long haul and that would make us have an experience of meaning.

46

There is a striking scene in the third Star Wars movie (not *Return of the Jedi*, but the third of the prequels). Anakin Skywalker is starting to have intense feelings for Padme (with whom he is having a secret relationship). He approaches master Yoda for advice: what should a Jedi do when they start to lose focus because they fear that something bad might happen to a person they love? Yoda is unambiguous in his response: what is important is not worldly pursuits and affairs, or the contingent attachments of embodied life, but attention to things of the spirit and soul. Yoda encourages Anakin to distance himself from Padme, and from worldly pursuits more generally, so that he can focus on what is important and be more ready to make the transition to the spirit-life beyond. He says,

Death is a natural part of life. Rejoice for those around you who transform into the Force. Mourn them, do not. Miss them, do not. Attachment leads to jealousy. The shadow of greed, that is. . . . Train yourself to let go of everything you fear to lose.[48]

The symmetries with Socrates here are striking. If we detach from the realm of bodies, we will not care about them as much, and when we transition to full immateriality we will attend more easily to things that are superior and merit our attention.

47

A worry also arises about the relative seriousness of our earthly pursuits if there is an eternal afterlife and if our embodied existence is intrinsically less valuable. Bertrand Russell put the worry like this:

> Immortality, if we could believe in it, would enable us to shake off this gloom about the physical world. We should say that although our souls, during their sojourn here on earth, are in bondage to matter and physical laws, they pass at death into an eternal world beyond the empire of decay which science seems to reveal in the sensible world.[49]

If there is an eternal afterlife, anything that is unfortunate or gloomy about a person's earthly existence can be regarded as an infinitesimally brief chapter in a much longer story. If our current embodied lives do not mean very much, things like poverty and riches do not matter much either, and we will be equals later on—in all the ways that are important. The early modern philosopher Mary Astell echoes Russell, though in most respects their thinking could not be farther apart. Astell was a social activist and reformer, working to enhance the opportunities of the women of her time. She was not working to promote suffrage or to expand employment opportunities, however; she is not arguing that earthly pursuits are especially valuable or that women's lives would be improved by participating in a wider range of them. For Astell, the best sort of life is the Platonic life in which we exercise our minds in readiness for the spirit life to come. She writes,

> And since our Happiness in the next World, depends so far on those dispositions which we carry along with us out of this, that without a right habitude and temper of mind we are not capable of Felicity; and seeing our Beatitude consists in the

contemplation of the divine Truth and Beauty, as well as in the fruition of his Goodness, can Ignorance be a fit preparative for Heaven? Is't likely that she whose Understanding has been busied about nothing but froth and trifles, shou'd be capable of delighting her self in noble and sublime Truths?[50]

Everyone is going to be busy at some earthly occupation—doctor, lawyer, priest, politician, scientist, mother, caretaker, teacher, seamstress—and God has given us different talents to mark out our individual purpose and task.[51] It is no loss if a person cannot be a lawyer or artist, Astell thinks, even if these bring worldly fame and reward. What is important is that society be reformed so that everybody has the leisure and opportunity to develop their ability at abstract thinking. As things stand, women are busied with froth and trifles, but that is not the highest sort of activity, and it is not the sort of activity that will facilitate a transition to the hereafter. Astell was a revolutionary in arguing that men and women have the same (God-given) ability to reason and think, and she promoted the corollary view that the education of girls should be upended to emphasize their rational nature.[52]

48

Astell is reflecting a fairly traditional view, but there is a way to take it to an extreme that is very unsettling. In the middle of *Revenge of the Sith*, Anakin Skywalker kills a number of young children. Then in the next movie, he blows up Alderaan. He wanted to test his death-ray system, and so he destroyed an entire planet and killed over a billion people. In addition, he lies to Princess Leia. He tells her that he will not blow up Alderaan if she answers his questions, but he then blows it up anyway, and seems to get a lot of satisfaction in doing so. But then in the sixth movie (*Return of the Jedi*), he rejects the dark side of the force and destroys the emperor, and all is forgiven. In the final scene, the spirit of Anakin appears alongside the spirits of Yoda and Ben Kenobi, and it is hard not to have a feeling of fuzziness and warmth. The implication (in the scene) is that beings move on to the eternal (and much better) spirit world, and that the children who were slaughtered by Anakin moved on to that world as well, along with most of the people who were killed by his death ray. Otherwise, the feeling of warmth and fuzziness would seem to be unconscionable.

49

A question on the table is whether or not a life of purely spiritual activity would be meaningful or fulfilling to us. If Wolf's view is right, the question is whether we could be actively engaged in projects, and if we could take these to have long-term value, in a situation in which there were absolutely no bodies. In our current situation, most of us would not enjoy the prospect of being put into a sensory-deprivation chamber for an extended period of time. We might find it horrifying if we were told that this would be our arrangement for eternity. The wrinkle of course is that a disembodied being is presumably very different from an embodied being, and so even though we would not find the arrangement fulfilling *right now*, we might find it wholly fulfilling once we are there.

50

Ernie (from Sesame Street) addresses the worry in song.* He imagines a number of places that he might want to visit, but where he would never want to live:

Oh, I'd like to visit the moon
in a rocketship high in the air.
Yes, I'd like to visit the moon,
but I don't think I'd like to live there.
Though I'd like to look down at the earth from above,
I would miss all the places and people I love.
So although I may like it for one afternoon,
I don't want to live on the moon.
Or I could travel under the sea.
I could meet all the fish everywhere.
Yes, I'd travel under the sea,
but I don't think I'd like to live there.
Though I'd stay for a day there if I had my wish.
But there's not much to do when you're friends are all fish.

And an oyster and clam aren't real family, so I don't want to
     live in the sea.
I'd like to go to the jungle, hear the lions roar.
Go back in time and meet a dinosaur.
There's so many strange places that I'd like to be.
But none of them permanently.[53]

If Ernie was told that he would be a very different sort of being on
the moon, with different projects and concerns, and ones that he
cannot adequately conceive in his current incarnation, he would no
doubt be intrigued but also perplexed.

51

So we have Socrates versus Ernie. Socrates would agree that
according to the standards of evaluation of most people, embodied
life is all that matters, but he thinks that the standards of evaluation
of most people are to be rejected. Socrates does not hide that in the
immaterial afterlife our activities would be nonsensory—we would
think of perfect circles and numbers and other abstractions, and
things like the elegance of the proof of the Pythagorean theorem. For
Socrates, this would be paradise, and as a philosopher it is hard not
to feel where he is coming from. Someone might argue in addition
that if God exists and there is an afterlife, we have a guarantee that
it will be fulfilling, even if we cannot simulate or estimate a purely
disembodied experience right now. But if we were stripped of our
embodiment, that sort of experience would be sublime.

52

We have been considering the question of whether or not there
would be projects that we would regard as meaningful in an
immaterial afterlife. We have been asking if we could be actively
immersed in pursuits and take them to have long-term value, if there
were absolutely no bodies. This is very difficult sort of question to
approach. We can hope that although the activities of an immaterial
afterlife might not offer us a lot right now, they would provide us
with an experience of meaning and significance in the future, when
we are different beings, with different concerns.

53

We have not considered alternative conceptions of the afterlife and whether or not those might be meaningful. Perhaps there is an afterlife and it is pretty much like the embodied life that we are living right now. In that case it would be easy to see how such a life could be meaningful. We could have all the things that matter to us—all the people with their quirks and passions, their voices and smiles and expressions, and all the ways that we like to spend time with them. We could have intimate conversations with our loved ones, and everything would be like it is now, only better. Or perhaps there are no bodies in the afterlife, but our immaterial minds are set up to have all of the meaningful experiences that we had before. The eighteenth-century philosopher George Berkeley defends a version of this view. He thought something even more extreme: that the perceptions that we have in the course of our "embodied" existence are caused directly by God, with no bodies anywhere to be found.[54] Berkeley took minds to be immaterial, and he assumed that since bodies and minds cannot interact, bodies are never the cause of our perceptions.The cause is not a Matrix machine, but a wise and efficient and extremely capable mind. We might insist (against Berkeley) that we do have bodies right now, but we might also be happy to accept a modification of his view to apply to the afterlife.

Possible discussion exercises

1　Epicurus thinks that desires for luxury are not as fulfilling as they might first seem, and that we can be just as fulfilled by desires that are simpler. Do you agree? Make sure to illustrate your response with an example.

2　Epictetus thinks that we should adjust and go along with pretty much everything that happens. Do you think his view is too extreme? Is there a version of his view that you find more plausible?

3　Imagine that we try to adjust to how things go, so that we feel less hatred and shame and regret. What do we do if we continue to feel these anyway—should we just be okay with that?

4 Do you think that Wolf is right that Blob is not living a meaningful life?

5 Imagine the case of a person who is very unsuccessful in their pursuit of a certain goal—for example, a civil rights activist who is killed for their activism 200 years before her society achieves any of the social changes for which she struggled. Did this person live a meaningless life?

6 This chapter has been supposing that Wolf's four criteria are sufficiently general that they would capture all examples of a meaningful life. Do you think that she is missing anything?

7 Someone might argue that we should live every day as if it were our last. What would Wolf say? Do you agree? Why or why not?

8 Do you think that Frankfurt is right that there is something demeaning about taking our first-order desires at face-value?

9 Can you think of a second-order inclination that it would be useful for you to have?

10 Do you have any second-order volitions that you have struggled to translate into first-order volitions?

11 Where do our second-order desires come from? Should we take *these* at face-value?

12 What happens if a person has a second-order desire but is unable to satisfy it—that is, they are not able to come to have the first-order desire that they seek? What are some of the things that might stand in the way? Come up with an example of a failed second-order desire for each of the three scenarios sketched in sections 34, 35, and 37.

13 Are there ways in which our current embodied life already involves purely spiritual activities? Would the activities still be the same (or better) if we had no bodies?

14 Consider some of the activities that human beings get excited about—playing sports, talking with each other, cooking, gardening, dancing, running a business, reading the newspaper (or a blog), playing cards, watching movies. Are there elements of these that could exist in a disembodied life and that could fulfill us?

15 Who do you think is right: Socrates or Ernie?

16 Assume that there is an eternal afterlife and that death is not the termination of our being. What would be some reasons for thinking that murder is bad?

17 What do you think is a conception of the afterlife that is very enticing?

18 Come up with your own everyday example for one of the views or arguments or objections presented in this chapter.

Notes

1 Epicurus, "To Monoeceus," in Cyril Bailey (trans. and ed.), *Epicurus: The Extant Remains*, New York: Georg Olms Verlag (1975), 87. Epicurus was a Greek philosopher who lived from 341–270 BC. He was enormously influential. The adjective term "epicurean" has been passed down to us and means roughly, "devoted to the pursuit of pleasure," but as we will see Epicurus had a more fine-grained view in which we are recommended to settle on pleasures whose pursuit is sustainable and that do not lead to significant pain.

2 Epicurus, *Principal Doctrines*, in Cyril Bailey (trans. and ed.), *Epicurus: The Extant Remains*, New York: Georg Olms Verlag (1975), 99.

3 Epicurus, "To Monoeceus," 89.

4 Epicurus, *Principal Doctrines*, 101.

5 Epictetus, *Encheiridion*, section 8. Epictetus was a Roman philosopher who lived AD 55–135. He was a slave for much of his early life, and it appears that part of his stoic attitude of acceptance was developed in his attempts to adapt to a terrible situation over which he had very little control.

6 Ibid., section 4.

7 Ibid., section 3.

8 Ibid., sections 11, 16.

9 Ibid., section 20.

10 Ibid., section 42.

11 Ibid., section 43.

12 Ibid., section 49.

13 Ibid., section 53.

14 Ibid., section 37.

15 See Wolf, "The Meanings of Lives," 794–805. Professor Wolf is a philosopher who teaches at the University of North Carolina, Chapel Hill. She has written on a number of interconnected issues including ethical responsibility and the attempt to reconcile human freedom with a deterministic picture of the universe. Among other things she is famous for defending the view that moral saints, or ideal ethical agents, do not provide the most appropriate model of a human life.

16 Ibid., 796.

17 Ibid.

18 Ibid.

19 Ibid. In her statement of the second criterion, Wolf combines (1) a discussion of the need for a person to be seriously committed to their pursuits and to take them to have value with (2) a discussion of the need for the person's pursuits to actually have value. This makes things a little bit confusing, I think, and so I will be separating the two here.

20 Ibid., 797–8.

21 Ibid., 798.

22 Ibid., 797–8.

23 Ibid., 798.

24 Ibid.

25 Friedrich Nietzsche, *On the Genealogy of Morality*, ed. Keith Ansell-Pearson, trans. Carol Diethe, Cambridge: Cambridge University Press (1997), preface, section 6.

26 Ibid., First Essay, esp. sections 10–12.

27 Harry Frankfurt, "Freedom of the Will and the Concept of a Person," *The Journal of Philosophy* 68 (1971), 5–20. Professor Frankfurt is a philosopher who currently teaches at Princeton University. He works on a broad range of issues including free will, responsibility, and as he expresses it in the title of one of his books, the importance of what we care about.

28 A nice example appears in the song "(When We Are Dancin') I Get Ideas" by Louis Armstrong,* Catalog Number 27720, Decca Records

(1951) (with a recent cover by M. Ward*). The song begins as follows: "When we are dancing / And you're dangerously close to me / I get ideas, I get ideas. / I want to hold you / So much closer than I dare do. / I want to scold you / 'Cause I care more than I care to.'"

29 Ibid., 8–10.

30 Ibid., 10–12.

31 Ibid., 11.

32 For purposes of clarity, then, we can say that first-order desires are desires that we actually have and that motivate us; first-order volitions are the strongest of these, the ones that win out in action; second-order desires are desires to have a desire, and these are either second-order inclinations or second-order volitions.

33 Wolf, "The Meanings of Lives," 794–5.

34 *Phaedo*, 74d.

35 Ibid., 80b–c.

36 Socrates glamorizes exactly this sort of scenario at the end of the dialogue, *Apology*.

37 This explanation is reminiscent of the externalist view about knowledge. In the same way that our word "knowledge" refers to something that we can name and encounter, so does our word "perfect." If we are suspicious of the idea that we encounter Socratic idealizations, we might look for another way that we might have formed ideas of them.

38 *Phaedo*, 65a–b.

39 This is also the thesis of Descartes' Second Meditation, CSM 2:16–21.

40 St Augustine, *On Free Choice of the Will*, 13.

41 *Phaedo*, 80a.

42 Ibid., 66a–69d.

43 Ibid., 64a.

44 Blaise Pascal was a mathematician and philosopher who lived in seventeenth-century France. He is most famous for Pascal's wager, in which he argues that even though we do not know that God exists, it is a more rational bet to believe that God exists than to believe that He does not.

45 Pascal, "The Wager," in *Pensées*, trans. A. J. Krailsheimer, London: Penguin Books (1966), 149–54.

46 Ibid., 150–1.

47 See, for example, Nagel, "The Absurd," 717.

48 This is in scene 77.

49 Russell, "The Faith of a Rationalist," 90.

50 Mary Astell, *A Serious Proposal to the Ladies. Parts I and II*, ed. P. Springborg, Ontario: Broadview Literary Texts (1696/2002), 80–1. Astell was an English philosopher and social reformer who wrote in the early eighteenth century. She is best known for her theories on education, and the education of women in particular, and for her critiques of the philosopher John Locke.

51 Ibid., 168.

52 See Alice Sowaal, "Mary Astell's *Serious Proposal*: Mind, Method, and Custom," *Philosophy Compass* 2 (2007), 227–43.

53 Jeff Moss and Damar Fehlau, *I Don't Want to Live on the Moon*, New York: Random House Books for Young Readers (2001).

54 George Berkeley, *A Treatise Concerning the Principles of Human Knowledge*, ed. Kenneth Winkler, Indianapolis and Cambridge: Hackett (1710/1982), 25, 30–1. Berkeley was an eighteenth-century philosopher and bishop who held that the most effective response to skepticism about the external world is to argue that tables and chairs and other "material objects" are just perceptions that exist in minds. We cannot doubt that these perceptions exist, and so skepticism cannot get off the ground.

CHAPTER FIVE

Uncaused eternal mind versus uncaused eternal matter

Abstract

This chapter considers the following: reasons for thinking that God exists; whether or not the current organization in the universe could be due to uncaused eternal matter; whether or not there is unconscious intelligence at work in the processes of nature; and whether or not human activity is often unreflective and "in the zone."

God as first cause

1

Philosophers have offered a number of proofs of the existence of God. No such proof is required for belief, of course, and many people throughout history have emphasized the importance of faith over attempts at proof. For example, the philosopher (or perhaps anti-philosopher) Søren Kierkegaard thought that a leap of faith was the much more impressive achievement.[1] But most philosophers tend to like arguments. Some of the earliest and most influential are from St Thomas Aquinas. One begins with the assumption that all creatures are such that their existence and nonexistence are equally possible. This argument

> is based on possibility and necessity and runs as follows: Among things we discover some for which both existing and not existing are possible, since some things are found to be generated and destroyed and as a result to exist and not to exist. But it is impossible that everything that exists is of this sort, because that for which not existing is possible, at some time does not exist. If then everything is such that not existing is possible for it, at some time there was nothing really existing. But if this were true, then right now there would be nothing, since what is not in existence begins to exist only in virtue of something which exists. If, then, there was nothing in existence, it was impossible for anything to begin to exist, and thus there would be nothing now, which is obviously false.[2]

We can reconstruct this argument in a couple of different ways. Aquinas might be saying that since for all existing creatures, their nonexistence is possible, there would have been some point in the past when the nonexistence of all creatures coincided. In that case, nothing would have been able to come into existence from that point forward. Nothing would exist now, but on the contrary things do exist now, and so there must be something whose existence is not such that its existence and nonexistence are possible. Clearly this thing's existence is possible, and so its nonexistence is not possible: "And this everybody says is God."[3]

2

We might take issue with the result that there must be a common moment in which all things fail to exist (if all creatures are such that their existence and nonexistence are equally possible). Even if time extends infinitely into the past, for all we know there are always a few objects whose existence overlaps. Presumably it is *possible* that there has been a singular moment when all objects were nonexistent, but that does not mean that there has actually been such a moment:

perhaps there is just a recurring pattern in which things go in and out of existence, but there is always something that exists. We might also worry about whether or not the argument is in a position to prove that *God* exists. There might be a being whose nonexistence is not possible, and we might call it "God," but that does not mean that the being is a divinity in any traditional sense.

3

Alternately, we could read the argument as supposing that since the existence and nonexistence of every creature are equally possible, there was a time before the existence of any creatures in which nothing existed—and the existence of creatures was merely possible (but not yet actual). This would be a moment before any creatures existed at all—a common moment in which no creatures existed. If at that moment all things were merely possible, then there had to exist something to move them from possibility to actuality, otherwise nothing would exist now. This something would have to be an actual existent, if merely possible things have no power, and it would have to be a thing that has always existed (or else it would have had to come from nothing). It has to be a necessary existent because if its nonexistence is possible, then something would have had to move *it* from nonexistence to existence, and so that would have been the necessary existent instead.

4

This reconstruction of the argument has problems also. One is that we are supposing that there was a moment when all creatures had merely possible existence—but perhaps the universe itself is a necessary existent, and presumably we do not want to call that "God." Another is that even if there was a moment when all creatures had merely possible existence, the being that moved them from nonexistence to actual existence does not have to be a god in any traditional sense. Perhaps Aquinas is thinking that the being would have to understand, and have ideas of, all the possibilities. It would also need to have enough power to actualize some, and have some good reason for preferring those over the others.

5

An additional argument that Aquinas offers for the existence of God begins from the assumption that the bodies in nature tend to act toward a goal or end. Since bodies do not have any kind of cognition or intelligence, there must be a being that does have cognition and intelligence and that directs them in an orderly way. This argument

> is based in the governance of things. For we see that some things which lack cognition, viz. natural bodies [i.e. the elemental bodies], function for an end. This is evident from the fact that they always or very frequently function in the same way and end up resulting in what is best. From this it is clear that it is not by chance but by purpose that they arrive at the end. But now those things which lack cognition do not tend towards an end unless they are directed by something with knowledge and intelligence, just as the arrow is directed by the archer. Therefore, there is some intelligent being who directs all natural beings to an end, and this being we say is God.[4]

Here the argument is a version of the argument from intelligent design that has been offered in contemporary times. The argument supposes that the bodies that surround us act for the sake of ends, but that beings only do this if they are guided by a mind. The bodies themselves do not have minds, and so they must be guided by a being or beings with a mind.

6

This argument also has potential problems. One is that it supposes without argument that the bodies that surround us do not have some form of cognition. For example, Cavendish (from Chapter Three) would argue that intelligence is spread throughout nature. Another potential problem is that, in concluding that God exists, the argument supposes that there is a single mind that guides the bodies in nature. Perhaps there are multiple minds that do this, and perhaps collectively they do not warrant the appellation "God."

7

Another medieval philosopher who weighs in with an argument for the existence of God is St Anselm. He offers an argument that assumes a traditional notion of God as infinite and perfect:

> [T]he Fool has said in his heart that God does not exist. . . . But surely when this very Fool hears the words "something than which nothing greater can be thought," he understands what he hears. And what he understands is in his understanding even if he does not understand [judge] it to exist. Indeed, for a thing to be in the understanding is different from understanding [judging] that thing exists. For when an artist envisions what he is about to paint, he has it in his understanding, but he does not yet understand [judge] that what he has painted exists. . . . But surely that than which a greater cannot be thought cannot be only in the understanding. For if it were only in the understanding, it could be thought to exist also in reality—which is greater [than only existing in the understanding].[5]

This is a version of what is known as the *ontological* argument for the existence of God. It can be difficult to know what to say about the argument, or to understand why it was once taken so seriously. The argument seems to be engaging in some sort of trickery—defining God into existence. Perhaps the problem is that we cannot in fact think a being than which nothing greater can be conceived—maybe we just make up a definition of the word "God" in terms of words like "being" and "greater," and we do not really have the idea that Anselm says we have. Or perhaps the problem is that things are not always greater if they exist in reality than if they exist in thought; or at least Anselm has not demonstrated as much. Perhaps the problem is that there are other things that we can think—like a hamburger greater than which cannot be thought—but we do not think that we should be able to include that any burger thereby exists. This sort of objection to Anselm is common. He would respond that we cannot think a hamburger greater than which cannot be thought, but we can think a *being* greater than which cannot be thought.

8

Descartes also offers an argument for the existence of God that starts from our idea of God. Descartes allows that for most ideas, if we have an idea of X, that does not entail that X exists. We have ideas of unicorns, for example, and there are many ideas that we make up, but these say more about us and our creativity than about actual objects in the world that our ideas represent. An idea of God is different. Ideas are mental pictures or representations, Descartes thinks, and since God is understood to be infinite, an idea of God would have to be a kind of infinite picture. Otherwise, it would not be an idea of *God* but of something else. Descartes writes,

> Now it is manifest by the natural light that there must be at least as much <reality> in the total and efficient cause as in the effect of that cause. For where, I ask, could the effect get its reality from, if not from the cause? . . . I must consider whether there is anything in the idea of God which could not have originated in myself. By the word "God" I understand a substance that is infinite, <eternal, immutable,> independent, supremely intelligent, supremely powerful, and which created both myself and everything else (if anything else there be) that exists. All these attributes are such that, the more carefully I concentrate on them, the less possible it seems that they could have originated from me alone. So from what has been said it must be concluded that God necessarily exists.[6]

Descartes says later to one of his correspondents that what he means when he says that there must be at least as much reality in a cause as is in its effect is that "Nothing comes from nothing."[7] He seems to be arguing that if we have an idea with an infinite amount of representational or pictorial content, an infinitely powerful being must have produced that idea. A finitely powerful being can produce some ideas, but its power can only result in a finite picture. If we have an infinite idea, and the only causes that existed were finite beings, then the leftover part of our infinite idea that was *not* caused by finite beings would have to have come from nothing. But that is impossible.

9

One of the worries for Descartes' argument is whether or not our idea of God really requires an infinitely powerful cause. Some people look into their own minds and think of a bearded man on a cloud when they think of God, and others think of something more abstract and difficult to nail down. Some might have a warm feeling, and some might think of God as infinite, but then think of infinity as the symbol ∞. Surely *these* ideas do not require an infinitely powerful being to produce. Here Descartes would respond that these ideas do not really capture infinitude, and so they are not ideas of God. Descartes goes so far as to say that if these are the only sorts of ideas of God that we have, then none of us has an idea of God after all, and thus we are atheists.[8]

10

Another potential worry for Descartes' argument is that even if we grant that an infinite idea can only be caused by an infinitely powerful being, a being that is infinitely powerful is not necessarily God. Perhaps there could be an infinitely powerful being that is not omniscient or omnibenevolent. Descartes would have to be able to make a case for the view that infinite power automatically involves these other divine attributes. Another worry for the argument is that perhaps there are infinitely many finite beings, and they are the collective cause of the infinite idea of God.

The argument from design

11

The eighteenth-century philosopher and theologian William Paley offered what is now a very famous argument for the existence of God—the argument from design. The argument is similar to the second argument from St Thomas Aquinas that we considered earlier, but Paley goes into much more detail. Paley considers two possible explanations of the order and organization that are exhibited in the universe. One is that the universe was designed by God. Another is that the universe came to exhibit order and organization on its own.

12

Paley asks us to imagine that we are on a walk and we see a watch on the ground. We wonder where it came from, and we would not be satisfied to hear that it has no cause and that it has just always existed. Paley sets up the case as follows:

> In crossing a heath, suppose I pitched my foot against a *stone*, and were asked how the stone came to be there; I might possibly answer, that, for anything I knew to the contrary, it had lain there forever: nor would it perhaps be very easy to show the absurdity of this answer. But suppose I had found a *watch* upon the ground, and it should be inquired how the watch happened to be in that place; I should hardly think of the answer which I had before given, that, for anything I knew, the watch might have always been there.[9]

Paley argues that the important difference between the watch and the stone is that the watch was created with a function in mind—it was created by a being that *had* a function in mind, and that had the wherewithal to convert its idea into a reality. Paley continues,

> The inference, we think, is inevitable; that the watch must have had a maker; that there must have existed, at some time and at some place or other, an artificer or artificers, who formed it for the purpose which we find it actually to answer; who apprehended its construction, and designed its use.[10]

Paley then asks us to imagine what we would say if the watch turned out to be even more sophisticated than we had assumed:

> Suppose, in the next place, that the person who found the watch, should, after sometime, discover, that, in addition to all the properties which he had hitherto observed in it, it possessed the unexpected property of producing, in the course of its

movement, another watch like itself, . . . that it contained within it a mechanism, a system of parts, a mould for instance, or a complex adjustment of lathes, files, and other tools, evidently and separately calculated for this purpose; let us inquire, what effect ought such a discovery to have upon his former conclusion.[11]

Paley argues that, upon *first* encountering the watch, we would be strongly inclined to say that it had a designer. But we would be *certain* that it had a designer upon learning that the watch was sophisticated and could also reproduce. A designer would need to have been present who had the function of the watch in mind; the designer would need to have been able to think about all of the intricacies that are involved in a watch-making watch; and finally the designer would need to have been able to execute the design and make it all happen.

13

Paley sees the case of the watch-making watch as on a par with the sorts of entities that we encounter throughout the natural world: beings that have coordinated functions and that are able to generate beings that have functions themselves. He concludes after a discussion of the watch and its wonders:

What effect would this discovery have, or ought it to have, upon our former inference? What, as hath already been said, but to increase, beyond measure, our admiration of the skill which had been employed in the formation of such a machine? Or shall it, instead of this, all at once turn us round to an opposite conclusion, viz., that no art or skill whatever has been concerned in the business, although all other evidences of art and skill remain as they were, and this last and supreme piece of art be now added to the rest? Can this be maintained without absurdity? Yet this is atheism.[12]

If we hold that the watch did not form without the assistance of an intelligent and capable designer, we should also conclude that the universe did not form without the assistance of an intelligent and capable designer. Indeed, the latter (designer) would be more intelligent, and extremely powerful. Therefore God exists, or at the very least there exists a being (or beings) with enough intelligence and power to have generated the order and organization in the universe that surrounds us.

14

An objection to Paley is that he may be right about the cause of watches, and even watch-making watches, but that he is wrong to extend his conclusion to apply to the order that we encounter in nature. The eighteenth-century philosopher David Hume argued that the elements of the natural world do not have the resources to bring about watches, but they *do* have the resources to bring about things like cells and plants and trees and neurons. For all we know, the latter have the wherewithal to bring about conscious human thinking, and only then would there appear watch-making watches. Hume argues that if we encountered a watch-making watch, we should conclude that it was created by sophisticated human intelligence, or something very much like it, but we are not in a position to conclude that human intelligence and other impressive phenomena are not produced by nature to begin with.

15

Hume frames the debate like this. On one view, God is the cause of the order and organization that we encounter, and God Himself is uncaused and eternal. An alternative view is that there is something else that is uncaused and eternal, and that is extremely powerful and sophisticated, but that this is just nature itself. Both views suppose the existence of something that is uncaused and that has the resources to bring about order. Hume writes,

> In like manner, when it is asked, what cause produces order in the ideas of the supreme Being, can any other reason be assigned by you, anthropomorphites, than that it is a *rational* faculty, and that such is the nature of the Deity? But why a similar answer will not be equally satisfactory in accounting for the order of the world, without having recourse to any such intelligent Creator as you insist on, may be difficult to determine. It is only to say,

that *such* is the nature of material objects, and that they are all originally possessed of a *faculty* of order and proportion.[13]

Hume is saying that on either view we have to posit the existence of something that is eternal, uncaused, and extremely sophisticated—that has a faculty of order and proportion.

16

Hume also feels the pull of Paley's conclusion that an intelligent being was behind the creation of the watch-making watch. He considers the example of an abandoned library that we might encounter, filled with a wide spectrum of books. The obvious inference to make is that the library was built by human beings (or by beings that are sufficiently like us):

> Suppose, therefore, that you enter your library, thus peopled by natural volumes, containing the most refined reason and most exquisite beauty: Could you possibly open one of them, and doubt, that its original cause bore the strongest analogy to mind and intelligence? When it reasons and discourses; when it expostulates, argues, and enforces its views and topics; when it applies sometimes to the pure intellect, sometimes to the affections; when it collects, disposes, and adorns every consideration suited to the subject: could you persist in asserting, that all this, at the bottom, had really no meaning, and that the first formation of this volume in the loins of its original parent proceeded not from thought and design? Your obstinacy, I know, reaches not that degree of firmness: Even your skeptical play and wantonness would be abashed at so glaring an absurdity.[14]

Hume agrees that a watch is the sort of thing that is produced by human art and intelligence. But he argues that the things that we encounter in nature are very different from watches. We encounter cells, ecosystems, amoeba, organs, trees, and plants. These entities are very sophisticated, and they lead to the development of entities that are impressive. Hume continues:

> You need only to look around you, . . . to satisfy yourself with regard to this question. A tree bestows order and organization on

that tree which springs from it, without knowing the order: an animal, in the same manner, on its offspring; a bird, on its nest: And instances of this kind are even more frequent in the world, than those of order, which arise from reason and contrivance.[15]

Presumably cells and other pieces of sophisticated matter are not conscious, and Paley would agree. He is assuming that things like nonconscious cells and trees and ecosystems compose the natural world. He is also assuming that these cannot be sophisticated and eternal and uncaused. Hume is asking why eternal sophisticated matter cannot exist uncaused, but eternal sophisticated mind can.

17

Hume argues that in the bulk of the natural world, we do not find things like watches or libraries. We find things that are produced by cells and sunlight and other nonhuman forces. He writes,

Now if we survey the universe, so far as it falls under our knowledge, it bears a great resemblance to an animal or organized body, and seems actuated with a like principle of life and motion. A continual circulation of matter in it produces no disorder: A continual waste in every part is incessantly repaired: The closest sympathy is perceived throughout the entire system: And each part or member, in performing its proper offices, operates both to its own preservation and to that of the whole. . . . And it must be confessed, that . . . the universe resembles more a human body than it does the works of human art and contrivance.[16]

The question for Hume is whether it is cells and other pieces of sophisticated matter that are the uncaused eternal entities that bring about the organization in the universe, or if the uncaused eternal entity is God.

18

Hume does not come down on any one side in the debate. *Dialogues Concerning Natural Religion* is a discussion with a narrator and three interlocutors—Philo, Cleanthes, Demea—and we do not know for sure which if any is Hume himself. He appears to be writing the dialogue as a way of fleshing out the subtleties and complexities of the different sides of the debate, and he says as much in his prefatory letter.[17] A theme of the dialogue more generally is that the atheistic and theistic positions are difficult to differentiate because neither can be conceived with much precision. Hume writes,

> Reason, in its internal fabric and structure, is really as little known to us as instinct or vegetation; and perhaps even that vague, undeterminate word, nature, to which the vulgar refer every thing is not at the bottom more inexplicable. The effects of these principles are all known to us from experience: But the principles themselves, and their manner of operation, are totally unknown: Nor is it less intelligible, or less conformable to experience to say, that the world arose by vegetation by a seed shed by another seed, than to say that it arose from a divine reason or contrivance.[18]

One view is that there is a mind with sophisticated faculties that exists and that has no cause or explanation. Another is that sophisticated bodies exist and have no cause or explanation. The suggestion in the dialogue is that we do not understand very well what we are thinking in either case. Either we are thinking that there is an eternal and perfect divine being—which is largely beyond us—or we are thinking that there was some matter or energy or force that was just sitting there a trillion years ago, and then forever before. Or perhaps there was no time at a certain point, and no space, but that can be hard to understand as well. In any case, it can be difficult to see how the two hypotheses specifically diverge if our conceptions of both are so hazy:

> These are only more learned and elaborate ways of confessing our ignorance; nor has the one hypothesis any real advantage above the other.[19]

Perhaps in an effort to be a diplomat, Hume is suggesting that so far as we can tell, what we have in mind when are thinking the one is not that much different from what we have in mind when we are thinking the other. He certainly had a political agenda: if we realize that we have hardly any idea what we are talking about, that "may teach, all of us, sobriety in condemning each other."[20] This was a common motivation in the early modern period, given a lot of the conflict that arose over religious disagreement.

19

Cavendish is even more blunt than Hume. She is a devout theist, but she argues that the human mind can form no accurate conception of a divine and perfect being, and so our piety should be humble:

> Man in this particular goes beyond others, as having not onely a natural, but also a revealed knowledg of the most Holy God; for he knows Gods Will, not onely by the light of Nature, but also by revelation, and so more then other Creatures do, whose knowledg of God is meerly Natural. But this Revealed Knowledg makes most men so presumptuous, that they will not be content with it, but search more and more into the hidden mysteries of the Incomprehensible Deity, and pretend to know God as perfectly, almost, as themselves; describing his Nature and Essence, his Attributes, his Counsels, his Actions, according to the revelation of God, (as they pretend) when as it is according to their own Fancies.[21]

> Theologie is a glorious study, but the way is difficult and dangerous, for though there are many pathes, yet there is but one that leads to heaven, and those that step awrie fall into the Gulph of damnation, and the deep study in this many times blindes the eyes, both of faith and reason, and instead of uniting mankind with love, to live in peace, it makes discords with controversies, raises up faction to uphold each-side, whose endlesse quarrels are followed with such hatred, and fought with such malice and envie, and the zeal spits so much blood, as if not onely several parties would be rased out, but the bulk of mankind.[22]

Cavendish thinks that Christianity is correct to posit that people have a proclivity for sin, and she thinks that one of the prominent misdeeds of the human race is to be arrogant and project onto scripture our own biases and aims.

Super-matter?

20

Hume is thinking that whether God exists or not, there exists matter that has the wherewithal to do some pretty remarkable things. Blood will rush to form a scab; a fetus will develop in utero along with the placenta that provides it support; microscopic cells pass on and receive messages from each other; bees protect their honey and seem to be able to inform the queen when there is a threat to the hive; ants constitute communities and behave in organized ways; the human body has an immune system that helps it to heal. On one hypothesis, God exists and is uncaused, and God produced matter. He also produced immaterial minds. On another hypothesis, there is something different that exists that is sophisticated and uncreated. Hume calls this "matter," but because of all of the baggage that comes with the term—that matter is lowly and unimpressive, for example—he might be happier to call it "super-matter." This would be stuff that is able to unfold in organized ways and bring about the organization that we witness in nature.

21

Hume argues that there are no serious incoherencies to either hypothesis—that an eternal God exists, or that the uncaused existent is super-matter. Some might suggest that if God exists and is perfect, then there should not be any evil or suffering, and that things like poverty and earthquakes would be nonexistent.[23] But Hume notes that if God exists and human minds are immaterial and immortal, then we do not die with the body but continue to exist for eternity upon its demise. If we do not think that a momentary headache is a horrific thing in the scheme of a single 80-year life, we cannot think that a life of poverty or devastation is so terrible when it is an even smaller (and a much much smaller) fraction of eternity.[24] Hume's view here might sound horrific, but his point is that it is not at all horrific within the framework of the hypothesis in question (that God exists and created us with eternal and immaterial minds). The super-matter hypothesis also makes sense of the existence of pain and poverty and random suffering, if super-matter is not as capable as God, but Hume is also suggesting that things are not so terrible if God exists and we are eternal. The philosopher Marilyn McCord Adams develops a version of this view, where the idea is that we get a much different perspective on the role of suffering in our lives if we consider it as part of a larger (and eternal) story.[25] We might note also that at funerals, a priest will sometimes say that a particular death may *seem* to be a tragedy, but that there is a larger point of view from which to take it in: the person has moved on to a better place, and we are selfish if we want them to return to the lesser sphere. The priest says this, and means it. In a similar vein, Descartes speaks of a private satisfaction that we feel when a loved one dies because their situation has so greatly improved, and for the rest of time.[26] We would miss a friend who leaves for another part of the world, and whom we will never see again, but if they are pursuing their dream, and if we know they will be successful, at least a part of us should rejoice. And that is if we expect that it is the last time we will see them.

22

Hume thinks that there are no insuperable problems with the thesis that God is the origin of the order in the universe. God is eternal and uncaused, and He created highly sophisticated bodies and also immaterial minds. Hume sees no more trouble for the view that sophisticated matter is the origin of the order in the universe. It is also eternal and uncaused. It is there, without explanation, just like God on the first hypothesis. If matter is sophisticated, and it appears to be capable of quite a lot, then it has the resources to bring about order on its own, and it may even have the resources to bring about thinking. It is no objection to say that matter cannot be uncaused, because the other hypothesis posits an uncaused being as well. It is no objection to say that matter is not sophisticated, if the other hypothesis grants that there exist (because God has created) sophisticated material creatures like cells, trees, ecosystems, and the placenta. Hume wants to say that we already know that super-matter exists—it is everywhere around us. If we sell it short, that is only because we do not pay attention to all of its wonders. It exists in plants, in simple organisms, and in utero. We have to posit it anyway, and so the question is whether it is the uncaused and not-further-explicable being, or if instead super-matter is created and something else is the uncaused and not-further-explicable being.[27]

Unconscious intelligence?

23

It is a very controversial thesis that matter is sophisticated enough that it has the resources to bring about order and organization on its own. Some philosophers have argued that there are such things as embodied intelligence and muscle memory—and that bodies exhibit mentality and intelligence. Cavendish is squarely in this camp.[28] She thinks that the best explanation of the orderly behavior of bodies is that bodies are intelligent and perceptive. She adds that much of human behavior is guided by embodied intelligence as well:

> most commonly, the Tongue runs by rote and custom, without the consent of the Heart, or knowledg of the Thoughts: for, the Tongue doth ofttimes like the Legs, which most commonly walk without the guidance of the sight, or the directions of the knowledg; for few measure each stride, or count or look at every several step they take, nor think they how they go, nor (many times) where they go; and the Mind, many times, is so deep in Contemplations, that the Thoughts are so fix'd upon some particular Object, or so busily employed on some Invention, or so delightfully taken with some Fantasm, that although the Legs walk themselves weary, yet the Mind and Thoughts do not consider or think whether the Body hath Legs or no.[29]

Cavendish also speaks at length about the behavior of spiders, ants, bees, plants, and other organisms. She that supposes that these do not think consciously, but still engage in intelligent and goal-directed activity, and with a significant amount of success.[30] We might think of other examples—driving a car with a manual transmission, dribbling a basketball, dancing, reacting to a soccer ball (e.g. as a goalie), or doodling an image as we listen or talk. There is also the kind of case cited by Cudworth—the movement of the fingers of the expert pianist. Or we might think of examples like picking up a social cue, even if we do not quite know what it is.

24

Cavendish and Hume would argue that there exists something that is very much like super-matter, whether it is created by God or not. There is the human placenta; there is the digestive system of an earthworm, also the eyes of a fly. And let us not forget the chameleon, the hummingbird, or the seahorse. In the short period of time between conception and birth, pieces of matter worked together to develop into these. There is also the caterpillar that will build a cocoon and become a butterfly. And then there is the human body and its brain. The human body might be the most sophisticated piece of machinery in the universe; if we did not have one, and we were given one for Christmas, we would be floored! One of the questions that was considered in Chapter Three was whether or not super-matter (though that term was not yet introduced) is sufficiently sophisticated to bring about thinking. It is difficult to settle this question once-and-for-all. If we notice an embodied human being who is thinking, we might say that that is evidence that super-matter thinks. Or, if we do not think that matter could do such a thing, we would say that the human being is composed of super-matter plus something else—mind or soul.

25

There is evidence that matter is sophisticated, though again the evidence can be interpreted differently. There was an interesting story* in the newspaper recently, with the subtitle: "Cancer appears to be even more willful and calculating than previously imagined." New research has shown that a cancer cell is able to reprogram its metabolism in the light of the nervous system's attempts to destroy it. The cell is responsive to the specifics of its attacker, and is able to adjust accordingly. If so, cancer is very sophisticated and (unfortunately) a high achiever. A similar example that has been put forward is that grass communicates when it is being cut (or mowed)—the cut blades of grass will inform the surrounding blades of grass to pull back nutrients from their topmost parts so that the negative impact of a mow is decreased.* But it is also possible to argue that all such talk is metaphorical.

26

Certainly some material things are less impressive than others—for example, a heap of poo is less sophisticated than a diamond, and a diamond is less sophisticated (at least in terms of powers and abilities) than a placenta, and also less sophisticated than the white blood cells that attack invaders of the human body, or the spider that weaves a web. But the fact that there are some unsophisticated material objects is not evidence that there is not a hierarchy of material objects or that many material objects are not remarkable. By the same token, there might be human minds that are relatively imperceptive, but that is no evidence that human thinking cannot be extraordinary, especially if we know that there have existed people like Socrates, Aquinas, Pascal, Einstein, Cavendish, and Descartes.

27

But Hume and Cavendish are not quite proponents of the doctrine of intelligent design. Both think that matter is very sophisticated, and both are reluctant to say anything positive about the divinity that might have created them. For example, Cavendish writes,

[W]hat Creature in the Universe is able to describe the Thoughts or Notions of God? For though I do humbly acknowledg God to be the Author of Nature; and with the greatest reverence and fear, adore that Infinite Deity; yet I dare not attribute any Notions or Ideas to God, nor in any manner or way express him like our humane condition; for I fear I should speak irreverently of that Incomprehensible Essence, which is above all finite Capacity, Reason, or Idea.[31]

Cavendish is worried that the more insistent we are in our proclamations about God and His specific aims and goals, the more likely we are guided by our own aims and goals instead. It is surprising that one of her plays is not entitled—"I know what God wants you to do, and He wants me to make you do it."

28

One way that a philosopher could flesh out the view that matter thinks and is intelligent is like this: to argue that material things like ants, fingers and cells are intelligent and that, because all intelligence is of the conscious sort that often occurs in human beings, ants and cells and other bodies in nature are conscious. The other way (and this is what Cavendish does) is to argue that generally speaking material things think and are intelligent, but that intelligence is often nonconscious as well.

29

An important objection to reported cases of embodied intelligence is that we are misdescribing things and that conscious intelligence *is* present in these cases. For example, a dancer or pianist might insist that they are always consciously thinking of their moves on some level, and a driver might insist that she is always conscious of switching gears. A related objection is to allow that there is no conscious awareness in these cases, but that there is no intelligence or cognition either. It is hard to know how to settle this sort of debate, though philosophers have tried.

30

One way to attempt to settle the debate is this. We could try to locate a bit of activity that is uncontroversially intelligent—for example, some intelligent conscious reasoning—and then argue that that activity cannot occur unless there is unconscious intelligent activity at work behind the scenes. If conscious intelligent activity in some way depends on the exercise of nonconscious intelligence, then the incidence of nonconscious intelligence would be just as common. Then it would not be a stretch to say that nonconscious intelligence is operating in other parts of nature as well.

31

Both Cavendish and Hume offer such an argument. Hume was struck by the way in which our thoughts tend to come to us in a helpful order; or how if they come to us in *dis*order, they are usually followed by a recognition that they are disordered, and followed again by a thought that specifies a way to emend them. There is presumably a process or faculty by which all of this happens—a preconscious faculty, by hypothesis, for it is a faculty that inserts thoughts into consciousness, from outside of consciousness. Arguably this faculty or process is intelligent: if we call a person intelligent when they express a clever or brilliant thought, presumably we should also identify as intelligent the process by which those thoughts came to enter the person's mind in the first place. That is, the person is brilliant not because they noticed the thoughts that came to them—that's easy—but because of the appearance of the particular thoughts to begin with.[32] Hume focuses on the way in which thoughts seem to come together by their own doing:

> Nothing is more admirable, than the readiness, with which the imagination suggests its ideas, and presents them at the very instant, in which they become necessary or useful. The fancy runs from one end of the universe to the other in collecting those ideas, which belong to any subject. One would think the whole intellectual world of ideas was at once subjected to our view and that we did nothing but pick out such as were most proper for our purpose. There may not, however, be any present, besides those very ideas, that are thus collected by a kind of magical faculty in the soul, which, though it be always most perfect in the greatest geniuses, and is properly what we call a genius, is however inexplicable by the utmost efforts of human understanding.[33]

We are thinking about something, and the next thought that we have is relevant in some way to the last. If it was not, and our thoughts just occurred to us in any old order, we would not be able to put them in order: we would first have to see the order in which we want them to form, and then make them form in that order, but in that case the right order would have already had to present itself. As Hume suggests, things are not usually so deliberate—where we consciously consider a full multitude of different thought-orderings, or different possible trains of thought, and notice that one is the *right* order, and then place that one at the forefront of our mind. In many cases what initially presents itself to us is just the thought-ordering that we go with—in a casual conversation, or when we are following a train of thought to wherever it might lead.

32

Cavendish puts the argument more playfully. She suggests that when we have a coherent train of thought, there is a process going on behind the scenes that makes our thoughts unfold as they do. She has no idea what the process is, so she attributes the work to fairies:

> Who knowes, but in the *Braine* may dwel
> Little small *Fairies;* who can tell?
> And by their severall actions they may make
> Those *formes* and *figures*, we for *fancy* take.
> And when we sleep, those *Visions*, *dreames* we call,
> By *their* industry may be raised all;
> And all the *objects*, which through *sens'es* get,
> Within the *Braine* they may in order set.
> And some pack up, as *Merchants* do each thing,
> Which out sometimes may to the *Memory* bring.
> Thus, besides our owne *imaginations*,
> *Fairies* in our *braine* beget *inventions*.[34]

Here Cavendish is referring to the common experience in which a train of thought unfolds in a person's mind, or a thought comes to us at exactly the moment that we need it to. I like to think of examples of late night talk show hosts who always seem to think of just the right funny thing to say, at just the right moment, where I am sure that in a similar situation I would draw a blank and have the desperate thought—think funny relevant thing! If our thoughts did not come to us in the right sort of order, we would be at a loss to put them into order ourselves—by hypothesis, we would not have that order consciously present to our mind. What customarily happens, though, is that we do not have to be so reflective about matters, and we think coherently and even with inspiration. What Cavendish and Hume are saying is that if we grant that there is intelligent conscious thinking (and we do), we have to admit that there is unconscious intelligence as well.

33

We might consider also the reasoning that seems to go on in sleep. Sometimes we fall asleep thinking about a problem, and we wake up with the answer. Or in the course of a day we sit on a problem or question, and then bingo the answer presents itself. In both cases it would seem that there was intelligence at work in the background and that it was (by hypothesis) unconscious.

34

The twentieth-century philosopher Martin Heidegger attempts to highlight ways in which human behavior can be highly skilled and intelligent without being monitored by consciousness. Heidegger argues that much of our behavior is intelligent, but is not mediated by conscious thought. He has a number of aims in proposing this view. One is to offer an account of human nature that (he thinks) is accurate and that emphasizes that we are not best described as *homo sapiens* (or thinking man, from the Latin). Another is to propose a view of the best way for human beings to live if they seek meaning and significance.[35]

In the zone . . .

35

Heidegger would be suspicious of the label *homo sapiens*. We took on that label in order to accentuate our more exalted side, or at least what philosophers might insist is our more exalted side, but

Heidegger is arguing that we are thereby missing an important component of who and what we are. First, he argues that

> Modern philosophy made a total turnabout of philosophical inquiry and started from the subject, the ego. It will be surmised and expected that, in conformity with this fundamental diversion of inquiry to the ego, the being now standing at the center would become decisive in its specific mode of being.[36]

Heidegger is talking specifically about Descartes' view that "I think, therefore I am" is the appropriate foundation and starting point for all knowledge because it is the result that is most indubitable. Heidegger agrees that "I think, therefore I am" is "unassailable,"[37] but he thinks that if we take it as our starting point in knowledge and inquiry, our subsequent results will be distorted. For example, we might reflect and ask what human behavior is characteristically like, and (in a highly reflective mode) conclude that it is always guided by conscious thought. We might enter a highly reflective state and inquire into our human nature, and conclude that first and foremost we are thinking things! Heidegger writes,

> *In what way is the self given?* Not—as might be thought in adherence to Kant [and Descartes]—in such a way that an "I think" accompanies all representations and goes along with the acts directed at extant (outer) beings, which would thus be a reflective act. . . . Formally, it is unassailable to speak of the ego as consciousness of something that is at the same time conscious of *itself*, and the description of res cogitans as cogito me cogitare, or self-consciousness, is correct. But these formal determinations . . . are nevertheless very far from an interpretation of the phenomenal circumstances of the Dasein [human being], from how this being shows itself to itself in its factual existence, if violence is not practiced on the Dasein by preconceived notions of ego and subject drawn from the theory of knowledge.[38]

Heidegger makes use of a different expression to pick out human beings—*Dasein*. The German expression translates to "being out there," and Heidegger uses it to try to capture that for the most part when we are engaging in our pursuits and activities, we are not in a reflective mode, detached from the world. That is, we are not stuck in our own heads. Heidegger is concerned that if he used expressions like "self" or "I" or "human being" or "*homo sapiens*," a number of misleading associations would cloud his point. It is true that one of the features that makes us distinctive is that we are conscious thinkers, and that is probably what differentiates us from a lot of animals, but it might not be the predominant feature of human life that philosophers have supposed it to be. Noteworthy perhaps is that when philosophers present Descartes' view on the primacy of the reflective *I* to individuals from non-Western cultures, they often express puzzlement and disbelief.[39] Heidegger might point to this (anecdotal) evidence as partial support for his view, if non-Western cultures make up a large part of the human population.

36

Heidegger considers the lectern that he approaches in his classroom. He argues that when he is actually *using* the lectern—perhaps moving it a little to the left in order to have a better stance toward his students—an accurate description of his experience is not as a conscious ego that is thinking about a lectern. He writes,

> Let us bring to mind again the environmental experience, my seeing of the lectern. In my comportment toward seeing the lectern . . ., do I find anything like an "I" in the pure sense of experience? In experiencing, in this living-toward, there is something of me: My "I" goes completely out beyond itself and resonates along in this "seeing." . . . Attending strictly to the experience, I do not see anything psychical.[40]

Heidegger is suggesting that when we are immersed in an activity and engaging in it skillfully, there is very little introverted conscious awareness. There might be such awareness if a breakdown of some kind occurs, but otherwise we are, so to speak, "in the zone." We might try to think of other examples to motivate Heidegger's point here. Maybe a pitcher in softball reflects very hard about exactly where she wants her pitch to land, and thinks about each of her arm movements along the way. What often happens in such a case is that if the pitcher cannot get back into her normal rhythm, she loses her ability to throw a strike.[41] Or perhaps a person is fleeing from a threat, and thinking very hard about how to fit the key into their door. Or a person might be staring at a word on the chalkboard, struggling to remember to spell it, when they might be better off to distract themselves for a moment, and just write.

37

Heidegger then wants to add our normal default mode is to be "in the zone." We are doing the things that we do regularly, and thus that we do expertly—writing words on paper, speaking to a friend, shifting gears as we drive, using utensils, typing, playing guitar (or the lute), or talking and moving our legs as we walk.

38

Heidegger is not arguing that most of the time human beings are unconscious. We are not zombies: we might be consciously attending to something at any given moment, but at the same time we are doing a lot of things unthinkingly. Heidegger thinks that we are doing these skillfully, but that a conscious ego is not monitoring our behavior. As a further defense (though he does not offer it explicitly himself), he might join Cavendish and Hume in pointing to organisms that are much simpler than us—and to which we do not attribute conscious intelligence—but that are able to do things skillfully. We have considered, for example, the spider, the ant, and the bee. Our nervous systems are much more potent than the nervous systems of these organisms, and one of the consequences is that we are able to engage in conscious thought. But another consequence is that, like these simpler entities, we should have the wherewithal to do things skillfully and unthinkingly as well. We might put an earthworm brain on a tray, with a list of the unthinking behaviors that it can direct, and also a magnifying glass and a scalpel. Then we could put a human brain on the tray as well. It would be odd to suggest that *it* cannot guide a lot of behavior unthinkingly, and with more organization and finesse.

39

Heidegger does not think that human beings are for the most part unconscious, and he also allows (as he should) that there are highly reflective activities at which we can be very skilled. He just thinks that our primary and default way of being is not to be a detached reflective mind.

Significance, reflection, and immersion

40

Heidegger is also concerned with the question of how our lives come to have a feel of meaning and significance. Heidegger does not talk much about anything like *objective* value or meaning; for reasons that we will consider, he is quite silent about Wolf's fourth criterion (from earlier in Chapter Four). We have seen that Heidegger holds that when we are in a highly reflective state, we do not function as well at many activities as when we are "in the zone." We fail to get the key into the door, to write a word correctly, or to throw a ball over the plate. Heidegger also thinks that when we are in a highly reflective state, we can easily lose sight of the significance and relevance of the projects in which we engage: they start to appear cold and out of context, unmotivated and absurd. Presumably there is a connection between the two, if our ability to engage in skillful and functional behavior would have to be tied to our sense of the relevance and significance of what we are doing.

41

Heidegger argues that there is a relation between, on the one hand, our ability to engage in unreflective skillful activity, and on the other hand, the significance (to us) of the objects and pursuits that we build our lives around. More specifically, he thinks that if we take the perspective of the reflective *I* and consider these objects and pursuits from a detached point of view, they appear cold and divorced of context:

> The world-like is extinguished there. . . . This grasping, this firmly placing observation of the object as such, occurs at the cost of forcing back my own "I". . . . I do not resonate along in its [the object's] determination, but . . . this resonating, this going-out-along-with, is prevented. The object-being as such does not touch me. The "I" that firmly places is not myself anymore. Observation, as an experience, is only a remnant of lived experience; it is a de-living.[42]

The language here is no doubt tricky, but Heidegger appears to be saying something like this: if we step back and stare at a lectern or baseball, for example, and think about the first as a piece of metal with a rectangular shape, or the second as a round thing that is white with red stitches, we are in an important sense no longer *experiencing* the lectern or the baseball. If we enter a highly reflective mode by forcing the presence of the conscious *I*, the object in question will be present without its surrounding context, and engagement with it will in an important sense be prevented. We extinguish the world of activity that a baseball inhabits, and it is as much a baseball to us as it would be to an alien.

42

Or we might be a committed fan, watching the game at the stadium. We are in the grip of the moment. We care about who wins, and we are engaging with our friends about the different things that might unfold. If we step back enough, and we stare at first base in its capacity as a white square object, and ask why a person would run around first base at all, or hit a ball over the fence, the significance of the activity can begin to recede. We might also step back and think reflectively about the noises that we are making when we use language to speak with the friend next to us, or about the squiggles on the scoreboard that are standing in for a player's name. This stepping back does not last very long, usually, and we return to the game in all its glory. Our ability to uncover significance and context—Heidegger would call it our ability to uncover worlds—is sort of like our ability to see the image in a magic-eye poster.[43] We can take a perspective in which we just see meaningless dots or pixels, and then all of a sudden, "we are *in*"—we see the dinosaur. From that point on we probably see the dinosaur right away, though we can still alter our vision and see the dots if we would like. The disanalogy, Heidegger would say, is that in the case of worlds it can be harder to retreat to a detached perspective for any extended period time. He would add that that means that a significant part of what we are is not a *homo sapiens*, but a *Dasein*.

43

Another example might be a specialized tool that is used to fix a car. Consider first someone who is really into cars, and who knows how to take one apart and put it back together. She would see a specialized wrench on the ground in her garage and know exactly what it was and what it was for. Then consider the neighbor who knows almost nothing about cars, and who walks by the garage and notices the wrench on the driveway. The person knows that it is something—perhaps that it is a tool—but does not know it fully for the object that it is. Now consider that the neighbor's toddler picks up the tool and starts playing with it. Heidegger would say that there is an important sense in which the person in the garage is closer to the wrench than the neighbor or the toddler, even though one of them is holding it. The object *as a wrench* is not anywhere on their radar.

44

On Heidegger's view, there is often an inverse relationship between the extent to which the conscious *I* is present in an activity and the extent to which the activity is being fully engaged. For example, the more that I am introspectively entertaining ideas when I am in the middle of a conversation, the less I am actually having the conversation. The more that I am reflecting on the chess pieces as mere blocks of wood, the less that I am actually in the game. In most cases, the more that there is a manifestation of the conscious *I*, the less it is that we are actually partaking in our activities and pursuits.[44] Instead, we are having a remnant of a lived experience, a de-living. If Heidegger is right, a person's self is not just (and not even primarily) their conscious *I* or ego, but an *I* in conjunction with an enormous set of embodied skills and capacities. If we overlook that larger nature, we might handicap our ability to uncover worlds, especially if we privilege and prioritize our reflective thinking side. Perhaps a person is not too concerned about seeing the significance of baseball. However, if their ability to uncover worlds was neutralized, and *nothing* showed up to the person as significant, that would be a loss. We can think of other things that matter to us—a national anthem, a dance performance or song that is integral to our culture or heritage, a hand signal or facial expression. An outsider would not see what all the fuss is about, and indeed these things might mean nothing to him. Heidegger is thinking that it would be sad if *we* became perennial outsiders ourselves.[45] Another example that people seem to find resonant is Nascar. If we are not Nascar fans, we might wonder how anyone could ever care about a bunch of cars going around, and around, and around, . . . a track. What if everything showed up to us like Nascar?

45

This is presumably one of the reasons why culture and heritage can be so important to individuals, even if we recognize that it is fairly random which culture we are born into. Our culture and heritage can provide orientation to us,[46] but show up as unmotivated to an outsider. Even categories that we might regard as highly artificial can be extremely grounding. For example, the philosopher Kathryn Gines has argued that even if the concept of race is biologically a fiction, a person's racial identification can be a large part of how they make sense of themselves, so we should think very carefully before the concept is abandoned.[47] Instead of abandoning the concept of race (like we might abandon the concept of phlogiston, or witch), it should be retained "for the purpose of maintaining the collective memory" of a given group—for example, for remembering distinctly African American achievements. Individuals can "remain connected by their collective memory, not only of the past, but also of present projects and future endeavors."[48] This is a source of energy, motivation, and Heidegger would say, orientation.

46

A worry of course is that some individuals or groups might unite around the concept of race in a very different way. For example, a quick Google image search will pull up thousands of scenes in which KKK members and other white supremacy groups are basking in the intimacy and orientation that comes with hating anyone who is the other. Such individuals get a lot of mileage out of their racist community, and that is probably where they feel most grounded.[49] The notion of race is not alone in being implicated here—we might also cite instances of nationality, religion, and culture, among others. But presumably all of these can be embraced in a way that does not do any harm to an outsider, Gines would note. If so, retaining the notion of race would not be objectionable either.

47

Heidegger thinks that worlds are the central provider of meaning for human beings. If we lost our ability to uncover worlds, everything would just seem absurd—like the lectern to an alien; like the car tool to the toddler; like a dance or ritual to a person from another culture; like Nascar or the Superbowl to a person who is not a fan.[50] To occupy these respective worlds is to appreciate the set of activities that constitute them and to take the nonreflective perspective that is required to engage in those activities skillfully and see them as significant. It is hard to define a world exactly—perhaps we know it when we see it—but it tends to be a set of activities and practices that a group participates in and that involves goals and ends that the participants take to be significant. We do use the term "world" in the way that Heidegger is supposing—for example, we have heard people thank the movie world in acceptance speeches at the Academy Awards; or a headline might read that "The fashion world was hit with a bombshell today when . . . ." We might also recall "The Wide World of Sports," a television show in the 1990s. A good barometer of whether or not something is a world is whether or not there is a magazine—for example, *Trains, Fine Gardening, Popular Mechanics, VideoGamer, Modern Farmer, Hit & Miss: A Roller Derby Magazine, Parenting, Stitch n' Bitch, Coin World, Bronies.*[51]

48

Returning for a moment to the material at the end of Chapter One, Heidegger is also worried about the impact of technology on our ability to uncover worlds and our ability to be immersed in significance. There is no question that it can take a lot of time to uncover a given world—other examples might be chess, dance, piano, cooking, letter-writing, friendship, comic books, stamp collecting, rock climbing, telling stories, conversing, eating, exercising. If the constant use of efficient technology affects our willingness to proceed slowly, we might not wait as long as it takes to register the significance of a world and the way that all of its facets are interconnected. We might give it 1 or 2 minutes, and then shrug our shoulders. Worlds that take any serious time to uncover might then become lost to us.[52] Or we might not lose these worlds, but participate in diminished or truncated versions of them.

49

Heidegger is worried that we are getting to the point where we can no longer enjoy things that take a lot of time, like reading a book or even a newspaper article, writing a letter, talking to another human being, being curious. Heidegger thinks that at core our freedom is at stake. Freedom is not just about willing or deciding among our options, he thinks, but is a matter of what options present themselves to us and what options we can enjoy or take seriously. He writes,

> The essence of freedom is not originally connected with the will or even with the causality of human willing. . . . Freedom governs the open in the sense of the cleared and lighted up, i.e. of the revealed.[53]

If there are certain options that are closed off from us in the sense that they would never occur to us, or in the sense that we would not take the time for the options to come to us on their own, then those are not options that are available for us to choose. Heidegger is thinking that we are getting to this point because of our constantly indulged desire for immediate satisfaction.[54] Here Frankfurt's view on second-order desires might be relevant again. If we are Enframed by technology, we will not take the time to assess our desires, and we will think that the best and most fulfilling desires to have are desires that involve immediate satisfaction. For example, we might not leave a lot of unstructured time in our schedule to allow for accidental and spontaneous interactions, but those sorts of interaction might in the end fulfill us more. We might not take the time to get to know people in a nonsuperficial way, and we might not take the time to discover the activities that are the best match for our skills and our deepest interests. Even for those individuals who do break free, Heidegger would worry about a larger societal issue if the majority of people are Enframed. A person cannot immerse as fully in the world of chess, bowling, Scrabble, a book club, or Fight Club, unless there are others who take part as well.

50

An important consequence if Heidegger is right is that we can pick up behaviors and practices (from our culture or surroundings) that are not screened by our conscious—and more reflective and critical— minds. Heidegger does not want to deny that it is important for us to indulge the conscious *I*, or that there is a lot of value in critical reflection. Indeed, a really problematic scenario would be one in which we spend so much time immersed in a world that we never step back to examine it or assess the behavior that it involves. But nor would we want to spend the bulk of our time in a mode of detachment, or to identify with the conscious *I*, if that would keep us from a deeper kind of involvement and significance.

Possible discussion exercises

1 Aquinas argues that God exists, but there is a worry that his arguments can only yield that there exists *some* uncaused cause of the universe. Do you think there is a way for him to say that the uncaused cause has all of the traditional attributes of the being that we call "God"? Do you think that Aquinas is even trying to prove the existence of that being?

2   Aquinas assumes that other arrangements of matter were possible before anything existed. Do we have any good reason for believing this, do you think?

3   Anselm says that we can conceive of a being than which nothing greater can be conceived. Can we have such a thing before our mind, do you think?

4   An objection to Anselm is that if his argument for the existence of God is successful, then we can define a whole lot of things into existence—like a piece of pizza than which no greater can be conceived. Can Anselm maneuver around this objection?

5   Paley argues that if we find a watch on the ground, the most plausible thing to say is that it was designed by a being with human intelligence (or something very much like it). Do you think this is right?

6   Are seahorses and chameleons the result of beings that are not conscious? What is at stake here?

7   Do you think Hume is right that we have equally cloudy conceptions of God and the matter that might have existed at the Big Bang?

8   Is it right to say that cells communicate?

9   Do you agree with Hume's suggestion that in some cases the thoughts that come to us are a matter of luck?

10 How much of our daily lives do you think we spend "in the zone" or "on autopilot"?

11 Come up with one example of a behavior that becomes awkward when we start thinking too much about what we are doing.

12 Describe an example of a world that you inhabit—it gets you out of bed in the morning, and you are invested in it at various points throughout the day. Are you able to take a detached perspective from which the world shows up as unimportant? How might you convince an outsider that the activities and objects of that world are important?

13   Are there worlds whose existence and perpetuation are predicated on the nonexistence of *other* worlds? Try to come up with one example.

14   Are there bad worlds? Does Heidegger have the resources to say so?

15   Do you agree with Heidegger that any activity can show up as wholly pointless and unmotivated from an outsider's perspective?

16   Imagine that Heidegger conceded that there are objective values. What role would he think that these play in a meaningful and fulfilling life?

17   Are you worried (with Heidegger) that significance is under threat?

18   Every generation has worried about the impact of the latest technology. Do you think that Heidegger is overstating his case?

19   Come up with your own everyday example for one of the views or arguments or objections presented in this chapter.

Notes

1   See, for example, Søren Kierkegaard, *Fear and Trembling*, trans. Sylvia Walsh, Cambridge: Cambridge University Press (2006), prologue. There will be some further discussion of Kierkegaard in Chapter Seven.

2   St Thomas Aquinas, *Summa Theologiae*, in Richard N. Bosley and Martin Tweedale (trans. and ed.), *Basic Issues in Medieval Philosophy*, Orchard Park, NY: Broadview Press (1997), Ia, question 2, article 3.

3   Ibid.

4   Ibid.

5   St Anselm, *Proslogion*, in Richard N. Bosley and Martin Tweedale (trans. and ed.), *Basic Issues in Medieval Philosophy*, Orchard Park, NY: Broadview Press (1997), ch. 2.

6   Descartes, The Third Meditation, CSM 2:29–31.

7   Descartes, *Second Replies*, CSM 2:97.

8 Descartes, *Appendix to Fifth Objections and Replies*, CSM 2:273.

9 William Paley, *Natural Theology, Volume I*, London: Charles Knight (1839), 1–3. Paley (1743–1805) was a philosopher and theologian at Cambridge University, known best for his watchmaker argument (discussed here). He was also a brilliant mathematician and an accomplished debater. He was ordained as a priest, but was unable to secure a distinguished ecclesiastical position upon his departure from Cambridge, in large part because of his critiques of property ownership.

10 Ibid., 4.

11 Ibid., 11.

12 Ibid., 19.

13 David Hume, *Dialogues Concerning Natural Religion*, in J. C. A. Gaskin (ed.), *David Hume: Principle Writings on Religion*, Indianapolis: Hackett (1779/1993), 65.

14 Ibid., 55.

15 Ibid., 81.

16 Ibid., 75.

17 David Hume, "To Gilbert Elliot of Minto, 10 March 1751: A Letter Concerning the Dialogues," in *David Hume: Principle Writings on Religion*, 25–6.

18 Hume, *Dialogues Concerning Natural Religion*, 80.

19 Ibid., 65.

20 Ibid., 88. See also Hume, *An Enquiry Concerning Human Understanding*, section 1.

21 Cavendish, *Philosophical Letters*, 318.

22 Cavendish, "An Epistle to My Reader, for my book of Philosophy," in *Philosophical and Physical Opinions*, unnumbered.

23 Hume, *Dialogues Concerning Natural Religion*, 95–115.

24 Ibid., 101.

25 Marilyn McCord Adams, "Horrendous Evils and the Goodness of God," *Proceedings of the Aristotelian Society*, Supplementary Volume 63 (1989), 297–310.

26 Descartes, *Passions of the Soul*, CSM 1:381.

27 Hume, *Dialogues Concerning Natural Religion*, 64–6. Yet a third hypothesis is that super-matter is not eternal and that it just came into existence from nothing. Physicists sometimes propose this, though they also report that when they use the word "nothing," they mean it in a different way than it is used in everyday

conversation. Hume would say that this hypothesis is also difficult to fully understand, along with the hypothesis that God came into existence from nothing.

28 See the discussion in Chapter Three, and also Cavendish, "Another Epistle to the Reader," in *Philosophical and Physical Opinions*, ii. See also *Grounds of Natural Philosophy*, 7, and *Philosophical Letters*, 531.

29 Margaret Cavendish, *Nature's Pictures*, London: printed by A. Maxwell (1671), 625.

30 See, for example, *Nature's Pictures*, 280–5.

31 Cavendish, "Observations Upon the Opinions of Some the Ancient Philosophers," in *Observations Upon Experimental Philosophy*, 10.

32 There are some interesting internet videos on this.*

33 Hume, *A Treatise of Human Nature*, I.i.7, 24.

34 Margaret Cavendish, *Poems and Fancies*, London: Printed by T. R. for J. Martin and J. Allestrye (1653), 162.

35 Part of this discussion might have been in Chapter Four, but it helps to first have the discussion of Cavendish and Hume on sophisticated bodies and unconscious intelligence.

36 Martin Heidegger, *Basic Problems of Phenomenology*, trans. and ed. Albert Hofstadter, Bloomington: Indiana University Press (1927/1988), 123.

37 Ibid., 158, quoted in full below.

38 Ibid., 158–9.

39 See, for example, the discussion in Kartsen J. Struhl, "No (More) Philosophy Without Cross-Cultural Philosophy," *Philosophy Compass* 5 (2010), esp. section 3.

40 Heidegger, "The Environmental Experience," in Günter Figal (ed.) and Jerome Veith (trans.), *The Heidegger Reader*, Bloomington: Indiana University Press (1922/2007), 35–7. A very helpful discussion of Heidegger's larger philosophy is in Hubert Dreyfus, *Being-in-the-World*, Cambridge, MA: MIT Press (1991).

41 There are famous cases of this—for example, Rich Ankiel, a former pitcher for the St Louis Cardinals, and also Chuck Knoblauch, a former second-baseman who could no longer make the throw to first, and had to move to the outfield. Ankiel become an outfielder and was successful once again, but he really struggled as a pitcher.*

42 Heidegger, "The Environmental Experience," 35–6.

43 These were popular in the 1990s and are still around today. The poster has a bunch of dots or images that do not add up to a

coherent picture, but if we look at the image long enough, a whale or dinosaur or solar system appears, and we see what all the fuss is about.*

44 The main exception here would be reflective activities themselves.

45 There is a lot of art and music that is dedicated to the situation in which the relevance of things no longer shows up to a person, and the person feels unmotivated and depressed, in part because of all the uphill labor that is involved in going through the motions and faking it. An example is "Life in Vain" by Daniel Johnston, *Fun*, Atlantic Records (1994).*

46 A nice illustration is in a *Simpsons* episode in which the character Apu tries to assimilate into American society by rejecting his Indian heritage and becoming (among other things) a Mets fan. He feels lost and disoriented. This is in season 7, episode 20.

47 Kathryn Gines, "Fanon and Sartre 50 Years Later: To Retain or Reject the Concept of Race," *Sartre Studies International* 9 (2003), esp. 64–6. Kathryn Gines is Assistant Professor of Philosophy at Penn State University and is Founding Director of the Collegium of Black Women Philosophers. Her writing focuses on issues in Continental Philosophy, Africana Philosophy, Philosophy of Race, and Black Feminist Philosophy. She recently published a book on Hannah Arendt.

48 Ibid., 66.

49 The movie *American History X* with Edward Norton tracks the disorientation of a racist who abandons his old community and its practices and tries to start a new life.

50 A song that illustrates this point nicely is "Ballad of a Thin Man" by Bob Dylan in *Highway 61 Revisited*, Columbia Records (1965). In the song, the character "Mr Jones" encounters a community of circus workers who have a common history and a common set of practices and references, but he cannot make sense of any of it.* The refrain in the song is, "You know something is happening, but you don't know what it is. Do you, Mr. Jones?"

51 There is a sample collection of magazine covers at the textbook website.

52 See Heidegger, "On the Question Concerning Technology," 3–35.

53 Ibid., 25.

54 A nice example that reflects this worry is in the movie *wall-E*.*

CHAPTER SIX

Free will: Mental energy that appears to poof into existence from scratch

Abstract

This chapter considers the following: whether our vivid experience of freedom and independence is proof that we always have a choice to do other than we do; whether we are in control of our ideas and decisions if thinking is produced by the brain; whether we are in control of our ideas and decisions if thinking is not produced by the brain; whether it is up to us to decide what we believe, or if beliefs form on their own; and also determinism and necessitarianism.

The experience of freedom

1

The philosopher John Searle—he is still at work in the early twenty-first century—makes some very controversial claims about free will and the control that we have over our thinking. Searle acknowledges that there is a vivid experience of freedom and independence that is built into everyday action—the experience that no matter what we are doing, it is always possible for us to do otherwise. He writes,

> If one tried to express it in words, the difference between the experience of perceiving and the experience of acting is that in perceiving one has the sense: "This is happening to me," and in acting one has the sense, "I am making this happen." But the sense that "I am making this happen" carries with it the sense that "I could be doing something else." In normal behavior, each thing we do carries with it the conviction, valid or invalid, that we could be doing something else right here and now, that is, all other conditions remaining the same.[1]

The first-person experience can be very pronounced, and there is no way that we could seriously give it up or deny it, no matter how strong the arguments might be that are presented from the other side. A psychologist might show us experiments that predict a person's behavior quite reliably, and marketers might show us the effects of various forms of advertising on the brain—effects that are very dependable—but these are not going to win out. If we try to decide to give up on the view that we are free, built into our decision is the sense that, we are free!

2

To raise worries about free will, Searle has to change the subject a bit. He points to other considerations that he suspects we are not going to give up either—considerations that would appear to be basic and obvious and uncontroversial. He argues that if we acknowledge these, we are forced to conclude that we are not free after all. First, he borrows from the likes of Cavendish and Mettrie and argues that mind-body interaction is evidence that minds and bodies are ultimately made of the same stuff.[2] For now, scientists say that this basic sort of stuff is the set of elements on the periodic table, though of course the list might be revised over time. Whatever the basic building blocks of the universe turn out to be, they will be physical, Searle thinks, and the existence of minds will be due to these building blocks if the building blocks are fundamental. Searle is on board with Cavendish, Mettrie, and

Hume in concluding that this is not a disappointing result: it is only disappointing on the assumption that matter is a low-grade being, but it appears to be quite sophisticated.[3]

3

Searle then proceeds to ask: if the basic building blocks of the universe are particles with properties like atomic weight and charge, how can they combine into larger objects that have very different features like thinking and consciousness and rationality? Searle addresses the question by arguing that most of the things that we encounter in nature are large-scale macroscopic objects that have features that are not had separately by the individual atoms and molecules that make them up:

> A common distinction in physics is between micro- and macro-properties of systems—the small and large scales. Consider, for example, the desk at which I am now sitting, or the glass of water in front of me. Each object is composed of micro-particles. The micro-particles have features at the level of molecules and atoms as well as at the deeper level of subatomic particles. But each object also has certain properties such as the solidity of the table, the liquidity of the water, and the transparency of the glass, which are surface or global features of physical systems.[4]

Water is a collection of hydrogen and oxygen atoms, and more precisely it is a collection of molecules each of which is composed of an oxygen atom and two hydrogen atoms. No individual hydrogen or oxygen atom is wet, but when the atoms all combine together (within a certain temperature range of course), they form a larger object that has the feature of wetness. Searle then posits that most of the properties and features with which we are familiar—properties and features at the macroscopic level—are features that are not had individually by the elements that give rise to them. These features are (as Searle calls them) "emergent properties."[5] They are properties that would not exist if the fundamental elements or building blocks of the universe existed in isolation from each other; they are properties that come into existence as a result of causal interactions between these elements.

In the spirit of Cavendish, Searle has to concede that we do not ultimately understand why the atoms that combine to form water are wet.[6] We might *say* that we understand it, because we say that H and O are such that when they combine together the larger collection is wet, but that is not to understand anything as much as just to repeat what happens.

4

Searle now turns back to the question of thinking. If the fundamental building blocks of the universe are the elements of the periodic table and these elements (presumably) do not think, then minds and their ideas would not exist if the elements of the periodic table existed in separation. Just like the wetness of water depends on the behavior of the atoms that make it up, our thoughts depend on, and owe their existence to, the atoms (and the neurons) that make up the brain. According to Searle, minds and ideas are emergent properties of collections of sophisticated bodies. If we take apart the H_2O molecules, the wetness is gone. The same applies in the case of the brain and our thinking. Searle writes,

> As long as we accept the bottom-up conception of physical explanation, and it is a conception on which the past three hundred years of science are based, then psychological facts about ourselves, like any other higher level facts, are entirely causally explicable in terms of and entirely realized in systems of elements at the fundamental micro-physical level.[7]

For example, the wetness of water could not stubbornly persist, if the underlying molecules reconfigured to make the water into ice.

Wiggle room?

5

Searle then turns (at last) to the question of free will. First, he notes that our brains are in a specific configuration any time we have a thought, or when any mental event is a constituent of our thinking life. We may not know the details of the configuration of our brain, but that is not the issue. The brain is always in some specific configuration or other; it is in a specific configuration at the moment that it is producing the emergent properties that (at that moment) are our specific thoughts or decisions. These emergent properties cannot go off and do their own thing while the neurons are in that configuration:

> Since all of the surface features of the world are entirely caused by and realized in systems of micro-elements, the behavior of the micro-elements is sufficient to determine everything that happens. Such a "bottom up" picture of the world allows for top-down causation (our minds, for example, can affect our bodies). But top-down causation only works because the top level is already caused by and realized in the bottom levels.[8]

Water cannot change from liquid to solid or steam if there are not first the relevant changes in the bonds at the microscopic level; nor (to consider the analogy from Chapter Three) can the music of a harp proceed in a way that is independent of the movement of the strings.

6

If Searle is right, our thinking depends—down to the very last detail—on the behavior of the elements that compose the brain and nervous system. We might have the thought—"Brain, have a different thought!"—but the brain was in a certain configuration at the moment before we had that thought, and if so, that is the only thought we could have had. The mind might make a difference, but only if the brain made the difference to begin with, in which case it is not mind over matter after all.

7

We might also think of the analogy of a light switch. If we flip the switch, and all of the intervening variables (in the wires and in the walls) are working properly, the light goes on. It *has* to go on. If at some point we flip the switch and the light does not turn on, one of the intervening variables must have become defective. If all of the variables were the same, the outcome would be the same. It could not be any different.

8

Searle realizes—as contemporary science seems to have shown— that sometimes there is randomness at the microscopic level of bodies, and hence that there might be some randomness at the level of our neurons. In that case, not all of our thinking would be necessitated or determined. Searle points out, however, that this sort of randomness would not give us any real freedom, or at least not the sort of freedom that we probably wanted. The (quantum) randomness in question—randomness at the microscopic level—rarely manifests itself at the macroscopic level. Much more important: even if it did, that would just mean that some of our thoughts and decisions are not necessitated by our brain configuration, but are due to random firings at the neuronal level. Most of the time when my brain is in state X, I have thought Y. But it may sometimes happen that I am in state X and then randomly there occurs mental event Z. A thought or decision might occur randomly as a part of a person's mental life, but random thoughts and decisions are not things over which we have any real control.[9]

9

Returning to the question of freedom and the control that we have over our thinking and our decisions, Searle just bites the bullet. We have a vivid experience of freedom, to be sure, but like all of our mental life, it is produced by the brain as well. Perhaps the experience is due to an evolutionary process, where beings died out, and hence did not reproduce, if they thought that their behavior was as deterministic as the inanimate bodies in nature.[10] In any case, "Our conception of physical reality simply does not allow for radical freedom."[11]

10

Searle allows that if we conceive of freedom very differently, decisions can still be identified as free even if they are the product of the brain. We might subscribe to the compatibilist view that we are free *and* our decisions are dictated by antecedent states. Note though that this is not the view that (1) our decisions are dictated by antecedent states and (2) we are always able to choose other than we do. Those two positions are not compatible at all. Compatibilism is instead the view that free action is action that is the result of our desires and preferences, and is not involuntary or counter to our will. Our desires and preferences are dictated by antecedent causes, on this view, but we can still be identified as free so long as our behavior is in line with our wishes. The compatibilist has in her favor that most of the time we use the word "free" to describe people who are doing what they want to do—who are not in chains, who are not being ordered by someone more powerful, and whose desires translate into action without interference.[12] So perhaps that is a central meaning of the word "free." Searle is worried that whatever compatibilist freedom amounts to, it is not the sort of freedom that we are craving when we want free will.[13]

11

In a recent survey* of philosophers, 59.1 percent accept or lean toward compatibilism; 13.7 percent accept or lean toward libertarianism (or the view that decisions are not dictated by prior causes); 12.2 percent accept or lean toward the view that there is no free will; and 14.9 percent indicated "other." We can imagine some of the reasons that put philosophers on the different sides of this debate. Libertarian philosophers might worry about the vivid sense of freedom that seems to be an undeniable fact of our experience, and they might also worry about how we can make sense of moral accountability if a person's decisions are always dictated by the state of the universe the moment before. On the other hand, compatibilist philosophers might worry about how we are supposed to have any serious control over our decisions, or about their coherence and stability, if they come into existence without a cause. There are theological considerations that arise as well. For example, a libertarian might worry that Judgment Day makes no sense if our decisions are causally determined. To throw more complication into the mix, the philosopher Lynne Rudder Baker has defended compatibilism on the ground that it makes the most sense of the doctrines of divine providence and divine foreknowledge.[14] The 12.2 percent of philosophers who *deny* that we have free will might think that our decisions have a prior cause but that we should therefore refrain from identifying them as "free."

12

Searle's is certainly not the only view of the relation between the mind and the body, but some version of the view has got to be right if it is true that there are such things as consciousness and introspective thinking and if it is true that the fundamental elements of reality are the elements of the periodic table. There is a dependence relationship between our mental life and the neurons that compose the larger nervous system, Searle is arguing, and if he is right about the extent of that dependence, thinking cannot go off in a direction of its own.

No control?

13

What is interesting though is that if we take the alternative view—that thinking is not a product of the brain—we do not appear to have a lot of control over our thinking either. The philosopher Peter Van Inwagen—a theistic philosopher who like Searle is also still at work[15]—sets up the problem like this. Our ideas and decisions and choices are clearly something even if they are immaterial, in that they can be vivid and pronounced and have an impact and make a difference. This is the sort of thing that Descartes was trying to advertise when he famously argued, "I am, I exist"—he was not just pointing out the obvious, but highlighting that there are things that are real but that are not overtly sensible or tangible.

He was reminding us that even though they are invisible and intangible, things like ideas and choices are something and have a not-insubstantial amount of reality. If so, there is a question about how they come into existence, and from where. If we think of our thinking as it exists from moment to moment, a decision or new idea is sort of like a new spike in mental energy; that is how we might simulate it on a chart or EKG machine. The spike had better not come from nowhere because then it would just poof into existence and into our minds, and we would not have been in control of putting it there. If it has a prior physical cause, it is difficult—for the reasons that Searle presented—to locate any space for (libertarian) freedom. But the problem is just as severe if minds are not physical. If minds are not physical and our ideas and decisions have a prior nonphysical cause—perhaps another decision or idea or some other mental item—it is equally difficult to make sense of how we could be free. If the mental effect is due to these prior causes, then given the causes, the effect has to follow. If our ideas and decisions are *not* due to prior causes, they just poof into our minds at random. We would not be in charge of putting them there in that case either.[16]

14

But perhaps we are thinking of things all wrong. Perhaps an idea or decision is not produced by prior mental events, but is produced by *us*. We are present in the background; each of us is a conscious *I*, and we produce our own decisions and thoughts. Here things start to get very tricky, however. To make ourselves have a thought—to be in control of putting an idea of X before our mind—we have to think, "Have an idea of X," but in that case we would have to already have the idea. It would have to already have been put there, and not by us. We would also have to make sense of the sudden emergence of the mental event, "Have an idea of X." A similar worry arises for the view that we freely produce our own decisions. In a decision there is a new appearance of mental energy, and the question is where that comes from. If it just poofs into our mind, then it is hard to see how we were in control of its generation. If we produce it—as a result of having the thought "I am going to make this decision"—we need to ask how *that* mental event arises. If it just appears from nowhere, then we do not produce it and do not control it, and if it does have a cause, then its cause would require a cause, or else *it* just appears from nowhere. A standard example might be the decision to eat a piece of pizza which is preceded by the thought—"I'm pretty sure I'm gonna eat that pizza"—which itself is preceded by a desire for pizza and an idea of eating pizza as an option. If we can tell a causal story about how all of these arise, it would appear that every aspect of our mental life is caused by prior events.

15

The thought boils down to this: our mental life is either caused by prior mental events, or else it initiates on its own and without a prior cause. If the latter, and my ideas and decisions are produced by an uncaused act, my mental life is not necessitated, but it would appear that I am just a loose cannon.

16

Or we might think of the mind as analogous to a transparent ball of jelly. This is not quite to imagine it as nonphysical, but at least it is somewhat invisible, and substantial. Then we could imagine some colored dots that appear on the ball's surface for various periods of time. At some moments there might be a hundred dots, at other moments no dots, and at other moments just a few. We could then ask about where these dots come from. One option would be to say that they pop into existence with no cause at all. Another would be to say that there is some complex activity taking place within the ball of jelly, and making the dots appear as they do. Suppose next that there is a moment in which the ball is presenting no dots at all, and then all of a sudden presents a dot that is red. We would probably think that the red dot has a cause that is somewhere inside the ball, or else we might say that the dot has poofed into being from scratch. In the case of an immaterial mind, we might be inclined to say that our decisions do not come from nowhere. We might say instead that they are produced by a prior mental act—"I am about to decide." But the question again is where *that* comes from. Perhaps it comes from yet a prior mental activity of revving up, and then Van Inwagen asks the same question one last time: if the decision manifests because of a prior mental act of thinking "I am about to decide," and that manifests by a prior mental revving, then what manifests *that*? The issue here is the difference between the production of the prior mental acts in an immaterial mind, and the sudden production of the red dot on the ball of transparent jelly. As Van Inwagen notes, there might be a sort of causation—"agent causation"—in which a person somehow produces a mental state that is not due to a prior cause:

> It has been suggested . . . that, although events do indeed cause other events, it is sometimes true that individuals, *persons* or *agents*, cause events. According to this suggestion, it might very well be that an event in Jane's brain—a current-pulse taking the left hand branch of a neural fork, say—had Jane as its cause. And not some event or change that occurred within Jane, not something Jane *did*, but Jane herself, the person Jane, the agent Jane, the individual thing Jane.[17]

But it is not clear how the person or agent or substance would be in any control of the production of such events, or how she would ever be in control of the generation of one mental event rather than another.

17

Another analogy might compare the having of a thought, or the making of a decision, with a spurt of lava that fires from within a volcano. The analogy is this: minds are things or substances that produce ideas and decisions, and volcanoes are substances that produce spurts of lava. One moment, the mind is not having a thought, or not making a decision, and the next moment things are very different—it is thinking something it was not thinking before, or it is deciding (for example) to vacation in Florida. One moment the volcano is not spurting any lava, and the next moment the lava appears with all its force and fury. The volcano analogy helps to illustrate Van Inwagen's worry. If we say that the spurt of lava does not emerge from the recesses of the volcano, then the appearance of the lava is a mystery, and it is uncaused and random. But if we say that the lava is due entirely to what was going on in the volcano, then the lava had to appear exactly when it did, in the light of these prior causes—the way that stubble emerges because of the sufficient causes that are already there beneath the skin. If we say that an idea or decision arises, but not as a result of what is happening in the recesses of the mind, then ideas and decisions would seem to just poof into existence as well, and it is hard to see how we would have any control over them.

18

We might explore further the hypothesis that our decisions and ideas are due to processes that occur beneath the threshold of consciousness and behind the scenes. Ideas and decisions would not be produced by nothing, and would not come from nowhere; they would come from an unconscious part of the mind where they in some sense already reside. We might think again of the analogy of the stubble that emerges on a person's face. It does not just poof into existence from nowhere, but instead there are causes beneath the skin that push the stubble through to the other side.

19

All of the earlier problems would still appear to be in play. However the process works, the unconscious agent is (by hypothesis) not the conscious *I*, and so we would not be aware of the manner by which thoughts and decisions manifest in our conscious mental life. It is hard to see how we could be said to be in control of them. Furthermore, if the activity of the unconscious agent behind the scenes has a prior cause itself and, if like most causes, that prior cause necessitates the existence of its effects, we are not free. If the unconscious agent behind the scenes produces our decisions and thoughts at random, we are not free. If the activity of the unconscious agent behind the scenes does not have a cause, but just poofs into existence, we are not free either.

20

Van Inwagen owns all of this. He thinks that free will makes absolutely no sense—that we have no idea what it is or how it works or how it *could* work. But we cannot shake our sense of freedom:

> I conclude that there is no position that one can take on the matter of free will that does not confront its adherents with mystery. I myself prefer the following mystery: I believe that the outcome of our deliberations about what to do is undetermined and that we—in some way that I have no shadow of an understanding of—nevertheless have a choice about the outcome of these deliberations. (And I do not believe that the concept of agent-causation is of the least help in explaining how this could be.)[18]

Van Inwagen thinks that the arguments show—across the board—that there is no way to make sense of human freedom,[19] but it is obvious and undeniable that we are free. He makes sure to note that, just like freedom, a lot of other things are mysterious—for example, the entities that have been posited as a result of experiments in quantum physics.[20] There would also appear to be things like numbers, perfect geometrical figures, and objective standards of morality. We should not deny the existence of these just because they are weird, and we should not deny the existence of freedom. As Van Inwagen puts it, a denial of freedom conflicts with things that we *know*, and that are *true*: for example, that Hitler did a lot of things that were bad, and that he should have done otherwise, and hence he could have done otherwise.[21] Searle agrees with Van Inwagen that we cannot deny that we are free. For Van Inwagen, it's because we really are free, and for Searle it is because we have a vivid experience of freedom that is produced by our brain.[22]

21

Other famous philosophers have considered the same data and concluded that (in effect) there is no free will. As we have seen, Searle concludes that there is no free will, though he also thinks that we are not capable of believing that freedom is an illusion. The seventeenth-century philosopher G. W. Leibniz defends the view that every aspect of our mental life is determined by the causes that were in place the moment before. He argues that there is no such thing as randomness and that if a given set of causes is in place, only one outcome can follow. With Spinoza and other philosophers in his tradition, he accepts the principle that whatever happens at a given moment, there is a set of prior causes that caused it to happen exactly as it did, otherwise it would not have happened that way. Leibniz thinks that, at any particular moment, there is a fact of the matter about all of a person's ideas and motivations, and all of the person's mental history. Any mental energy that arises in the next moment, in the form of a decision or thought, must have the person's prior states as their complete and determining cause.[23] If a new decision or thought *did* just appear at random, that would not be a meaningful sort of freedom anyway. But that is irrelevant, Leibniz thinks. Everything has a prior sufficient cause that makes it be exactly as it is; otherwise it would not be that way. There is no randomness, and a person's prior states, fully described, lead to a unique and singular result. If we want to object that what leads to the decision or thought is the person's mind—the person has the thought, "I am going to introduce a decision"—Leibniz again wants to know where *that* comes from. It is a new blip of mental life, and it has a cause.

22

Hume anticipates some of Van Inwagen's concerns about the control that we have over our thinking. As we have seen, he speaks with admiration of the "magic" by which thoughts seem to come together by their own doing. They enter the conscious mind already ordered, or if we arrange them in the right order ourselves, it is with an eye to an order that presented itself just before. Presumably there is a faculty in the back of our mind that lines up our thinking, and a question is how it operates. Perhaps our thoughts are ordered in part by an unconscious self that is in the background, or the needs of the nervous system, or a number of other partial causes: the way that our grammar and language operate, or our culture, our more local cognitive history, or who knows. Or perhaps thoughts line up in our mind, but with no cause at all. That would be remarkable if there was absolutely no mechanism at work in such a complicated and subtle and successful process. If there *is* a mechanism at work behind the scenes, Hume is right that it is a remarkable one. But even if thoughts just poof into our mind without a cause, that is not to suggest that we put them before our mind or that we have much control over their appearance.

23

The mental life of any given individual is obviously complicated. There are thought patterns that a person might exhibit habitually, and, on the other end of the spectrum, there are mental events that a person might wish to generate but that do not come easily. For example, we might try hard to be charming or charismatic, or to come up with the perfect thing to say. The actor Neil Patrick Harris plays a television character that illustrates how these different attempts can play out. The show is *How I Met Your Mother*, and the character (Barney Stinson) is often in a situation where he does not see what he will say next. But he is confident that something will come to him—he says, "Wait for it, wait for it . . .," and (perhaps because it is television) the perfect thought comes to him indeed. Then he expresses it, and gets a laugh. But his thought does not come to him because he puts it before his mind; instead, he is very honest that he has to "wait for it." Even if he very energetically tries to think of the right thing—or as Van Inwagen would say, even if there is a mysterious process of agent causation and something is behind the scenes that is in control of the manifestation of his mental efforts and his acts of will—the appropriate thought either comes to him or it does not. If he described himself as generating the thought on his own, the description would be misleading.

24

Another show illustrates attempts that are less successful. On *Food Network Star*, contestants are required to exhibit their prowess at cooking, but also (and perhaps more importantly) their prowess at talking to the camera. They must be interesting, funny, energetic, poised, and in a word, compelling. Almost all of the contestants are terrific at cooking; that is not where the challenge lies. The difficulty is almost always with the camera. Some of the contestants become awkward and deliberate: spontaneous charm does not come, even if the contestants wait for it. In some cases, they find themselves attempting to *perform* it. When they do, it becomes transparently clear to the judges (and also to the audience) that the contestants are not being natural—that they are trying too hard, and even overacting. The contestant will then say things (in the more candid one-on-one interview) like that they *try* to be natural, or to be friendly or charming or clever. If they are repeatedly unsuccessful, they report that they need to find a way to tap into something, a sort of groove. In some cases, as with Barney Stinson, the contestant wills or decides to be natural and easy and clever, and it comes. Thoughts come to them while they are presenting their food, and they are relaxed and energetic and smooth. In other cases: nothing.

25

On a particularly telling episode of *Food Network Star*, a very gifted contestant (Jeff) came up with a comment that was funny and charming, just in time for the onlooking judges.[24] Four contestants were cooking in front of a distinguished panel, and they all had to describe their food and answer questions. The eventual winner has to be able to cook while talking and telling stories and responding to whatever the moment may bring, and so the episode was featuring (and testing) an important skill. The kitchen was hot, and Jeff was sweating a fair amount. At one point he sweat into the spring rolls that he was preparing. A judge called him on it—"You need to clean yourself; just clean yourself." His initial response was (or at least appeared to be) mild mortification. But then: "Usually I wear a headband, but I didn't want to today; sometimes my hair is the only thing I've got going for me." The judges laughed, and pretty hard. The other contestants were noticeably annoyed, wishing that something similar had come to them in their own moment of need. There were numerous instances on the show when they were in a similar circumstance, but nothing. It is not that an extremely clever comment or response came to them, and they saw how completely appropriate the comment was, and they just randomly decided not to take advantage. Or perhaps a good thought did come to the competitors in these cases, but the overriding thought also came to them that for whatever reason it would be best not to express it. But not Jeff. The right thought did come to him, and he expressed it and won the day. Presumably his cognitive history was helping him out here, where a thought came to him that did not come to others. Or if (contra Leibniz) the thought came to him at random, it is still hard to see how he was in control of its production.

26

There is a similarly telling episode of *How I Met Your Mother*. Barney experiences a trauma, and he struggles to have the charming thoughts that had always come to him automatically.[25] He is at a bar with his friends, and he approaches a woman he does not know, with the expectation that he will have interesting things to say once they start talking. He says something to her that appears to be a lead-up to a remark that is witty and compelling. He says in his characteristic manner, "Wait for it; wait for it . . .," but nothing comes. He is abandoned in his moment of need. He says with even more volume and force—"Wait for it!"—but in this instance things do not work out. To be sure, when the right thoughts come to him he *is* being witty, and his wittiness is a part of him, but that is not to say that he has a lot of control over whether he is witty or that his thoughts and decisions are solely the product of his will.

27

Perhaps the correct thing to say here is that Barney and others are empowered because of steps that they have taken in the past to make sure that the right sorts of thoughts occur to them now. This seems right, and there is no question that Barney and individuals like him have played a role in their own cognitive histories. At the same time, we have to ask about the specific moments that are a part of such a history. These moments have a history themselves, or else they were due to agent causation (or something similar).

28

We might also raise the question of whether a person's causal history is limiting, or if in fact it is just the opposite. Perhaps a person's causal history makes it possible for the person to have thoughts when otherwise they would not. Still, we might get frustrated that only certain thoughts come to us, and wish that our thinking would unfold differently. Perhaps we only think of things to say that are highly conventional, or relatively uninteresting, and we wish we could do better. With this might come the drive to get exposure to new inputs and habits and skills. We might try to overcome our regular cognitive trajectory—and be more original and authentic, for example[26]—but there can be a puzzle about how we could do this unless a new cause intervened. And in that case it can seem as though the whole process—and indeed as though the pursuit of any sort of goal—is entirely out of our hands. This is one of the reasons that Van Inwagen thinks that there has to be at least some level of radical freedom, however inconceivable and inexplicable it may be. Otherwise we could not even make sense of ourselves as setting goals and aims.[27]

Do beliefs form on their own?

29

Spinoza was also worried about the extent to which we control our ideas and our decisions. We sometimes use this sort of locution— "Here is the information; it is up to you to decide what to believe." The locution is perfectly sensible; and it would be off-putting, and also a step in the direction of tyranny, if we were told what to think and why. But Spinoza is worried that the locution is misleading. He thinks that for the most part our beliefs tend to form on their own—as a result of the information that comes into our view, in conjunction with our existing background beliefs. He puts it like this:

> It is never we who affirm or deny something of a thing, but it is the thing itself that affirms or denies, in us, something of itself.[28]

Spinoza's point appears to be that as new information comes in, our beliefs form on their own. We say—"I decided what to believe"— but we are just capturing that our belief does not feel forced (by an outside authority, for example), and that it squares with the beliefs and assumptions that we already have.[29]

30

For Spinoza, all beliefs and decisions have a prior causal history. Consider, for example, that we are a juror in a courtroom, perhaps in a murder trial. Let's say that the defendant's wife was found dead, and the defendant is accused of having killed her. We learn that he has no alibi, that he and his wife were having marital problems, and that they had been in counseling. We learn also that she had a large life-insurance policy. In addition, a neighbor testifies that she saw him rolling up a large carpet outside of the house on the day that his wife disappeared, and stuffing it into a truck. At this point we might start to notice a belief forming in ourselves about the defendant's innocence or guilt. We might find ourselves believing that he probably did something terrible. Spinoza would ask us to describe the details of the formation of the belief—whether we *decided* to believe that the defendant is guilty, or if the belief just started to form as the different pieces of evidence came in.

31

But of course we might not arrive at this conclusion at all, or at least not yet. We might have the antecedent belief that a person should not come to any conclusions about a case until they are in possession of all of the relevant information. If so, we might still be neutral or ambivalent.

32

Now imagine that we learn (from the cross-examination) that the defendant works in the carpet business and that he rolls up carpets in his yard on a daily basis. We learn in addition that the defendant had a large life-insurance policy himself, and that he and his wife had purchased these together, years before. We learn also that although they participated in couples therapy on a regular basis, they had been doing this since the start of their marriage, out of a commitment to keep it strong for the long haul.

33

Some final information comes in. We learn that the defendant had been having an affair for five years and that he told his mistress that he wished his wife was out of the picture. We learn that the defendant had used bleach to scrub clean the living room of the house that he had shared with his wife, and we learn that on the day of the killing he had searched a number of websites to find out how best to do this. Our beliefs might change dramatically at this point. Or perhaps a juror is still inclined to vote "not guilty." Perhaps he has antecedent beliefs in the prevalence of conspiracies, or perhaps he is a rabid sexist who holds that women always have it coming. But Spinoza would argue that even so, the beliefs that form—they form on their own.[30] They form in the light of the information that we take in, against the background of our existing beliefs and assumptions. We like to say that we are in control of deciding what we believe, but for Spinoza that is because we tend to have the antecedent background belief that human beings are self-determining and independent.[31]

34

We might attempt to refute Spinoza by forming a belief at will. For example, we might decide to believe that the sun is blue, without any evidence. We can say out-loud that it is blue, and we can even yell and exclaim it. But it is not clear that that means that we thereby believe it. Spinoza would say that what is true of us in that case is that we have exclaimed some things and that we still have the belief that the sun is yellow. If an authority that we really trust tells us that the sun is not yellow, but that it just *seems* yellow on the horizon, then belief-formation might be very different. Perhaps Stephen Hawking tells us that the sun is really blue and that it looks yellow to us because of the way that the light interacts with our retinas. Or perhaps the pope offers a theological analogue. But in such a case Spinoza would ask us to feel if the belief has formed as a result of a decision or act of will, or if it has formed on its own in the light of the new input.

35

A similar case is where we are told that we will be given one million dollars if we believe that two and two add to seven, or that three equals nine, or that forced child prostitution is morally acceptable. For a million dollars, a person might be able to say that they believe these things, and perhaps they could even commit to broadcasting the views in public for the remainder of their lives, but it is not clear that the beliefs would actually form.

36

Spinoza also subscribes to the view that at any given moment the bodies in the universe are in a specific configuration and that that configuration dictates exactly what will come next. He would add that if we had all the information about a situation that we confront, and knew all of the causal variables involved, a belief would form in us about how things have to unfold. This is not what happens in most cases, when our information is incomplete. But Spinoza thinks that there is an ideal to which we can aspire. When we acquire information,

[O]ur soul is changed in such a way that it receives other modes of thought, which it did not have before. Now when someone, in consequence of the whole object having acted upon him, receives corresponding forms or modes of thought, then it is clear that he receives a totally different feeling of the form or character of the object than does another who has not had so many causes [acting upon him], and is therefore moved to make an affirmation or denial about that thing by a different and slighter action (because he becomes aware of it only through a few, or the less important, attributes). From this, then, we see the perfection of one who takes his stand upon Truth, as contrasted with the one who does not take his stand upon it.[32]

Falsity arising thus, namely, because when we happen to know something or a part of an object, we imagine that the object (although we only know very little of it) nevertheless affirms or denies that of itself as a whole; this takes place mostly in feeble souls, which receive very easily a mode or an idea through a slight action of the object, and make no further affirmation or denial apart from this.[33]

If our snapshot of a situation is composed of a small amount of information, or if it only takes into account the information that is relevant to our needs and concerns, and does so to the exclusion of other information that is present, then our snapshot is incomplete and skewed. If so, there is a radical gap between the scene that we are representing to ourselves and the world that is really out there and that we are navigating. For example, we might say, "It just started raining," or "The object is not making a sound." Or we might note that Tuesday is trash day and wonder how the city can pick up the whole town's garbage in a single morning and afternoon. With more information, and from a more disinterested perspective, we might say later that it did not start raining, but that it was already raining in the next town over; or we might learn that the object in question is making a high-pitch sound that can be easily heard by a dog. Spinoza is not pulling any punches in his description of the person who is content to paint their picture of the world on the basis of incomplete information: their experience is fiction. Of course, the controversial issue for Spinoza—and indeed there are a lot of controversial issues for Spinoza—is who is in a position to say that they have a complete picture, and when.

Determinism and necessitarianism

37

Determinism is the view that things have to unfold in one specific way given the causes that are in place at the prior moment. Still, the view leaves open that at some juncture the prior causes could have been different. Necessitarianism is basically determinism *plus* the view that there does not exist the possibility that the prior causes could have been different. Spinoza motivates necessitarianism along the following lines. Possibilities would have to be something in order to be able to do anything or make a difference, but all that really exists at any moment is the actual universe. Outside of this universe, there is no alternative reality that could be extracted or tapped, in a way that would allow the prior causes to ever have been different. Spinoza thinks that the infinite universe is all that there is; he calls it alternately "God" or "Nature." As an infinite being, it has no limits and constitutes all of reality. Spinoza says this:

> God, or substance consisting of infinite attributes, each of which expresses eternal and infinite essence, necessarily exists.[34]
>
> Whatever is, is in God. . . .[35]
>
> The eternal and infinite being, whom we call God, or Nature, acts by the same necessity whereby it exists.[36]
>
> Nothing in nature is contingent, but all things are from the necessity of the divine nature determined to exist and to act in a definite way.[37]
>
> Things could not have been produced by God in any other way or in any other order than is the case.[38]

God or Nature is all of reality. It includes the entirety of the physical universe, and it includes the set of ideas that are a complete picture of that universe. That of course means that our own minds and ideas are a component of God or Nature; or as Spinoza puts it, that they are "in God." Our ideas would seem to be incomplete and gappy representations of reality, and so Spinoza is forced to say that our minds contain unconscious elements and that when the conscious and unconscious elements of all minds are considered together, they are a picture of reality from a God's-eye point of view.[39]

38

For Spinoza, the prospect that things could ever happen other than they do supposes that there are alternative causal variables that could swoop in from outside the universe and make things happen differently. But he would add that there is no outside to the universe. We might think, for example, of a hockey arena that has a penalty box. A player in the box is outside of the game and so is not on the ice, but when he swoops back in he is able to make an important difference. It is not as though there is a similar box on the outside of the universe, containing bodies that might enter and make things happen differently, or that might stay put where they are. If there was such a box, Spinoza would say that we have drawn the boundary of the universe wrong: the box is also part of the universe, along with the things inside of it, and if they make a causal difference they do so in the specific region where they are located—as a function of their actual powers and energies, and as a function of the properties and features of the bodies that surround them.

39

Spinoza might say something more rhetorical like this: when things happen, they happen in the light of the variables that actually exist and not in the light of variables that do not. If we had more information about the bodies that surround us, and the bodies that are pressing upon them, and the bodies that are pressing upon *them*, it would be much clearer what is possible and what is ruled out. It would also be clearer that our sense of what is possible is often a function of the limited information that we have taken in. To consider another example, let's say that we drop a toy boat into the Iowa River from the middle of the student pedestrian bridge. We might say that it is *possible* for the boat to veer to the left and end up on shore next to the student union. We might say that it is also possible for the boat to float down the middle of the river and be swallowed by the machinery at the hydroplant. However, or at least this is Spinoza's thought, there is a fact of the matter about the current of the river, the weight and constitution of the boat, the rate and force of the wind that presses against the boat as it falls from the bridge, and the current upstream in nearby Coralville. There are also a number of other variables that are in place at the given moment—the ones that surround Coralville and the ones that surround the ones that surround Coralville—and any variables that are *not* in place do not exist and so cannot do anything, and cannot make a difference. Spinoza's thought is that the boat's movements will be a function of the variables that are present, and so there is a fact of the matter about where the boat will end up, even if we do not know it because of the incompleteness in our information. If we had all the information, we would see where the boat will go—where it *has* to go. Spinoza would respond to Aquinas's initial argument for the existence of God by saying that it is not true that before anything was actual, there were a lot of different possible ways that things could be. There is no unactualized possible reality now, and there was no unactualized possible reality then.

40

Of course, Spinoza is forced to a remarkable extreme. He has to concede that necessitarianism reaches all the way down and applies even to our ideas and decisions. Van Inwagen would insist that that cannot be right. Spinoza would insist that the alternative is loose-cannon freedom and that that is not freedom at all.

Possible discussion exercises

1   Is an experience of freedom all that we need for practical purposes? Are we free so long as it is impossible for anyone to predict our own behavior?

2   How do Searle and Heidegger disagree on the issue of human freedom and the control that we have over our behavior? Which do you think is the more plausible view?

3   Searle thinks that whatever the fundamental building blocks of the universe turn out to be, they are going to be physical. Is this a fair thing to say? Why or why not?

4   Do you think that Van Inwagen is right that Hitler could have done otherwise? What can Van Inwagen's determinist opponent say here about holding Hitler accountable?

5   Do you think that everything requires a prior and sufficient cause, even a decision? Why or why not?

6   Do you think that the compatibilist view of freedom is a cop-out? Why or why not?

7   Do you think that we do not have a lot of control over the unfolding of our mental lives? Why or why not?

8   Someone might allow that our ideas and decisions at any given moment are due in large part to our cognitive history, but insist that at earlier moments we had control over how our cognitive history developed. Do you think this is right? Why or why not?

9   Are there any cases in which we can decide to believe something, and the belief thereby forms?

10 Come up with an example of something that you believe is possible, but where Spinoza would say the belief is based on incomplete information.

11 Come up with an example of something that you believe is possible, but where the belief cannot be explained in terms of incomplete information.

12 One view is that there is real randomness, and another is that things just appear random sometimes, when we don't know all the causes that were in play to bring about some effect. Which do you think is right?

13 Is Spinoza right to hold that if two people had all the same information about an issue, and all the same background beliefs, they would form the same beliefs about it?

14 Do you think that there are such things as possibilities? What are they?

15 Spinoza will go on to argue that human beings would be much happier, and much better off emotionally, if we were successful in remembering that things have to happen exactly as they do. What might be an example? Is he right, do you think?

16 Is it better to have loose-cannon freedom, or is it better to be causally determined to make the decisions that we do? Is there a third option that has not been considered?

17 Come up with your own everyday example for one of the views or arguments or objections presented in this chapter.

Notes

1 Searle, *Minds, Brains and Science*, 95.

2 Ibid., 17, 25–6.

3 Ibid., 24.

4 Ibid., 20–2.

5 See also John Searle, *The Rediscovery of the Mind*, Cambridge, MA, and London: MIT Press (1992), 14.

6 Searle, *Minds, Brains and Science*, 24.

7 Ibid., 98.

8 Ibid., 94.

9 There are a number of interesting web videos that address this and other issues surrounding free will.*

10 Ibid., 98.

11 Ibid.

12 Again, this is similar to the move that an externalist might make in defining the word "knowledge," or that Socrates' opponent might make in defining the word "perfect."

13 Searle, *Minds, Brains and Science*, 89.

14 Lynne Rudder Baker, "Why Christians Should Not Be Libertarians: An Augustinian Challenge," *Faith & Philosophy* 20 (2003), 460–78. Lynne Rudder Baker is Distinguished Professor of Philosophy at the University of Massachusetts, Amherst. She has written numerous books and articles on metaphysics, philosophy of mind, philosophy of action, and philosophy of religion.

15 Peter Van Inwagen is a distinguished professor of philosophy at Notre Dame University. He is a leading figure in metaphysics, philosophy of action, and philosophy of religion, especially the problem of evil. He is perhaps most famous for his argument that compatibilist freedom is not a kind of freedom at all because it does not leave room for agents to have control over their decisions.

16 Peter Van Inwagen, "The Powers of Rational Beings: Freedom of the Will," in John Perry, Michael Bratman, and John Martin Fischer (eds), *Introduction to Philosophy: Classical and Contemporary Readings*, Fifth Edition, Oxford and New York: Oxford University Press (2010), 406–8.

17 Ibid., 407.

18 Ibid., 410.

19 That is—that there is no way to make sense of noncompatibilist freedom.

20 Ibid., 408.

21 Ibid., 409–10.

22 Searle, *Minds, Brains, and Science*, 98.

23 Leibniz, *Discourse on Metaphysics*, sections 13–14; *Monadology*, sections 7–22. Spinoza's view will be considered in more detail below on pp. 198–205.

24 This is season 7, episode 2.

25 This is season 3, episode 10.

26 Nietzsche and Heidegger seemed to want to promote the benefits of this sort of endeavor.

27 Van Inwagen, "The Powers of Rational Beings," 409–10.

28 Baruch Spinoza, *Short Treatise on God, Man, and His Well-Being*, in Samuel Shirley (trans.) and Michael Morgan (ed.), *Spinoza: Complete Works*, Indianapolis: Hackett (1662/2002), 82.

29 Baruch Spinoza, *Ethics*, in Samuel Shirley (trans.) and Michael Morgan (ed.), *Spinoza: Complete Works*, Indianapolis: Hackett (1677/2002), part 2, propositions 48–9.

30 We have been considering a made-up court case, but there are number of real-life instances that we might consider as well.*

31 Spinoza, *Ethics*, appendix to part 1.

32 Spinoza, *Short Treatise on God*, 80.

33 Ibid., 83.

34 Spinoza, *Ethics*, part 1, proposition 11.

35 Ibid., part 1, proposition 15.

36 Ibid., part 4, preface.

37 Ibid., part 1, proposition 29.

38 Ibid., part 1, proposition 33.

39 Ibid., part 2, corollary to proposition 10; propositions 32 and 33.

CHAPTER SEVEN

Agency, authority, and difference

Abstract

This chapter considers the following: the control that we have over our decisions as opposed to the power and authority that we have to implement those decisions; whether or not an individual's power and authority in a given environment is a function of the power and authority of the other beings in that environment; and whether or not we are ever under an obligation to modify our desires or preferences if they lead us to behave in ways that limit the possibilities of others.

Free choice and effective choice

1

Cavendish had a number of aims in life, one of which was to be a scientist. But of course a person cannot just declare—"I am a scientist"—and have it be true. A person can say "I am a news reporter," but if they are not actually employed as a news reporter, or if no one will read or take seriously the person's stories, then the person is not actually a news reporter. If they run around town saying that they are, we have another name for them instead. The same presumably applies in the case of a surgeon, a musician, a professor, a banker, a carpenter, a secretary, a personal trainer. Cavendish was not a scientist; she would say that she was an aspiring scientist and that whether or not she would be an *actual* scientist was up to more than her free decisions.[1] She might have had a lot more success today, where the circumstances of the surrounding world have altered. But by hypothesis that would not be due to anything different happening on her end. Her decisions and mental life could be entirely the same in both the seventeenth century and today. In her own time, there was corrosion in the interface between her decisions and the world.

2

Cavendish subscribes to the larger view that every body in the universe depends on the bodies that surround it for its properties and its structural integrity. She writes,

> no seeds can produce of themselves if they be not assisted by some other matter, which proves, that seeds are not the prime or principal Creatures in Nature, by reason they depend upon some other matter which helps them in their productions; for if seeds of Vegetables did lie never so long in a store-house, or any other place, they would never produce until they were put into some proper and convenient ground: It is also an argument, that no Creature or part of Nature can subsist singly and precise from all the rest, but that all parts must live together; and since no part can subsist and live without the other, no part can also be called prime or principal.[2]

We might think of other examples. We say that a solid in a beaker (in a chemistry lab) turns blue because of the solution that we added to it, but the reaction would not have occurred if the atmospheric pressure or temperature was much different than what it is, or if the laws of nature were very different. The glass would not retain the form of a beaker; the solution would not have been a solution. Part of what is motivating Cavendish is the view that the universe is a plenum, with no empty space, and so each thing stands in causal relations with all others, however distant.[3] The "empty space" that we encounter is filled with bodies that are not familiar to our macroscopic senses—perhaps what we might call "energy" or a "field" today.

3

Cavendish takes this view—that we depend on other beings for our properties and features—to apply across the board. For example, she remarks that (in her time at least) a woman's social capital is largely dependent on her marital status:

> [I]t is an Honour for Maids to get good Husbands, because it is a kind of Reproach to live unmarried, for Marriage is Honourable, and gives a Respect to Women, unless they be incloystered, which all Constitutions will not agree withal.[4]

One of the roles that was not fitting for a woman in Cavendish's time was the role of philosopher. This is not to say that Cavendish thought that women like herself were incapable of generating important philosophical results, or that women were not free to attempt to become philosophers, but instead that women were doomed to be unsuccessful in such attempts because of the interface between their decisions and the world. Cavendish satirizes the situation in one of her plays, in which a group of men at first have a traditional view of the role of women, but where in the end, and unrealistically, they come full circle. But first:

> 1. *Philosopher*: Come my learned brothers, are we come now to hear a girle to read lectures of naturall Philosophy to teach us? Are all our studyes come to this?
>
> 2. *Philosopher*: Her doting father is to blame, he should be punished for this great affront, to us that's learned men.
>
> 3. *Philosopher*: Philosophers should be men of yeares, with grave and Auster lookes, whose countenances should like rigid lawes affright men from vanityes; with long wise beards, sprinkled with gray, that every hair might teach, the bare young Chins for to obey. And every sentence to be delivered like the Law, in flames and lightning, and flashes with great thunder, a foolish girle to offer for to read: O times! O manners!

1. *Philosopher*: Beauty and favour and tender years, a female which nature hath denied hair on her Chin, so smooth her brow, as not to admit one Philosophycall wrinckle, and she to teach, a Monster tis in Nature; since Nature hath denied that sex that fortitude of brain.[5]

When the aspiring philosopher Sansparella finally enters, philosopher #1 says, "Sir, we perceive now, you have invited us to feast our eyes, not our eares."[6] Then they listen to Sansparella, and they react very differently than people had reacted to Cavendish in real life:

1. *Philosopher*: No, no, we will all now send for Barbers, and in our great Philosophies despair, shave of[f] our reverend beards, as excrements, which once did make us all esteemed as wi[s]e, and stuff boyes foot-balls with them.

2. *Philosopher*: Nature, thou dost us wrong, and art too prodigall to the effeminate Sex; but I forgive thee, for thou art a she, dame Nature thou art; but never shewed thy malice untill now, what shall we do?[7]

The fictional world that Cavendish is representing in the play is a hybrid between her actual world—in which traditional gender norms are firmly in place—and an alternative possible world that in her time is quite distant. Cavendish likes to employ this maneuver—situating us in other worlds—to describe how the selfsame person can be surrounded by different audiences and environments, and straightaway have different amounts of ability and power.

4

Cavendish is interested in shining a light on the interface between our decisions and the world. To show just how far away is the world of *Youth's Glory and Death's Banquet*, Cavendish has one of Sansparella's admirers state an unexpected wish:

1. *Gentleman*: Certainly, Nature was never so bountifull, to any of that Sex, as she hath been to her.

2. *Gentleman*: The truth is, she favours the Female Sex, for the most part, more than she doth the Masculine Sex; because she is of the Female kind herself.

1. *Gentleman*: Faith, I could wish that I never wisht before.

2. *Gentleman*: What wish is that?

1. *Gentleman*: Why, I wish, I were a Woman, but such a Woman as the Lady *Sanspareille*.[8]

In Cavendish's time, women were not capable of making philosophical contributions, and so they would not make an impact, and they would not be philosophers. Cavendish is writing playfully, but at the same time she is very serious. She is concerned that there are forces at work that are making it impossible for women to do the things that might constitute their passion and that might also add to the larger good. In an introduction to her book of plays, she speaks to some of the forces in question:

2. *Gentleman*: No, for a womans wit is too weak and too conceived to write a Play.

1. *Gentleman*: But if a woman hath wit, or can write a good Play, what will you say then.

2. *Gentleman*: Why, I will say no body will believe it, for if it be good, they will think she did not write it, or at least say she did not, besides the very being a woman condemnes it, were it never so excellent and care, for men will not allow women to have wit, or we men to have reason, for if we allow them wit, we shall lose our prehemency.[9]

Cavendish is worried that a specific group has used its power to overtake a large mass of physical and emotional and psychological territory, to the point where a different group that also inhabits that territory is thereby constrained.

5

Cavendish was regarded as something of a nut in her time. People called her "Mad Madge." But the very same person would not have been universally regarded as crazy in 2014. Cavendish (if she were living today) would be seen by many as quite accomplished: she authored novels, plays, and philosophical treatises, and she read practically everybody and everything. One of her most important books was *Philosophical Letters*. The philosophers and scientists of her time would not correspond with Cavendish in print, and so *Philosophical Letters* is a fictional depiction of a correspondence in which she engages with their views and arguments. In a different work, *Blazing World*, Cavendish has her main character transported to another planet, one on which she is the same person in terms of her beliefs and choices and talents and skills, but where the objects and "people" in her environment are very different from the beings that she encounters on earth. They are more open than their earthly counterparts to the prospect of a female scientist, a female philosopher, a female military leader, a female barrister, a female anything. On the Blazing World, the main character is taken seriously as an authority figure, and that is part of what allows her to be Empress. Similarly, in *Bell in Campo*, a group of women form an army and become "co-partners" in government, and "help rule the World."[10] The women submit to a powerful "generalless," and together they use their weapons to defeat the enemy and save the male army as well. In Cavendish's own society, a woman might give an order, but it would not lead to anything, and it would not be authoritative, and the woman would not be a general. The surrounding world is different in *Bell in Campo*.

6

In the current day, Cavendish might cite the recent Yale University study in which scientists evaluated identical job application materials from male and female "applicants" for a laboratory manager position. A broad sample of physics, chemistry, and biology professors were asked to evaluate a cross-section of the applications. The study was set up so that half of the "applications" were from (traditionally . . .) male-named "applicants," half were from female-named "applicants," and pairs of male and female "applications" were made to be identical except for the specification of gender. The resumés, the letters of recommendation, and everything else was word for word the same.[11] The results of the study were remarkable, though perhaps this depends on who is asked. Across the board, the male "applicants" were rated as superior to the females. They were rated as more hirable, and were thought to merit higher pay packages. The bias appeared equally on the part of the male and female scientists who served as evaluators. One of the upshots of the study was that the existence of bias might help to explain the uneven ratio of men and women in the STEM disciplines and also the classroom dynamics that might be contributing to it. Cavendish would reference the Yale study and say that the application materials were identical but that the applicants are differently interfaced with the world.

7

Albert Camus's novel *The Stranger* offers another interesting example of an individual who is in control of his decisions, but who comes to find that there is corrosion in the interface between his decisions and the world. At the midpoint of the book, the main character—Mersault—kills a man. He is put on trial and convicted, but there is reason to believe that if he had behaved differently in life and on trial, he would have been found innocent by reason of self-defense. Mersault killed a man who swung a knife at him: "The scorching blade slashed at my eyelashes and stabbed at my stinging eyes."[12] Mersault shot the man once, and then four more times as he lay wounded on the ground. Mersault could have told the jury that he was in shock after the man came at him, but he offered no such explanation of his behavior. Instead he comes across to the jury as unusual and odd. In the opening sentence of the book, we found him reporting, "Maman died today. Or yesterday maybe. I don't know."[13] The jury discovers that Mersault does not know when his mother died, and also that he went on a date on the day after the funeral. Just *before* the funeral, he smoked a cigarette and drank coffee as he sat with his mother's body. Here is his own description of the experience of the jury:

> To another question he [the funeral director] replied that he had been surprised by my calm the day of the funeral. He was asked what he meant by "calm." The director then looked down at the tips of his shoes and said that I hadn't wanted to see Maman,

that I hadn't cried once, and that I had left right after the funeral without paying my last respects at her grave. And one other thing had surprised him: one of the men who worked for the undertaker had told him I didn't know how old Maman was. There was a brief silence, and then the judge asked him if he was sure I was the man he had just been speaking of. . . . As he took the stand the caretaker glanced at me and then looked away. He answered the questions put to him. He said I hadn't wanted to see Maman, that I had smoked and slept some, and that I had had some coffee. It was then I felt a stirring go through the room and for the first time I realized that I was guilty.[14]

At one point, the prosecutor sums up his case without any reference to the details of the killing. He says,

Gentlemen of the jury, the day after his mother's death, this man was out swimming, starting up a dubious liaison, and going to the movies, a comedy, for laughs. I have nothing further to say.[15]

Mersault was definitely a stranger or outsider. If he had not been so odd, and if the jury had been able to identify with him, his desire to seek companionship and see a film the day after the funeral might have been more explicable. None of this is to suggest that he did not do a horrible thing, but only that the guilty verdict had more to do with his lack of social and political capital than with the actual facts of the case. Especially relevant (and extremely horrifying) is that since Mersault was a Frenchman in colonial Algeria, and the man that he killed was an Arab, the jury might have regarded the loss of life as less momentous. Or perhaps it would have been inclined to assume that the man must have done something to deserve his fate. Here Camus is featuring two instances of corrosion in the interface between a person's decisions and the world—not just the case of Mersault, but also his victim.

8

We might imagine an alternate book that someone might write— *The Vegan*—about a character who lives in a meatpacking town and who attempts to be active on the local school board. The person weighs in with an objection about the latest curriculum proposal, and remarks they are there as a representative from "Vegan Citizens of America." Eyes roll over, and the school board moves on to the next issue. To extend the example, there is two-car accident a few months later in which the vegan survives but the driver in the other car does not, and the vegan sits in fear as she recalls the events of *The Stranger*.

9

A similar (but very much opposite) case was in the news in February 2014. A teenager in Texas drove drunk and caused an accident in which four people were killed and two were seriously injured. The teenager's blood-alcohol level was tested at three times the legal limit after the crash. The penalty for the crime was no jail time, ten-years probation, and therapy. Some have alleged that the reason for the light punishment is that the white upper-middle-class teenager was "one of us" and did not have it in him to be fully behind the horrific consequences of his actions. The teenager was instead a victim of *affluenza*.*

10

If Cavendish is right, freedom has at least two components: the control that we have over our thinking and our decisions, but also the interface between our decisions and the world. It is fairly clear from her personal experience why Cavendish would regard this as obvious. Spinoza had a similar view, and it is interesting to wonder if Spinoza's thinking was informed by his personal experience as well, and in particular by his excommunication. Here is an excerpt of the judgment against him:

> The Lords of the *ma'amad*, having long known of the evil opinions and acts of Baruch de Spinoza, have endeavored by various means and promises, to turn him from his evil ways. But having failed to make him mend his wicked ways, and, on the contrary, daily receiving more and more serious information

about the abominable heresies which he practiced and taught and about his monstrous deeds, and having for this numerous trustworthy witnesses who have deposed and born witness to this effect in the presence of the said Espinoza, they became convinced of the truth of the matter; and after all of this has been investigated in the presence of the honorable *chachamin*, they have decided, with their consent, that the said Espinoza should be excommunicated and expelled from the people of Israel. By the decree of the angels, and by the command of the holy men, we excommunicate, expel, curse and damn Baruch de Espinoza, with the consent of God. . . . Cursed be he by day and cursed be he by night; cursed be he when he lies down, and cursed be he when he rises up; cursed be he when he goes out, and cursed be he when he comes in. The Lord will not spare him; the anger and wrath of the Lord will rage against this man, and bring upon him all the curses which are written in this book, and the Lord will blot out his name from under heaven.[16]

There is not a lot of space that is left for Spinoza to maneuver here. He would say, though, that there is a way in which his situation is not unique to a person who is excommunicated. At every moment a given object or person is in a fully specific situation or configuration, and the surroundings are in a configuration, and also *their* surroundings, and that is the extent of the universe. Spinoza goes so far as to argue that even our decisions are necessitated. Cavendish holds that decisions are free and that (somehow) we have control over them.[17] Part of the intervention that she is attempting to make is to highlight that individuals may be equally free with respect to their decisions, but differently free with respect to the amount of corrosion in the interface between their decisions and the world.

11

To consider another analogy, Cavendish might grant that the acceleration of a car is due to the depression of the gas pedal, but then insist that that is only when surrounding variables are functioning correctly. A car that is sitting in a junkyard, and that has no tires or engine—it will not accelerate when the pedal is pressed. Cavendish is thinking that a person's will is not a stand-alone cause either.

12

An extremely important objection to keep in mind throughout the rest of the chapter is whether it is up to the individual to use their free will and energy to eradicate any corrosion that is present in the interface between their decisions and the world, or if it is the business of the larger community, or if it is both. Someone might argue that if in fact there is corrosion, and if there is more corrosion in the case of some people than others, *we* did not put it there, and so it is not our responsibility to attend to it.[18] Furthermore, it might be argued that it is healthy for the individual to be the one who attends to the corrosion; the effort would help to exercise and strengthen their resolve. It might be argued finally that the individual had better be the one who attends to the corrosion, because no one else is going to do it. Some of these objections will be discussed more fully in Chapter Eight, "The Individual and Society."

13

Cavendish was happy to get science-fictional, and we might come up with examples of our own. There is the extreme case of Smith, who had the unfortunate lot of being a human born on the Planet of the Apes. Humans had been released from jail a few generations ago, but if freedom is in part a matter of the decisions that we make, and in part a matter of the interface between our decisions and the world, Smith was not nearly as free as the apes that surrounded him. He was in control of his ideas and decisions—while in prison, one of his ancestors had the time to come up with a refutation of Searle—but still his freedom was very limited. He did not have a lot of social or political capital. People were very unlikely to hire or do business with him, either because they hated his kind or because they anticipated that there would be fallout for their own business or personal relations. Smith had trouble getting customers from the ape population, and other humans had very little money, so he could not run a successful hardware store, or a marketing firm, or a lumber company, or much else. He was not allowed to squat on land and convert it into wealth. No one would sell him property, and he also had trouble renting. He could not get hired as a pilot, and he could not get into medical school. He tried to be an attorney, but he lost his first 20 cases when he did not come across as authoritative to the jury. People were unlikely to hire him before, and there was little chance that they would hire him now. His great-grandchildren did not inherit much money down the road, and they did not have much social or political capital, and even worse they had to compete in a free market with the descendants of apes.

14

Of course, this is a not-too-subtle allusion to the situation of the majority of African Americans in the twenty-first-century United States, or to the situation as Cavendish would understand it, from slavery through Jim Crow, to the civil rights violence of the 1960s, to today. The humans on the Planet of the Apes are somewhat analogous to African Americans in the mid-nineteenth century, if we assume that the former were denied employment, education, land, and legal rights for the hundred years after their release. The analogy is made more precise if we stipulate that the apes are very resourceful and control all of the existing weaponry, the military and the police, the courts, the schools, the financial institutions and banks, most of the (Heideggerian) worlds, any chambers of commerce, and all internal and external borders.

15

Cavendish holds that freedom is a function of the interface between a person's decisions and the world. In our own time, she might ask about the kinds of roles that people are hired to play in a television series or movie, and whether or not it is important that the audience find their performance believable. There is a sense in which anyone is free to choose to pursue whatever role they want, but there is an equally important question about the circumstances in which a given actor would attract a paying audience. For example, if the audience does not take seriously that a given individual could be a lead, then that individual will not be successful as a lead, or will not be a lead in a successful movie. For a long time Asian men have been sidekicks in American movies, but not leading men. It is not necessarily a producer's *fault* not to hire an Asian actor to play a leading role, as the producer might be under a lot of pressure to bring in a certain purse.[19] An individual producer might be motivated to change the shape of the movie world, but if their movie is a flop at the box office, another producer might be found to take their place.[20]

16

Another example from the entertainment world might be the actor or actress who is vocally pro-life. Hollywood is known for being more liberal than conservative, and an actor might find that a producer is less likely to work with them if they have views that are not in line with the larger community. A producer might not refuse to work with whoever is best for the part, but there is such an abundance of talented actors that there would be no trouble locating an acceptable alternative. The actor Kirk Cameron (at his peak in the 1980s) has insisted on many occasions that he was blacklisted as a result of his religious views. It is tempting to counter that he was not a good actor, but he was extremely successful when his views were not yet public.[21] A vocally Christian actor who has had a lot more success is Mark Wahlberg.

17

Teachers and coaches sometimes report that they have less authority to do their job effectively if they are not seen as authoritative in the eyes of their audience. Nonwhite college professors have had an experience* in which they are sitting at their desk, reading or working on the computer, and a student knocks on their door to ask, "Are you Professor (so and so)?" Apparently the student knows the office number—maybe even looks at the placard outside the door—but still needs to confirm that the person before them is a professor.

18

An example from the world of sports is the great tennis player, Billie Jean King. She was the number-one ranking female player in the world for many years; she won (among other titles) a total of 20 titles at Wimbledon. When her homosexuality became public in 1981, she lost all of her endorsements within 24 hours.*

19

Cavendish is thinking that a person's freedom to do something—to own land, to secure a job, to start a business, to have customers, to seem authoritative in front of a jury, to maintain a scientific lab, to be a member of the philosophical community—is due in part to the configuration and receptivity of the surrounding world. The philosopher Naomi Zack has addressed the question of whether or not African Americans today are due compensation as a result of their historical connection to the institution of slavery. Her idea is not so much to compensate people for the horrific treatment of their ancestors, but to compensate them for injustices that are in place today and that grew and developed since the time that the institution ended. Zack argues that as a legal issue, there are reasons that reparations are not feasible, for example: statutes of limitations; the question of whether there are particular African Americans who have an alternate history that exempts them from the biases in question; and the issue of how a group (nineteenth-century slave-owners) can be said to be legally at fault for performing actions that were not against the law at the time that they were performed. But Zack argues that there is an alternative to reparations that is still very important—what she calls rectification, in which the depth of the injustice to the victims of slavery is acknowledged, along with the economic, social, and political advantage that whites have tended to have in the 150 years since the injustice was formally put to a stop. Zack argues that as a result of a steady (and Spinozistically tight) chain of events since the mid-nineteenth century, African Americans are now at a tremendous disadvantage with respect to their social, political, and economic capital.[22] Cavendish would say that this amounts to an unusual amount of corrosion in the interface between their decisions and the world.

20

An interesting test for the view that people of different ethnic groups encounter different amounts of corrosion in the interface between their decisions and the world is the individual who is the member of one ethnic group, but who can pass as the member of another. The philosopher Ron Mallon has discussed the metaphysical implications of the phenomenon of passing—where an individual is received very differently in their professional and personal interactions when others think that she is white.[23] If the person is found out, they often lose capital and authority, and are not able to navigate the world so well.[24]

21

The philosopher George Yancy has attempted to characterize a distinctive visual and cognitive experience that white people have as they approach and encounter a black person, especially a black male. Yancy writes,

> [T]he woman on the elevator does not really "see" me, and she makes no effort to challenge how she sees me. To begin to see me from a perspective that effectively challenges her racism, however, would involve more than a *cognitive* shift in her perspective. It would involve a continuous effort at performing her body's racialized interactions with the world differently. This additional shift resides at the somatic level as well. After all, she may come to judge her perception of the Black body as epistemologically false, but her racism may still have a hold on her lived body. I walk into the elevator and she feels apprehension. Her body shifts nervously and her heart beats more quickly as she clutches her purse more closely to her. She feels anxiety in the pit of her stomach. Her perception of time in the elevator may feel like an eternity. The space within the elevator is surrounded from all sides with my Black presence.[25]

To the extent that Yancy is correct, the experience that he is describing would place limits on the kinds of personal and professional dealings that are available to black Americans. This is not to say that there are not many exceptions in terms of classes of white people having little social and economic capital and versa, but that things would appear to be uneven as a matter of statistical average. We might note that an analogous jolt to the structure of awareness is sometimes effected when an individual with a disability is encountered, or when an individual is encountered who is regarded as "the other."

22

The political philosopher Harold Cruse has argued that for these and other reasons it is important for members of a social group to retain their cohesion as a group, and to act in concert, for purposes of power and backing.[26] Dominant groups tend to do this, and to benefit from the social and political and economic capital that ensues. Cruse is suggesting that members of less dominant groups would be wise to follow their lead (and not proceed as isolated individuals). His view calls to mind the situation in medieval times when a person would travel with documents from the king, specifying that the person should be afforded safe travel.[27] It was not just out of kindness or decency that the traveler would be treated with respect, but out of a recognition of the practical consequences to anyone who might have other plans. Cruse is thinking in large part about the integrationist policies of the 1960s, where (he argues) the most talented individuals were sent from African American communities to live in isolation. With a different kind of intervention, these communities would have retained their most skilled members and hastened the speed of community development, and they would now be better able to work as a group to leverage economic and political might. Like many, Cruse rejected the policy of "separate but equal," but thought that "plural but equal" should be put in its place: individuals from different groups would participate in all aspects of a country's economy and society, but also have a base of power and strength in the form of their specific community. He was in favor of civil rights legislation, of course, and he thought that our laws should reflect that everyone is equal, but he also thought that equality under the law was only a small fraction of what makes people autonomous and free.

Is there something in the water?

23

A (fairly) recent author who has taken up some of the same themes as Cavendish is the philosopher Simone De Beauvoir. Beauvoir argues that, generally speaking, boys and girls are raised in such a way that they form the belief that males and females have very delineated roles and talents. These beliefs then end up guiding our behavior in a way that limits the freedom of us all (but especially women). Beauvoir writes,

> Almost nowhere is her [woman's] legal status the same as man's, and frequently it is much to her disadvantage. Even when her rights are legally recognized in the abstract, long-standing custom prevents their full expression in the mores. In the economic sphere men and women can almost be said to make up two castes; other things being equal, the former hold the better jobs, get higher wages, and have more opportunity for success than their new competitors. In industry and politics men have a great many more positions and they monopolize the most important jobs. In addition to all this, they enjoy a traditional prestige that the education of children tends in every way to support, for the present enshrines the past.[28]

Beauvoir allows that we are free to make the decisions that we make, but she is concerned that men and women encounter different amounts of seamlessness and corrosion in the interface between their decisions and the world. Because of the way we are raised, later in life we will feel more comfortable with the prospect of a male as our mechanic, carpenter, money-manager, referee, surgeon, pilot, engineer, etc. This level of comfort will then inform our free-market purchasing decisions and have a dramatic impact on who can do what for a living.

24

Beauvoir traces our adult preferences to entrenched beliefs and expectations that form when we are young. Girls are validated for things like being pretty, helping in domestic affairs, and caretaking, and boys are validated for climbing trees, exploring, and being independent.[29] Girls read fairy tales about women who are rescued by men, and they read histories in which men have been the primary difference-makers. Forces are then in place that keep these beliefs and expectations from doing an about-face. Beauvoir writes,

> Everything helps to confirm this hierarchy in the eyes of the little girl [and the little boy]. The historical and literary culture to which she belongs, the songs and legends with which she is lulled to sleep, are one long exaltation of man. . . . The superiority of the male is, indeed, overwhelming: Perseus, Hercules, David, Achilles, Lancelot, the old French warriors Du Guesclin and Bayard, Napoleon—so many men for one Joan of Arc.[30]

Boys and girls are punished when they step out of line of our expectations for them, and on the flipside there are rewards. Boys get rewarded for being active, expressive, powerful, and independent, Beauvoir argues. For a girl to be any of those, she faces judgment, isolation, and rebuke.[31]

25

It is not that traditional gender norms are part of the natural order of things, Beauvoir thinks. Women are able to act counter to type, but in that case "we are exhorted to be women, remain women, become women."[32] Beauvoir would cite the example from the post-World-War-II United States in which women took over work in domestic factories while the men were off at war. Propaganda videos were produced to convince women that women "had it in them," and to announce that it was acceptable to put traditional gender norms on hold, at least for the moment. Even with their delicate fingers, one of the videos explains, women are capable of the work of men.* Then the war ended and women were made to return to the home.

26

The economic consequences of traditional gender norms are enormous, Beauvoir thinks. By later life, men and women have internalized these, and in addition we identify with being masculine or feminine. We will not all of a sudden act in ways that we take to be inappropriate, and we will make our purchasing (and other) decisions accordingly. Indeed, some men will report that when they encounter a woman they see her first and foremost as a physical object. The more virtuous among these might deliberately induce a shift in their awareness in order to see the woman as a person or agent, but they had their initial thought nonetheless. Individuals can have similar thoughts when they encounter a man, but Beauvoir would say that statistically speaking women are regarded as objects or things and that there are implications for the professional (and personal) stage. The philosopher Rae Langton has argued that in the extreme case of pornography, women are seen as objects alone. They are silenced—not because they are prevented from speaking, but because they are not heard and because they are seen as things; and a mere thing has nothing to say.[33] Cavendish would argue that insofar as there is a strong consumer market for pornography, there is a large amount of corrosion in the interface between a woman's decisions and the world. There is something in the water, Beauvoir and Langton would add, and if we care about freedom we need to see that it is removed.

27

Things have changed in the past 60 years certainly, but Beauvoir would point to recent US census statistics that expose how the professions are still very segregated.* Even though women are working more than before, they tend to be clustered in jobs that emphasize caretaking: women tend to be nurses, schoolteachers, secretaries, flight attendants, counselors, nannies, and support staff; men are judges, professors, doctors, pilots, construction workers, accountants, politicians, surgeons, and lawyers. Women and men choose to enter these professions—otherwise they would not be in them—but Beauvoir would argue that an equally important factor in the breakdown of professions is how the larger society of consumers makes its purchasing decisions: who they are willing to pay to do what. For example, we tend to be more comfortable hiring a female, rather than a male, nanny. A man is not a nanny unless he chooses to be a nanny, but he is not a nanny *just because* he chooses to be a nanny, and he might be wise to make a different choice altogether. Beauvoir would argue that the same analysis applies across the board. In some professions (like the law), women now constitute almost 50 percent of the workforce, but the breakdown within the profession is gendered. For example, women are paralegals, assistants, and legal secretaries in much larger numbers than men, and the work that is characteristically done by males tends to involve higher pay. Beauvoir wants to point to questions like—who will come across as most authoritative to a jury, but without seeming too aggressive; or, who is the client most comfortable encountering at the front desk.

28

Beauvoir would offer a number of contemporary examples of corrosion in the interface between decisions and the world. There is the case of the female construction worker. Women might appear on a given crew, but often they are holding a stop sign, and not operating any machinery. The woman might request to operate such machinery, but the foreman might see the request as silly, or as an instance of rabble-rousing. Even if the foreman does not dismiss the request straightaway, there might be other factors that incline toward a negative decision: perhaps there are complicated issues about the cohesion of the crew, and not as much work will get done if the men want to see themselves as the exclusive machine operators. Wolf would chime in at this point and argue that there is an important issue here about who has the most opportunity for a meaningful life. On her view, to lead such a life we need to locate pursuits that we take to be of value for the long haul, and in which we can be actively engaged. These need to be activities that we enjoy, at least to some degree, and that we have the talent and ability to pursue with at least occasional success. Cavendish and Beauvoir would chime in and say that whether or not person is able to engage in their pursuits with success is in large part due to the interface between their decisions and the world. Wolf would then conclude that that means that some people are not nearly as well positioned as others to lead meaningful lives.[34]

29

Another example is the case of professional female boxers. The financial purse for women is not nearly what it is for men, and the main reason is that generally speaking consumers do not pay to watch female boxing, either live or pay-per-view. None of this is to suggest that women and men should be treated as exactly equal (as boxers) or that women should be scheduled to fight the men's reigning heavyweight champ. But there are plenty of men who make a living as professional boxers and who do not fight the heavyweight champ either. Instead, there are divisions for middleweight, lightweight, featherweight, even flyweight. Boxers fight opponents within the same weight class, and they have a paying audience. Women could have their own weight classes as well, but since they do not have the same sort of paying audience, there is less opportunity to fight professionally.[35] We can speculate as to the reasons why people pay for what they do, but one reason is presumably that consumers like to see women behave in certain ways and recoil to see them behaving in others.

30

A recent development in the sport's world is the participation of women in Ultimate Fighting Championship.* Women like Ronda Rousey and Sara McCann have been featured in bouts on prime-time television, and the viewership has been significant. A question that Beauvoir and Cavendish might raise is whether or not women will be better received in traditionally male professions if images of athletes like Rousey and McCann become more regular and routine.

31

We might also consider the significant difference between the National Football League and female leagues like the Women's Football Alliance and the International Women's Football League. The latter offer opportunities for women to play football at the professional level, but at the same time it is extremely difficult for women to make a living at it. There is full contact, and the women appear to be very good athletes, but there is not much of a paying audience. A quick look at any YouTube clip of a game from either league will show a mostly empty stadium, and usually it is not a stadium but a high-school or junior-college venue.* This is not to suggest that people should pay to attend these games even if they are not interested, but instead it is to point out that our preferences might be due in part to larger forces, and to point out an example in which a person's freedom to do something professionally is in part a function of the interface between their decisions and the world. Cavendish and Spinoza would argue that there is always an interface, but that the interface is more corroded in some cases than in others.

32

There is a professional women's football league that is actually very successful. It is the Lingerie Football League, offering what it calls "True Fantasy Football."[36] The women play full-contact in their underwear. These women are tremendous athletes, and clearly they are opting to play.* But it seems that there are certain possibilities that are open to women who want to make a living at football, and there are certain possibilities that are not.

33

An extremely difficult question for Cavendish and Beauvoir is whether freedom is best promoted by encouraging consumers to modify their first-order attitudes and desires, or if that would instead be a freedom-squashing imposition. We might imagine a policy—everyone who likes the NFL should be forced to watch 2 hours of IWFL or WFA per week. In the spirit of Frankfurt, we could make sure that, as we watch, we are eating a food that we love, or listening to our favorite music, so that gradually we might become interested in the games on their own. If it turns out that we are too set in our ways, we might continue to watch NFL games only, but pay some kind of levy that helps the next generation of youth to be more flexible—sort of like a carbon credit. These proposals might sound ridiculous—indeed they do sound ridiculous—but they might seem like a viable option to anyone who is interested in promoting freedom and who allows that there is sometimes a massive amount of corrosion in the interface between decisions and the world. Cavendish and Beauvoir are concerned to increase the amount of freedom and agency that is had by human beings, and the issue is whether such proposals celebrate freedom, or inhibit it.

34

Cavendish used fiction to sketch scenarios in which the selfsame people all of a sudden had newfound abilities and powers, just because the interface between their decisions and the world was wiped clean. She would presumably allow that the individuals who are most successful are the ones whose features are best suited to their environment. That is to say, the fittest survive. But Cavendish is arguing that whether or not a being is fit in its environment depends itself on what the environment is like. Charles Darwin offers the extreme example of the domestic pet of a powerful species:

> If there exist savages so barbarous as never to think of the inherited character of the offspring of their domestic animals, yet any one animal particularly useful to them, for any special purpose, would be carefully preserved during famines and other accidents, to which savages are so liable, and such choice animals would generally leave more offspring than the inferior ones; so that in this case there would be a kind of unconscious selection going on.[37]

The beloved pet of the savage is strong in its environment, though it would not be strong if it retained all its features but was no longer regarded with favor. More generally, a being that is strong in an environment would not be strong in that environment if that environment changed in certain ways. If the being was so strong that it could guarantee that its environment would suit them, that would be something, but presumably the being could only do this if it constituted the environment itself. Spinoza and Cavendish would argue that no person is an island and that, given the ocean and other things that surround it, not even an island is an island!

35

An important objection to consider is that a person can always move to an environment that is more accommodating, in which there is less corrosion in the interface between their decisions and the world. Here Cavendish would attempt to defend the view that a person can only make a home in an environment (of other people) if that environment is amenable.

36

An objection *here* is that an individual has a lot of control over whether they are able to adapt to an environment. Cavendish would disagree and say that an individual has only some control and that another crucial factor is whether or not there is corrosion in the interface between the individual's decisions and the world. She would then worry about who is required to move in order to locate a better interface, and who has the luxury of staying put. She would also worry about whether or not different people have a radically different number of environments that respond well to them, and whether or not these environments afford prospects that are similarly fulfilling.

37

Another objection to Cavendish is that the individual has the ability to change the amount of corrosion in the interface between their decisions and the world. Here Cavendish would probably pound her fist and say that whether or not a person has the agency and authority to affect the interface between their decisions and the world is itself a function of whether or not there is corrosion in the interface between their decisions and the world. She might argue in addition that whether or not a person is in a position to notice that there is corrosion in the interface between their decisions and the world is in part a function of whether or not there is corrosion in the interface between their decisions and the world.

Responsibility for self

38

The philosopher Jean-Paul Sartre would raise these and other objections against Cavendish and Beauvoir. Sartre interpretation is difficult, given the many strands in his thought, but one of these strands is an emphasis on the profound freedom and responsibility of the individual. He writes,

> [E]xistence precedes essence. . . . Let us consider some object that is manufactured, for example a book or a paper-cutter; here is an object which has been made by an artisan whose inspiration came from a concept. . . . Therefore, let us say that for the paper-cutter, essence precedes existence. . . . What is meant here by saying [instead] that existence precedes essence? It means that, first of all, man exists, turns up, appears on the scene, and only afterwards, defines himself. Man is nothing else but what he makes of himself. . . . [M]an is responsible for what he is. Thus, existentialism's first move is to make every man aware of what he is and to make the full responsibility of his existence rest on him.[38]

One of Sartre's arguments for the view that what we are is completely up to us is that even if we tried to avoid our decision-making responsibility, that would be a choice itself. He says,

> [W]hat is not possible is not to choose. I can always choose, but I ought to know that if I do not choose, I am still choosing.[39]
>
> [M]an is condemned to be free.[40]

Another argument that Sartre offers is based on the consideration that at the moment of decision or action, we always have a vivid sense that our choice is up to us. Here he is assuming the Cartesian view that what we know best are not external bodies but our own internal conscious states, and he is assuming that we have a vivid internal awareness of our freedom:

> There can be no other truth to take off from than this: *I think; therefore, I exist.* There we have the absolute truth of consciousness becoming aware of itself. Every theory which takes man out of the moment in which he becomes aware of himself is, at its very beginning, a theory which confounds truth, for outside the Cartesian cogito, all truths are only probable.[41]

Sartre has a response to the deterministic arguments of Searle and others: the evidence that a philosopher puts forward for determinism is never more than probable; since it conflicts with evidence that is *undeniable*, human beings always have the libertarian ability to do otherwise.

39

If we are as free as Sartre says we are, and what we are is entirely up to us, we might feel a lot of responsibility for the decisions that we make, and we might feel a corresponding amount of anguish. Sartre indeed thinks that a constant companion of our freedom is a sense of anguish, but it makes us uncomfortable, and so we divert our attention:

> [Man] cannot help escape the feeling of his total and deep responsibility; of course, there are many people who are not anxious; but we claim that they are hiding from their anxiety, fleeing from it.[42]

Many of us have had the feeling of wanting to raise our hand in class to express our point of view, or even just to ask a question, but then we hold back and refrain from expressing our freedom. Later in the day we might feel a sense of regret or self-violation—the sense that we have sold ourselves short. Or perhaps we have a recurring desire to pursue a career or hobby that is unconventional, but instead we do what people normally do, and live with quiet desperation. Another example might be more common and mundane: we want to talk to the person next to us on the bus, or in the elevator, but we stay quiet; or we want to sing, but we thwart our freedom out of fear of how others will respond.

40

Sartre has to be right that we sometimes (or perhaps often) choose to thwart our freedom, and that we feel a sense of self-violation when we do. We might fail to speak up in some context, or hold off on pursuing a dream or passion—all in ways that lead to a less fulfilling experience. But Cavendish would object to Sartre that even if we are in control of our decisions, that does not mean that we are in control of whether or not those decisions are effective. She would say that, to some degree, that is up to the amount of corrosion in the interface between our decisions and the world. We should note however that Sartre does not think that *everything* about us is up to our choice—for example, our height, eye color, and other elements of what he calls our *facticity*.[43] With respect to the rest of our features, though, Sartre would argue that people need to take things into their own hands. At the very least, we need to try, and to take a stand. He would also argue that since we are radically free, we are in charge of choosing our values, and so we are in charge of whether or not we care about how our decisions pan out. He writes,

> [W]e find no values or commands to turn to which legitimize our conduct. So, in the bright realm of values, we have no excuse behind us, nor justification before us. We are alone, with no excuses.[44]

> It follows that my freedom is the unique foundation of values and that *nothing*, absolutely nothing, justifies me in adopting this or that particular value, this or that particular scale of values. As a being by whom values exist, I am unjustifiable.[45]

Sartre thinks that we should not automatically accept our gut verdict about whether or not failure at a given endeavor is significant. Perhaps we have attempted and failed at some pursuit, but the pursuit is only valuable according to standards that we have never stepped back to evaluate. Perhaps we just internalized these, and if so, our immediate reaction to failure is just another betrayal of our freedom. Sartre might sound cold and callous here, but presumably he is right that we sometimes feel the pull of values over which we never had much of a say. If freedom is so important, we might want to exercise our freedom to locate values that are more our own. Indeed, it is easy to wonder if Sartre thought that the most fulfilling life was one in which we pursued goals that were arbitrary and unconventional—in order to be sure that our acceptance of them was due to our freedom alone.

41

We might worry though that if we did live such a life, every moment would feel unmotivated and absurd. If we settle on values that feel arbitrary, our pursuits will seem ridiculous. But if we settle on values that do not feel arbitrary, it is not clear that we *chose* them as much as we uncovered them. Sartre might add though that a looming concern is that there are all sorts of influences that might be at play in the historical formation of our values, and so we might as well choose from scratch.

42

A third objection to Sartre would come from Heidegger: just because there are many occasions in which we are not choosing, that does not mean that we are choosing not to choose. Our behavior is not always highly conscious. Instead, we are in the zone, and no choosing is going on.

43

Van Inwagen might raise a fourth objection. Sartre thinks that we have libertarian freedom, in which our decisions do not have a prior cause. He argues, for example, that there is a gap of nothingness that separates our present and our past—such that our past does not cause or bind our present decision[46]—but in that case it sounds as though our decisions arise from nothingness.

Van Inwagen would say that it is a mystery how any such decision would be within our control. Van Inwagen thinks that decisions *are* within our control, though he is a mysterian about how that is possible. Sartre thinks that it is an absolute certainty that we are free, and he might have to accept the mysterian conclusion as well.

44

A worry about Sartre's view is that if we choose our values, and we choose the basis on which we choose our values, then they are utterly arbitrary. It is hard to see how we would take such values seriously, or how they would ever get a foothold. I might choose freely to value collecting coins, or climbing mountains, or talking on the phone, but I might find that in the course of pursuing these activities I am really going against the grain. I *hate* the activities. Sartre might respond that my existing values were not due to my free choice and that since freedom is so important, I should keep trying to identify with my new values, come what may. In that case, though, there is a question about whether I am accurately described as *valuing* the things in question. I am accurately described as wanting to value them, but that would appear to be a separate issue.

Choosing our deepest desires and values

45

Nietzsche has a view that is in many ways non-Sartrean. He thinks that human beings are a species of animal and therefore have strong animal impulses, but that we have kept these at bay as a result of acculturation. He speaks of the "blond beast" or lion that finds an outlet in dominant groups in history:

> At the centre of all these noble races we cannot fail to see the beast of prey, the magnificent blond beast avidly prowling around for spoil and victory; this hidden centre needs release

from time to time, the beast must get out again, must return to the wild:—Roman, Arabian, Germanic, Japanese nobility, Homeric heroes, Scandinavian nobility. . . . This "daring" of the noble races, mad, absurd, and sudden in the way it manifests itself, the unpredictability and even improbability of their undertakings.[47]

Nietzsche supposes that the repression of our instincts has been especially pronounced due to the influence of Christianity and its devaluation of the body in comparison to the soul.[48] A more satisfying sort of life, he posits, would be one in which we express the more animalistic side of ourselves—whether by engaging in chaos and violence, or by expressing our energy in pursuit of a creative ability or passion:

> That something is a hundred times more important than the question of whether we feel well or not. . . . In sum, that we have a goal for which one does not hesitate to offer human sacrifices, to risk every danger, to take upon oneself whatever is bad and worst: the *great passion*.[49]

He thinks that we do not express our passionate side, however, because we have developed an evil eye toward our impulses. We have developed a meta-impulse to keep our impulses in check, and we have overdone it:

> This instinct of freedom, forcibly made latent—. . . this instinct for freedom forced back, repressed, incarcerated within itself and finally able to discharge and unleash itself only against itself. . . . For too long, man has viewed his natural inclinations with an "evil eye.". . . A reverse experiment should be possible *in principle*—but who has sufficient strength?[50]

Nietzsche anticipates that we would find ourselves more fulfilled if we turned an evil eye instead toward our inclination to thwart our impulses. He is non-Sartrean in the sense that he does not think that we choose what will satisfy us. There is a fact of the matter about what will satisfy us, if we would just allow it to find expression.

46

The philosopher Søren Kierkegaard has a very, very different view of Christianity, but a similar critique of the Sartrean view that we should choose our values and goals at random. Kierkegaard agrees with Sartre (and Nietzsche) on the importance of freedom-expression, but he does not think that our interests and goals are (or should be) a matter of arbitrary choice. Instead, he thinks that every human being has a passion *already*—even if it is fairly flexible and has to be channeled into the offerings that are available to the person at the historical time that they are alive. Kierkegaard spends a lot of time discussing the situation of individuals who pursue their passion. Such individuals have to be extremely strong given the pull of other forces, especially what Kierkegaard calls the Public—which is basically the "they" in "That's what they say," or the "one" in "That's just what one does." The Public presents a set of norms that tells us what sorts of activity are acceptable, and that tells us what are the acceptable ways of engaging in them. The Public is indeed a force:

> [N]o majority has ever been so certain of being right and victorious as the public. . . .[51]
>
> [T]he public levels. . . . The really terrible thing is the thought of all the lives that are or easily may be wasted. . . . That is the leveling process at its lowest, for it always equates itself to the divisor by means of which everyone is reduced to a lowest common denominator.[52]

There are important differences between individuals, Kierkegaard thinks, but those differences are hacked away in the generic models of behavior that the Public endorses.

47

There is no denying that we gain something by pursuing a career or hobby or lifestyle that is endorsed by the Public: our behavior is intelligible to others insofar as others have their home in the Public as well. We can explain ourselves, and we are never alone:

> [I]t is refreshing to become intelligible to oneself in the universal . . ., and every individual who understands him understands the universal through him, and both rejoice in the security of the universal. He knows it is beautiful to be born as the particular individual who has his home in the universal, his friendly abode, which immediately receives him with open arms when he wants to remain in it.[53]

At the same time, there is a great cost:

> [L]evelling is eo ipso the destruction of the individual.[54]
>
> [I]t is only the lower natures that have the law governing their actions in another person, the premises for their actions outside of themselves.[55]

To the extent that we limit our practices and pursuits to the generic and leveled activities that are publicly sanctioned, we are not acting on the uncontainable passions that we have and that desperately want to find expression.

48

Kierkegaard conjures two characters who are supposed to help us to appreciate the importance of passion in human life. One is a person who recognizes all of the struggle that will be involved in pursuing their passion, and who recognizes that it is just too much, and is horrified to take the plunge, but they pursue their passion anyway:

> [H]igher than this [the public and the universal] there winds a lonely trail, narrow and steep; he knows that it is frightful to be born solitary, outside the universal, to walk without meeting a single traveler. He knows very well where he is and how he relates to people. Humanly speaking, he is mad and cannot make himself intelligible to anyone. And yet it is the mildest expression to say that he is mad.[56]

Faith is this paradox, and the single individual is utterly unable to make himself intelligible to anyone.[57]

The knight of faith has simply and solely himself, and therein lies the frightfulness. . . . The true knight of faith is always absolute isolation.[58]

[T]he one who goes faith's narrow way, him no one can advise, no one can understand.[59]

Kierkegaard does not mean that a person who pursues their passion will never be in the company of others. His examples of knights of faith are a philosophy professor, a servant girl, a tax collector, a man who lives his dream of spending his life with a princess, and the biblical Abraham. These individuals live amidst others, but they are isolated in the sense that they cannot explain or justify their life-defining pursuits and relationships in terms of the standards of the "they." A knight of faith is almost superhuman, or more precisely, she is able to emphasize the part of herself that is divine. Kierkegaard speaks of the knight as standing toward God as an equal:

the wondrous glory that knight attains in becoming God's confidant, the Lord's friend, and, to speak very humanly, in saying "You" to God in heaven, whereas even the tragic hero only addresses him in the third person.[60]

On this view, we are made in the image of a being that is infinite and finite, and part of our task is to put the two factors into balance.

49

Kierkegaard describes the tax collector as fully immersed in his earthly life with his family and friends, barely able to contain his passion in a finite frame. But he does, and with no remainder:

In the afternoon he takes a walk in the woods. He enjoys everything he sees, the throngs of people, the new omnibuses, the Sound. . . . Towards evening he goes home, his gait as undaunted as a postman's. On the way he thinks about an appetizing little dish of warm food his wife surely has for him when he comes home, for example a roast head of lamb with vegetables. If he were to meet a kindred spirit, he would continue conversing with him all the way to Osterport about this dish with a passion befitting a restaurateur. . . . If she has it, to see him eat would be an enviable sight for distinguished people and an inspiring one for the common man, for his appetite is heartier than Esau's. . . . On the way he goes past a building site and meets another man. They talk a moment together; in no time he erects a building, having at his disposal all the resources required for that purpose. . . . Everything that happens—a rat scurrying under a gutter plank, children playing—everything engages him with a composure in existence as if he were a girl of sixteen.[61]

Kierkegaard is describing an individual who has a tremendous amount of energy and passion, and who expends all of this energy toward his worldly pursuits, come what may. We can almost hear someone taking issue with the tax collector: "You are *too* into things. Chill out." Some everyday examples of individuals like Kierkegaard's tax collector might include Quint (the fisherman from the movie *Jaws*), Emmett Brown (the "mad" scientist from *Back to the Future*), Sheldon Cooper (from the show *The Big Bang Theory*), Steve Irwin (the animal expert and crocodile hunter), Willy Wonka a Star Trek Trekkie, or a committed Brony. What is always tricky about identifying a knight of faith is that because a central component of their behavior is not explicable or justifiable in terms of the standards of the Public, there is a fine line between showing up as impassioned and showing up as crazy.*

50

Kierkegaard appears to want to say that in order to overcome the force of the public an individual has to be godlike—a hybrid between the human and the divine. He writes,

The God-man is the unity of God and an individual human being. That the human race is or is supposed to be in kinship with God is ancient paganism; but that an individual human being is God is Christianity, and this particular human being is the God-man. Humanly speaking, there is no possibility of a crazier composite than this either in heaven or on earth or in the abyss or in the most fantastic aberrations of thought.[62]

There is, namely, an infinite chasmic difference between God and man, and therefore it became clear in the situation of contemporaneity that to become a Christian (to be *transformed into likeness with God*) is, humanly speaking, an even greater torment and misery and pain than the greatest human torment, and in addition a crime in the eyes of one's contemporaries. And so it will always prove to be if becoming a Christian truly comes to mean becoming contemporary with Christ. And if becoming a Christian does not come to mean this, then all this talk about becoming a Christian is futility and fancy and vanity, and in part blasphemy and sin against the Second Commandment of the Law and sin against the Holy Spirit.[63]

Part of what is so distinctive about the religion of Christianity, Kierkegaard thinks, is that it posits the ideal of a being that is a combination of earthly and divine. This is a being who recognizes fully all that he is up against, but he taps into his infinite passion, and is steadfast.

51

A very different person might have the same amount of passion and energy, but not channel it into their daily life, and instead be more of a dreamer. This is a person who might recognize how important their passion is to them, but who also appreciates how strenuous it would be to live it. Kierkegaard calls this person a knight of resignation. They live their day-to-day life in submission to the standards of the Public, and their passion is channeled instead toward their imagination. They realize how great their life could be, and so they experience resignation—indeed, Kierkegaard calls this individual a knight of *infinite* resignation.[64] Knights of resignation "are really strangers in the world,"[65] whereas the knight of faith

> constantly makes the movement of infinity, but he does it with such precision and proficiency that he constantly gets finitude out of it and at no second does one suspect anything else. . . .

[T]o transform the leap of life into a gait, absolutely to express the sublime in the pedestrian—that only the knight of faith can do—and that is the only miracle.[66]

The relevance here of Christianity is apparent. Kierkegaard rejects the life of the knight of infinite resignation and thinks instead that "Temporality, finitude is what it is all about."[67] However, to channel our passion we need to tap into an enormous amount of strength—to be able to counter the pull of the Public. According to Christianity, all of us are created in the image of a being that is earthly and divine and whose divinity is somehow contained in a finite frame. Kierkegaard writes,

> Faith is a miracle, and yet no human being is excluded from it, for that which unites all human life is passion. . . .[68]
>
> [A]t every moment [there is a] chasmic abyss between the single individual and the God-man over which faith and faith alone reaches.[69]
>
> [T]he common denominator is that every one should really and essentially be a man in a religious sense.[70]

For Kierkegaard, Christ is a model, an inspiration, and a source of strength. Unlike Sartre, Kierkegaard thinks that all of us have a passion that we need to uncover and express. He worries though that most of us worship the Public, or that at best we are knights of resignation. Kierkegaard is an absurdist not in the sense that he thinks that we should be random and absurd and ridiculous, but in the sense that our most passionate pursuits and concerns should not require a publicly intelligible rationale or sanction. They *cannot* require such a sanction, or else they would be leveled down to a common denominator, and they would not be passions. The committed pursuit of a passion requires instead a leap of faith.

51

A concern for Kierkegaard is that the knight of faith will inevitably be crushed by adherents of the Public, just like Mersault in *The Stranger*. Kierkegaard seems to be thinking that we can express enough of our passion to be fulfilled, but still navigate the minefields that would thereby surround us. Maybe if we have the passion that he says we do, we could do it, and just not care about the repercussions. But he also thinks (from the title of his masterpiece) that such a life is lived in fear and trembling:

> [T]hat single individual who teaches the most humble and yet also the most human doctrine about what it means to be a human being, the established order will intimidate by charging him with being guilty of blasphemy.[71]

> Even if one comprehended, fully comprehended, the purely human, this understanding is still a misunderstanding in regard to the God-man.—What responsibility I bear, no one understands as I do. Let no one take the trouble to terrify me on this account, for to him who can terrify me in a totally different way I relate myself in fear and trembling. But then, too, not very many understand as I do that Christianity has been abolished in Christendom.[72]

Kierkegaard is in the tradition of thinkers who identify as Christian but think that Christianity has been misunderstood.

52

If Cavendish is right, there are at least two components to freedom. One is to have control over our thoughts and decisions. The other is to be interfaced with the world in such a way that our thoughts and decisions are effective. We are supposing (for the sake of argument) that we have freedom in the first sense; otherwise it would be hard to take ourselves seriously as agents and decision-makers, and it would be hard to make sense of the project of assessing our beliefs about freedom (or anything else). There are at least two components to freedom, and accordingly there are two different kinds of obstacles to freedom. One is where, for whatever reason, we are not sufficiently smart or charming or resourceful to think the things that it would behoove us to think at exactly the moment that we need to think them. The other sort of obstacle in the way of freedom is where a person's will and mind are in good order, but the interface between their decisions and the world is corroded and their choices are not effective.

Possible discussion exercises

1 Are there some radical steps that Cavendish might have taken to become a scientist or philosopher in her time?

2 Come up with a real-life case in which a person commits a crime but is set free—because the jury identifies with the person and does not believe the person "had it in them."

3 Do you know anyone who is an outsider and who does not have a lot of social capital? (No need to name the person of course.) State one way in which the person's lack of social capital is a liability in their life.

4 Are there any respects in which you are taken to be an outsider?

5 Tom Hanks was the star of *Castaway* (2000), in which his character is stranded alone on an island for many years. The movie was very successful at the box office, earning well over $400 million worldwide. Could Denzel Washington have successfully played the lead in this movie, or (at an earlier time) Billy Dee Williams or Sidney Poitier?

6 Imagine that a given female appeals to her desires and interests and insists that she does not want to be a construction worker. Or perhaps a man does not want to try ballet. Can Beauvoir take issue here?

7 Would you hire a "manny" to take care of your child?

8 If people do not have a first-order desire to watch professional female football, are they under any obligation to have a second-order desire to watch it? Why or why not?

9 Do you think that Darwin is right that what it is to have strength in an environment is in part a function of what the environment is like itself? Come up with a potential example of an individual who would be strong in one environment but weak in another.

10 Assume that a person does develop a first-order desire to watch professional female football, in place of their desire to watch NFL football. What would be some of the other

effects on the person's life? Is this too much of a sacrifice for a person to make? Would the person's new life actually be better for them? Why or why not?

11 Come up with an historical example in which women attempted to wipe away some of the corrosion in the interface between their decisions and the world, but they were unsuccessful because of corrosion in the interface between their decisions and the world.

12 Come up with an historical example in which a different group attempted to wipe away some of the corrosion in the interface between their decisions and the world, but they were unsuccessful because of corrosion in the interface between their decisions and the world.

13 Cavendish argues that the effectiveness of our decisions is due in part to the interface between our decisions and the world. How might we argue (against Cavendish) that the interface between our decisions and the world is up to us and the decisions that we made in the past?

14 Is the structure of your awareness ever affected when you encounter a person who is not familiar to you?

15 Sartre argues that we sometimes thwart our desire to express freedom, and we feel a sense of violation as a result. Come up with an example of your own.

16 Do you agree with Sartre that we are not expressing our freedom fully unless we arbitrarily choose our values?

17 Do you agree with Kierkegaard that there is such a force as the Public?

18 Are there any respects in which you are a knight of resignation? Do you agree with Kierkegaard on the amount of energy that is required to pursue a passion come what may?

19 Are there other individuals—from television, film, literature, or real life—who are so into their pursuits that they seem kind of crazy?

20 Come up with your own everyday example for one of the views or arguments or objections presented in this chapter.

Notes

1 For the moment let's assume that Van Inwagen has got to be right that we have at least some control over our thinking and our decisions.

2 Cavendish, *Observations Upon Experimental Philosophy*, 40–1.

3 See, for example, *Grounds of Natural Philosophy*, 217.

4 Margaret Cavendish, *The World's Olio*, London: printed for J. Martin and J. Allestrye (1655), 85.

5 Cavendish, *Youth's Glory and Death's Banquet*, 134.

6 Ibid., 136.

7 Ibid., 140.

8 Ibid., 136.

9 Margaret Cavendish, "An Introduction," in *Playes*, London: John Martyn, James Allestrye, and Tho. Dicas (1662), 2.

10 Margaret Cavendish, *Bell in Campo*, in *Playes*, London: John Martyn, James Allestrye, and Tho. Dicas (1662), 588–9.

11 See Corinne A. Moss-Racusin, John F. Dovidio, Victoria L. Brescoll, Mark J. Graham, and Jo Handelsman, "Science faculty's subtle gender biases favor male students," in *Proceedings of the National Academy of the Sciences* (2012), www.pnas.org/cgi/doi/10.1073/pnas.1211286109.

12 Albert Camus, *The Stranger*, trans. Matthew Ward, New York: Vintage (1942/1989), 59.

13 Ibid., 3.

14 Ibid., 90.

15 Ibid., 94.

16 Spinoza's excommunication, as translated in Steven Nadler, *Spinoza: A Life*, Cambridge: Cambridge University Press (1999), 120.

17 Cavendish's view on the control that we have over our decisions is very complicated, and perhaps even unsettled, but most commentators think that she grants a two-way power to the will by which we always have the ability to do otherwise. I am assuming that here.

18 Here we might think of the classic Billy Joel* song, "We didn't start the fire."

19 Another example is from the first season of the television show, M.A.S.H. The original three-man cohort of doctor buddies included

"Hawkeye" Pierce, "Trapper," and an African American character. The latter character was not believable as a member of the group; because of various racial dynamics at the time, he was not able to have an emotional connection with the other two characters. The scenes are quite painful to watch actually. The actor (Timothy Brown) was quickly replaced. The cited reason was that Brown's character was unrealistic because in fact there were no African American doctors who served in the Korean War. That turns out not to be true, but in any case it is hard to believe that that could have been the whole reason, given the viewer-awkwardness of the scenes in question.

20 Attempts at such intervention might be successful over the long haul, but in the short term can lead to enormous fallout for the cause and for individuals who work toward it.*

21 Or perhaps it's that most people were not able to be entertained by him when he started to say things that were charged.*

22 Naomi Zack, "Reparations and the Rectification of Race," *The Journal of Ethics* 7 (2003), 139–51. Naomi Zack is Professor of Philosophy at the University of Oregon. She is the author of eight books, three edited volumes, and numerous articles. She specializes in philosophy of race, feminist theory and politics, disaster ethics, and history of modern philosophy.

23 Ron Mallon, "Passing, Traveling and Reality: Social Constructionism and the Metaphysics of Race," *Nous* 38 (2004), esp. section 2. Ron Mallon is Associate Professor of Philosophy and Director of the Philosophy-Neuroscience-Psychology Program at Washington University in St Louis. He has published numerous articles in moral psychology, experimental philosophy, social construction, and philosophy of race.

24 A movie about this is *Imitation of Life*—the original in 1934, and another version in 1959.

25 George Yancy, *Black Bodies, White Gazes: The Continuing Significance of Race*, Lanham, MD: Rowman and Littlefield (2008), 5.

26 Harold Cruse, *Plural but Equal*, New York: William Morrow (1987), esp. part 4. Harold Cruse was Professor of African American Studies at the University of Michigan. He was the author of numerous books and articles, with a focus on politics, race, culture, and music.

27 This turned into our contemporary institution of the passport.

28 Simone De Beauvoir, "Introduction," in *The Second Sex*, trans. and ed. H. M. Parshley, New York: Random House, Vintage Books

(1989), xxvi–xxvii. Simone De Beauvoir was a twentieth-century philosopher and writer who wrote numerous books, essays, and novels. Her areas of focus were feminism, politics, and social activism.

29 Ibid., 279–86.

30 Ibid., 288.

31 Consider, for example, the Ban Bossy campaign.*

32 "Introduction," xix.

33 Rae Langton, *Sexual Solipsism: Philosophical Essays on Pornography and Objectification*, Oxford: Oxford University Press (1998), esp. ch. 1. Rae Langton is Professor of Philosophy at the University of Cambridge. Her research has focused on issues in the history of philosophy, ethics, political philosophy, metaphysics, and feminist philosophy. She has published numerous articles and (in addition to *Sexual Solipsism*) is the author of *Kantian Humility: Our Ignorance of Things in Themselves*, Oxford: Oxford University Press (1998).

34 Heidegger might put the issue in terms of whether or not there are worlds that are predominant and that rule out the possibility of other worlds.*

35 There are a number of examples that could be cited, but one is the case of Gail Grandchamp.*

36 An interesting development is that the league recently changed its name to "Legends Football League."

37 Charles Darwin, *The Origin of Species*, Oxford and New York: Oxford University Press (1996), 31–2. Darwin of course is famous for defending the theory of evolution.

38 Jean-Paul Sartre, "The Humanism of Existentialism," in Charles Guignon and Derk Pereboom (eds), *Existentialism: Basic Writings*, Indianapolis: Hackett (2001), 292–3. Jean-Paul Sartre was a twentieth-century philosopher, novelist, playwright, and political activist. He was awarded the Nobel Prize in Literature in 1964, but turned it down. A noteworthy tidbit is that Sartre and Beauvoir were romantic and intellectual partners for much of their lives.

39 Ibid., 304.

40 Ibid., 296.

41 Ibid., 302. Note that Searle (from the discussion in Chapter Six) would agree that we have a vivid experience of freedom, but he thinks that it is caused by the brain.

42 Ibid., 294.

43 Jean-Paul Sartre, *Being and Nothingness*, trans. Hazel E. Barnes, New York: Washington Square Press (1956), 98.

44 Sartre, "The Humanism of Existentialism," 296.

45 Sartre, *Being and Nothingness*, 76.

46 Ibid., 56–64.

47 Nietzsche, *On the Genealogy of Morality*, First Essay, section 11, 23.

48 Ibid., First Essay.

49 Nietzsche, *The Will to Power*, section 26, 19.

50 *On the Genealogy of Morality*, Second Essay, section 17, 24. The movie *Fight Club* explores this theme, though hopefully it does not present the only route for people to channel their energies.

51 Søren Kierkegaard, *The Present Age*, trans. Alexander Dru, ed. Walter Kaufmann, New York: Harper & Row (1962), 61.

52 Ibid., 65–7.

53 Kierkegaard, *Fear and Trembling*, 66.

54 Kierkegaard, *The Present Age*, 54.

55 Kierkegaard, *Fear and Trembling*, 37.

56 Ibid., 66–7.

57 Ibid., 62.

58 Ibid., 69.

59 Ibid., 58.

60 Ibid., 68.

61 Ibid., 33.

62 Søren Kierkegaard, *Practice in Christianity*, ed. and trans. Howard V. Hong and Edna H. Hong, Princeton: Princeton University Press (1991), 82.

63 Ibid., 63, emphasis added.

64 See the discussion in *Fear and Trembling*, 36–40.

65 Indeed they would seem to be stuck in their own head.*

66 *Fear and Trembling*, 34.

67 Ibid., 42.

68 Ibid., 59.

69 *Practice in Christianity*, 139.

70 Kierkegaard, *The Present Age*, 67.

71 *Practice in Christianity*, 91.

72 Ibid., 139.

CHAPTER EIGHT

The individual and society

Abstract

This chapter considers the following: who is responsible for eliminating corrosion in the interface between decisions and the world; the different ways in which our projects and pursuits might interfere with the projects and pursuits of others; and the question of when we should step aside for the sake of the other's freedom, and when we should stand firm for the sake of our own.

Liberalism and libertarianism

1

One way to frame a discussion of the relationship between the individual and society is to ask about the extent to which individuals interfere with each other's ability to pursue a fulfilling life and about the extent to which it is society's obligation to intervene.

2

One of the central issues that arises in thinking about corrosion in the interface between decisions and the world is social welfare programs and whether they are necessary, or even helpful, in promoting freedom and agency. Some might argue that social welfare programs enhance the freedom and agency of the less fortunate, and others might argue that they in fact hinder the freedom of the less fortunate, along with the freedom of those who are footing the bill. The philosopher John Rawls offers a number of arguments in favor of the liberal welfare state. He argued this: if before we were born, we did not know how smart, attractive, charming, or strong we would be, or whether we would be born into crushing poverty or wealth, or (to borrow the language of Cavendish) how much social and political capital we would be granted by virtue of the interface between our decisions and the world, we would want the range of starting points in life to be less random than they are at the moment.[1] Rawls is assuming the obvious point that there are a number of things that are not up to us before we are parachuted into the world: for example, whether or not we are smart, talented, beautiful, quick-witted, or charming; and whether or not we are born into poverty, or into a group that is blacklisted and has a disproportionate amount of trouble developing a customer base, or into a group whose predecessors were not allowed to acquire and pass on wealth. If we have little to no say in these, then if we know that we will have to compete with others who are more lucky, we will hope that there is more evenness in where we are placed. Rawls is thinking that we would prefer this for self-interested reasons, but that we would also just think that it is more equitable and fair.

3

Rawls is worried about a situation where we find ourselves with a radically uneven amount of energy and power and credits at birth—sort of like a malfunctioning *Dungeons and Dragons* or *Life Force* game—but we say that our trajectory is entirely up to us. He proposes that we attempt a fictional thought experiment: we imagine ourselves behind a "veil of ignorance" before we are transported to our situation on earth. Rawls writes,

> Among the essential features of this situation is that no one knows his place in society, his class position or social status,

nor does anyone know his fortune in the distribution of natural assets and abilities, his intelligence, strength and the like. I shall even assume that the parties do not know their conceptions of the good or their special psychological propensities. The principles of justice are chosen behind a veil of ignorance. This ensures that no one is advantaged or disadvantaged in the choice of principles by the outcome of natural chance or the contingency of social circumstances.[2]

In the "original position," we do not know where we will end up, and we are asked what we would want the range of possible destinations to be. Rawls speculates that we would want to land in a world that has a not radically uneven birth-distribution of wealth, talents, and social and political capital.[3] It is true that the distribution would eventually become wide again, as some people would work harder than others and some would rather surf. Some would also be smarter and more talented than others, but Rawls would add that in our current situation, with its thick history of violence and subjugation, the intelligence and talent of a large number of people do not have a chance to develop. Rawls is thinking that, behind a "veil of ignorance," we would vote against distributions that are too much the result of luck. We would also put into place laws and norms that make it unacceptable for the relevant kinds of violence and subjugation to crop up anew, so that uneven distributions that are the result of such things would not have a chance to take root again.

4

An objection to Rawls is that his "veil of ignorance" thought experiment is totally incoherent. If we are not yet born and do not have any features, it makes no sense to talk about what we would or would not prefer. Rawls is assuming that we already have some features, and a worry is that he is stacking the deck in order to get the result that he wants. For example, he is assuming that we are not gamblers or risk-takers, ready to roll the dice, and he is also assuming that we are concerned about fairness. Rawls would seem to be building these assumptions into his theory and then getting his results for free.

5

Rawls is also assuming that we are not sufficiently free and in control of our trajectory that we would be able to overcome our initial placement, no matter how bad it was. What we say here will probably depend on what we want to say in response to the arguments in Chapters Six and Seven. On the one hand, it can seem as though we have very little control over our ideas and decisions, and also that our freedom is in large part a function of the interface between our decisions and the world. On the other hand, it seems that we have to have some control over our trajectory if we are going to take ourselves seriously as agents. So a pivotal question is how much control and autonomy we in fact have, and whether it is enough to keep the Rawls experiment from being applicable.

6

Indeed, there is no question that an important part of the dignity of a person lies in their autonomy. Rawls himself would have to admit that one of the reasons that his "veil of ignorance" exercise is so time-sensitive is that human beings have a special kind of value and dignity, and that there is a lot at stake if we do not take action now. The libertarian philosopher Robert Nozick has taken issue with Rawls along these lines. In this passage he quotes from Rawls and takes issue with his view:

> Here we have *Rawls'* reason for rejecting a system of natural liberty: it "permits" distributive shares to be improperly influenced by factors that are so arbitrary from a moral point of view. These factors are: "prior distribution . . . of natural talents and abilities as these have been developed over time by social circumstances and such chance contingencies as accident and good fortune." Notice that there is no mention at all of how persons have chosen to develop their natural assets. Why is that simply left out? Perhaps because such choices also are viewed as being the products of factors outside the person's control, and hence as "arbitrary from a moral point of view." "The assertion

that a man deserves the superior character that enables him to make the effort to cultivate his abilities is equally problematic; for his character depends in large part upon fortunate family and social circumstances for which he can claim no credit." . . . This line of argument can succeed in blocking the introduction of a person's autonomous choices and actions (and their results) only by attributing everything noteworthy about the person completely to certain sorts of "external" factors. So denigrating a person's autonomy and prime responsibility for his actions is a risky line to take for a theory that otherwise wishes to buttress the dignity and self-respect of autonomous beings; especially for a theory that founds so much (including a theory of the good) upon persons' choices. One doubts that the unexalted picture of human beings Rawls' theory presupposes and rests upon can be made to fit together with the view of human dignity it is designed to lead to and embody.[4]

The objection here is very telling. Rawls supposes that there is something that is very special about human beings and that we are, so to speak, worth all the fuss. Part of what is most special about us is our autonomy and dignity, and our faculty of choice. If so, however, we do not need to go to all the lengths that Rawls lays out to level the playing field. We can do a lot of that work ourselves. Indeed, if our society or government takes on the task—by imposing rules and regulations and structure—autonomy and freedom would be inhibited even more.

7

A related objection to Rawls is that it is good for us to use our freedom in the attempt to determine our own trajectory. More specifically, if he had his way there would be a lot less motivation and exertion. We get excited watching movies like *Rambo* or *Die Hard*, or any movie in which the individual conquers all, and presumably that is because we value the hard work and determined will of a person who can make it on his own. The debate here turns in part on the question of whether or not Searle or Van Inwagen or Cavendish is right about the extent of freedom and agency.

8

Nozick offers a thought experiment to motivate the view that dramatically uneven distributions of wealth and capital are acceptable. He argues that in fact we find them acceptable—and much more acceptable than the distributions that Rawls thinks would arise from the "original position." Nozick asks us to consider a situation in which the initial distribution of holdings (D_1) is our favorite—"perhaps everyone has an equal share, perhaps shares vary in accordance with some dimension you treasure."[5] Then he asks whether we should also find acceptable the updated distribution (D_2) that arises along the following lines. Suppose we are basketball fans, and we have the option of paying extra so that Wilt Chamberlain can play on the local professional team. As we walk through the gate, we hand off our ticket, and we add an additional 25 cents into a bin that goes directly to Mr Chamberlain. Nozick says of such basketball fans:

> They are excited about seeing him play; it is worth the total admission price to them. Let us suppose that in one season one million persons attend his home games, and Wilt Chamberlain winds up with $250,000, a much larger sum than the average income and larger even than anyone else has. Is he entitled to this new income? Is this new distribution D_2, unjust? If so, why? There is *no* question about whether each of the people was entitled to the control over the resources they held in D_1; because that was the distribution (your favorite) that (for the purposes of argument) we assumed was acceptable. Each of these persons *chose* to give twenty-five cents of their money to Chamberlain. They could have spent it on going to the movies, or on candy bars, or on copies of Dissent magazine, or of Monthly Review. But they all, at least one million of them, converged on giving it to Wilt Chamberlain in exchange for watching him play basketball. If D_1 was a just distribution, and people voluntarily moved from it to D_2, . . . isn't D_2 also just?[6]

An opponent might respond that the thought experiment is not actually an objection to Rawls if it does not allow our favorite initial distribution to include facts about the distribution of skills and talents. Mr Chamberlain is clearly ahead of the game. Nozick would respond that our skills and talents are to some degree up to us, but in addition he is worried that our freedom would end up highly constrained if the distribution of skills and talents was included in the presumptive Rawlsean algorithm. He concludes his book with a description of utopia:

> The minimal state treats us as inviolate individuals, who may not be used in certain ways by others as means or tools or instruments or resources; it treats us as persons having individual rights with the dignity this constitutes. Treating us with respect by respecting our rights, it allows us, individually or with whom we choose, to choose our life and to realize our ends and our conception of ourselves, insofar as we can, aided by the voluntary cooperation of other individuals possessing the same dignity. How *dare* any state or group of individuals do more. Or less.[7]

Rawls would disagree and argue that for historical and biological reasons there is a dramatic unevenness in the ability of people to live the life that they would choose to lead. He thinks that in the original position we would freely choose to put steps into place that would reduce some freedoms, so long as they maximized others. The scenario of the original position is fictional of course, or it is long past, but government and society can at least take action in the present.

9

We might put the debate between Rawls and Nozick in terms of examples of our own. A worry for Rawls is that he is inevitably proposing a kind of interference in free-market commerce, and that governmental regulation as a rule has proven to be inefficient. We could point to numerous examples. There is the county firefighter who retires with a full pension at age 50. There is the life-saving drug that cannot make it to market because still more regulatory testing is required. There is the company that will not locate its job-producing factory in a given city because of high taxes, or strict zoning laws. There is the long line at the local Department of Motor Vehicles; the annual deficit of the US postal service; and the restaurant that goes out of business because it could not afford to get its wheelchair ramp up to code. In addition, it can take years for any given regulation to be properly formulated and become law, in ways that make it hard for the business world to adjust. The government interference that would be inevitable in a Rawlsean society is bound to inhibit the freedom of the marketplace. It would be inefficient, and in addition, it would give people a disincentive to exercise their willpower, creativity, and initiative. It would lead to more bad than good.

10

One response would be to deny that there are government inefficiencies. That would be a tough case to make. Another would be to try to argue that when we compare the overall inefficiencies that would ensue on the Rawlsean picture with the amount of freedom and fairness that would be promoted, the inefficiencies are tolerable. It would be extremely hard to do the math, and probably impossible, but Rawls would argue that the resultant inefficiencies might be well worth the cost, given the alternative. On this line of reasoning, it might be argued that all things considered the policies of a social welfare state do not stifle freedom or initiative or creativity, but instead they are on a par with the nurturing that is often received by those who are born into families that are wealthy or resourceful. Certainly there are exceptions, but youth who are raised with a lot of resources and opportunity are often successful and hardworking. It might then be argued that there is more creativity and initiative in the world if everyone is a dependent for at least a while. A Rawlsean might offer this analogy: there will always be traffic so long as there are drivers and roads; and if we are to retain all the benefits of the institution of driving, some amount of traffic will have to be tolerated. A Nozickean might argue that the highway system would be in a lot better shape if it was limited to drivers who were responsible.

11

A Rawlsean might also try to tackle some of the particular worries about regulation. The thinking might go like this: the reason why it takes so long for regulations to be formulated is that industry attorneys make sure to hold up the passage of regulations, so that it can be said that they take too long to implement; or legislators slash the funding of departments that are in charge of enforcing regulations, so that the departments cannot help but appear inefficient; the life-saving drug requires further testing because companies would otherwise rush their drug to the market, and they would just feign ignorance (and hire more attorneys) if people died as a result; the firefighter gets a good deal because firefighting is dangerous; the company that bypasses a given city or country because of taxes or regulation relocates in an area in which there is enforced child labor, or in which factory doors are not unlocked in the case of a fire.* It is difficult to confirm some of these—therein lies a problem—and how we understand the data might depend on whether we are a Rawlsean or Nozickean in the first place.

12

A Rawlsean might also argue that free markets do not promote freedom as much as is often thought. It is possible to think very abstractly about a paradise that would ensue if unfettered free markets were the norm. It could be argued however that if the free market is left to its own devices, companies will do whatever they have to do, and whatever they can get away with, to have a competitive edge. There are worries about loose regulations with respect to oil rigs, health supplements, and for-profit halfway houses; there is the apparent lack of oversight in the banking crisis of 2008; and there were the compounding-pharmacy drugs of fall 2012. Just as individuals would tend to drive a lot faster if there were no speed limits—and there would be an increase in the number of accidents—companies would attempt to get away with a lot if there were no regulations. They would do this out of the same motivation that drives companies in a regulated economy to work *around* regulations. Such a company might engage in highly problematic behavior but still thrive in a free market; they might have a high enough profit margin to hire lawyers, lobbyists, and public relations experts to project a better corporate image than the regulation-respecting competition. So a question is whether or not—all things considered—regulations enhance freedom, or limit it. Rawls might point to regulations surrounding Kentucky bourbon, for example, and argue that the customer's freedom is promoted when the customer can be sure that she is paying for genuine Kentucky bourbon, and not a diluted (or otherwise problematic) imitation. The company benefits as well, when its competition is not allowed to break the rules and lower costs.

13

Rawls might continue to make the case: some of the work to enforce norms of fairness could be done by free-market consumers who incorporate norms of fairness into their free-market purchasing decisions. For example, if we value freedom, and if a person or group tries to corrode the interface between an individual's decisions and the world, we can dislike the person or group, and make our purchases accordingly. People do this sort of thing with some frequency—refuse to vacation in a country that practices apartheid, or they pay a little extra for a product with the label, *Made in the U.S.A.*, or purchase fair-trade coffee so that the growers can make a living wage. In a similar vein, Pee-Wee Herman has been blacklisted since 1991 for performing an act that consumers regard as unseemly; only now is the consumer giving him a second chance. The former US presidential candidate John Edwards is now ostracized. Nor do we buy products that have the endorsement of the former Olympic sprinter and steroid-user Marion Jones. Companies then make a corresponding free-market decision not to hire her as a spokesperson. Michael Vick suffered a similar free-market penalty, at least for a while.[8] There is another case that is highly problematic but that still makes the point: individual business owners refused African Americans as paying customers for a long stretch in US History. That is, free-market businesses placed something else at a higher value than money. So there is Pee-Wee Herman and John Edwards, and also the doctor who came to the aid of an injured John Wilkes Booth. (His name was Mudd.)

14

A Nozickean objection is that it is not our responsibility to rectify the situation of the coffee growers in another country. We would probably mess things up if we intervened, but in any case we should let the workers sort things out for themselves. Furthermore, we should not feel that we are under any obligation to pay more for products if in fact they are available for less. We would be holding off on the satisfaction of other desires that we have, and that would be going against the grain. It would be a kind of violation—especially if we are committed to the ethical principle that people should take care of themselves. If we *want* to act on the desire to help the coffee grower rather than on the desire to pay less for coffee, that is our choice. Or, if we have a relatively weak desire to help the coffee grower, but we want to make that desire stronger than our desire to pay less for coffee, that is our choice as well. Frankfurt would say that that would be a matter of taking a stand on our desires and not being automatically motivated by the first-order desires that we happen to find ourselves with. But there is a difference between having a second-order desire voluntarily, and suggesting that it is our obligation. There is also a question about how much we can modify the structure of our desires and aims and projects without doing violence to our sense of orientation and self.

15

Furthermore, it is *naïve* to think that people are going to make purchasing decisions that take into account the well-being of the producer. The recent case of Apple is telling here (though there are numerous examples in addition). Many iPhones and iPads are produced by Foxconn Technology in China, and some would identify the factory working conditions as very problematic.* Nonetheless, Apple has continued to secure profits in the billions. If consumers were in fact concerned about the conditions of the makers of Apple products, they would hold off on buying such products until changes were made, or they would switch to a different brand altogether. But the lines for the latest iPhone are always out the door. On a related note, Michael Vick signed a $100-million contract with the Philadelphia Eagles in 2011, and fans at the stadium cheered him on. So a potential objection against the Rawlsean is that we do not care so much about the conditions of any actual worker, but about being able to feel as though we care, or about being able to say that we care, or about being able to talk in ways that project an image of concern that might benefit us in our personal lives and at work. That is, when I help someone who has fallen down on my university campus, I do so because I know that someone might be watching—perhaps even the Dean or Provost—and it is in my interest that I be seen as good. So part of what we need to know in adjudicating between the views in Rawls and Nozick is the extent to which human beings are (or at least can be) genuinely concerned about the well-being of others, and whether or not we are almost entirely self-interested.

Mind versus body again?

16

Another benefit of free markets, a Nozickean might argue, is that even if individuals would have to struggle, the upside is that—individuals would have to struggle! This is not always a bad thing. Exerting willpower is by itself very important, and it would result in more initiative and creativity, with likely material consequences. We might be compelled by some of the arguments against human freedom, but all sides (presumably) have to admit that we have at least some control over our decisions and our trajectory.

17

A cultural or historical reason why a vigorous exercise of will might be regarded as important is because it is our will and our efforts that are considered when each of us is standing before God as a solitary individual on Judgment Day. St Augustine reflects this position. He assumes that there is a Judgment Day and argues that each individual is alone responsible for their decisions. That is the only way that punishment or praise would be fair:

> If you know or believe that God is good—and it is not right to believe otherwise—then he does no evil. On the other hand, if we acknowledge that God is just—and it is impious to deny it—then he rewards the good and punishes the wicked. . . . Evil

deeds are punished by the justice of God. They would not be punished justly if they had not been performed voluntarily.[9]

It is not as if we can say to God—"You know, the buck doesn't stop here; there were causal variables surrounding my brain and my decisions, and variables surrounding those variables, and variables surrounding *those*. Didn't you read Spinoza?" Augustine then adds that even though we are completely in control of our will, there are some things that we do not control:

> [People are] utterly miserable, even if they have all these things [a splendid reputation, great wealth, and various goods of the body], when they cleave to things they can quite easily lose, things that they do not have simply in virtue of willing them. . . . Then consider those who have this good will whose excellence we have been discussing for so long now. They lovingly embrace this one unsurpassable good and delight in its presence. They enjoy it to the full and rejoice when they consider that so great a good is theirs and cannot be stolen or taken away from them against their will. Can we doubt that they will resist everything that is inimical to this one good?[10]

For Augustine, the only thing that is really up to us is our decisions and our will, but the silver lining is that success in the external world of bodies in not important anyway. This is a version of the Socratic view that what is most significant about a person is their soul and their mental activity. If mental activity is what matters, as well as mental discipline and determination, we are hurting people in the earthly domain when we keep them from exerting their will in their effort to help themselves.

18

The idea (contra Rawls) is that people will benefit if they are *not* given social assistance. This could be for two reasons. With Socrates, Augustine, and Astell, it could be argued that even if we are not materially successful, we are successful in all the ways that matter—so long as we exercise our wills in the proper way. Or, it could be argued that God makes sure that we are rewarded here on earth if we do exert our wills correctly, and that we receive material compensation. Social assistance gets in the way no matter what.

19

We might also consider Rawlsean and Nozickean angles on the nature and causes of crime, and the relation between crime and the question of the interface between decisions and the world. Some might argue that crime and other sorts of aberrant behavior are the result of people using their free will incorrectly, end of story. Some might argue that there is a much longer story and that crime is largely a matter of social factors. Cavendish would argue that in many cases people engage in criminal behavior out of frustration and contempt when the interface between their decisions and the world is disproportionately corroded. She would note that even in the case of normal (noncriminal) behavior, we can get quite frustrated when the deck is stacked against us. For example, we would be very frustrated at the community of rule-enforcers, and also at our competition, if we were participating in a horse race, and our gate opened only 20 percent of the time—or if we pushed the elevator button and the elevator came just sporadically. We might be inclined to have a lot less respect for the rules and for our competitors, and we might seek out a different game, where the connection between the world and our will is more even. To use another metaphor, we might decide to play in another sandbox, or take our ball and go home, or take someone else's ball and go home. We might think that this is actually the right thing to do. The philosopher Cornell West speaks in these terms in describing the rage that is present in the members of some African American communities who are frustrated at causal forces that delimit their options:

> The accumulated effect of the black wounds and scars suffered in a white-dominated society is a deep-seated anger, a boiling sense of rage, and a passionate pessimism regarding America's will to justice. Under conditions of slavery and Jim Crow segregation, this anger, rage, and pessimism remained relatively muted because of a well-justified fear of brutal white retaliation.

The major breakthroughs of the sixties—more physically than politically—swept this fear away. Sadly, the combination of the market way of life, poverty-ridden conditions, black existential *angst*, and the lessening fear of white authorities has directed most of the anger, rage, and despair toward fellow black citizens. . . . Only recently has this nihilistic threat—and its ugly inhumane outlook and actions—surfaced in the larger American society.[11]

Cavendish (along with Rawls) has argued that we should work to promote evenness in the interface between decisions and the world, so that we are not guilty of depraved indifference. If Cavendish is right, we had better hope that there are not extraterrestrials who are extremely powerful and have a strong sense of justice.

20

Or an opponent might argue that historically speaking human beings have tended to treat each other terribly no matter what, and there is nothing that can be done about it. That is to say, there will never be a time in which the dominant group is composed of individuals who are invested in the well-being of others and who are interested in eradicating the corrosion in the interface between decisions and the world. To think otherwise is to have a foolish view of human nature. For example, there are the many individuals who want to project an image of kindness and decency, but only because such an image will further their self-interest. And then there are the very extreme cases. There is the horrible man who kidnapped three young girls in Cleveland, held them hostage for more than a decade, and forced one of the girls to have his child. He knew that the families of the girls were desperately searching for them, but he simply boarded up his windows. He was doing what he wanted to do. There is the husband and wife in Antioch, California, who kidnapped an 11-year-old girl and kept her locked in a shelter for almost 20 years. There is the sociopathic man who killed children and teachers in Sandy Hook, Connecticut. There is the man who threw his 3-year-old son from the top of a high-rise in Manhattan to make his ex-wife suffer. There are the characters in *Lord of the Flies* who basically become vicious and cruel when the law enforcement mechanisms of society are no longer in play. There were the citizens of Nazi Germany, and the citizens of most of the pre-civil war United States, who implicitly (if not explicitly) supported the behavior that took place in their midst. And there are the numerous social-science experiments in which human subjects are given the authority and latitude to dominate and subordinate other participants; in due course the subjects are so horrifically cruel and vicious that the experiment has to be stopped early, before things get out of hand.* The worry in the latter few cases is that the people would not appear to be especially sociopathic or unusual; and it can be hard to say for sure that we would not do the same thing if we found ourselves in identical circumstances.

21

There is also the story in Plato about Gyges' ring: its wearer becomes invisible, and is thereby able to get away with anything.[12] We might ask what we would do in that situation, or what we think others would do. An opponent of Rawls and Cavendish might argue that there is no fantasy situation in which human beings are especially concerned about the well-being of others and that instead of trying to fix things, we should team up with the well-meaning among us, but also sit on our own gold.

Getting in each other's way

22

Another issue that bears on the question of individual freedom and the way in which it can interfere with the freedom of others is gay marriage. This issue is being debated in the United States and elsewhere, and it is an important instance of the many debates about who should be allowed to do what and when. It is just one debate, but it might be seen as representative in various ways. The individuals on both sides have strong and sincere feelings, and it is difficult to isolate a common denominator from which they could build consensus. There are a number of varied strands to the debate: for example, some homosexual individuals have no interest in marriage, and there are some individuals (both homosexual and not) who think that the institution of marriage should be abolished altogether. The discussion here will focus on the strand of the debate that has been most prominent in the public sphere: the disagreement between those who hold that homosexual activity is immoral and thus should not be sanctified in the law, and those who (perhaps irrespective of their views on the morality of homosexual behavior) hold that gay marriage should be permitted.

23

On one side of the debate, some might appeal to their faith and argue that God forbids homosexual behavior and that therefore it should not be allowed. In addition, some might feel disgust or nausea at the appearance of homosexual affection, and then take that disgust to be tracking a fact about the indecency or immorality of the behavior in question. It is a lot to ask an individual to vote to codify into law practices that they take to be abominable. There might also be some impact on the ability of some individuals to live meaningful lives if they are living in a context in which they have to see themselves as implicitly condoning practices that they regard as unacceptable. An analogy might be with a taxpayer who can no longer stand that their government is supporting a dictator in a country far away. An opponent of gay marriage might also argue that heterosexuality is the norm in nature, enabling species to continue to exist, and that homosexual behavior is therefore unnatural and wrong.

24

Here we have two groups that would have an impact on each other's freedom. An opponent of gay marriage might point to the passages in Leviticus 18.22–4 and 20.13 in which homosexual activity is regarded as an abomination:

Thou shalt not lie with mankinde, as with womankinde: it is abomination.

If a man also lie with mankind, as he lieth with a woman, both of them have committed an abomination: they shall surely be put to death; their blood shall be upon them.[13]

Picking up on some of the material from Chapter Two, an opponent of gay marriage might argue that God has not just arbitrarily decreed that homosexual behavior is an abomination: instead, God reports to us that it is an abomination after He consults an independent standard of morality that entails that homosexual behavior is objectively bad. For example, homosexual behavior might be bad because it does not result in the production of offspring, and because sexual activity that does not result in offspring is frivolous. This is not to say that all human beings should engage in procreational activity—for example, priests and nuns have more important things to do—but the argument would be that if we do engage in sexual activity, it should result in children.

25

Supporters of gay marriage might agree that whatever God reports about moral matters has to be true, but disagree that God says anything decisive about homosexual behavior. There are the above-cited passages in Leviticus, but the supporter of gay marriage might worry that if we interpret those as the literal word of God, then there are other passages that we would have to read literally as well:

For euery one that curseth his father or his mother, shalbe surely put to death: hee hath cursed his father or his mother; his blood shalbe vpon him.[14]

Both thy bondmen, and thy bondmaids, which thou shalt haue, shall be of the Heathen, that are round about you: of them shall ye buy bondmen and bondmaids. . . . Moreouer, of the children of the strangers that do soiourne among you, of them shall ye buy, and of their families that are with you, which they begat in your land: and they shalbe your possession.[15]

Giue them, O Lord: what wilt thou giue? giue them a miscarying wombe, and drie breasts.[16]

There is no question that there are alternative ways to read these, but a worry is that if human minds start picking and choosing how the various passages of scripture are to be interpreted, then we are no longer basing our morality on what an infallible God reports, but on what fallible beings say that He reports. Galileo made this point in the early seventeenth century. He argued that the Bible cannot err, but that it is such a deep and profound document that it is often hard to know exactly what it is telling us:

> I think in the first place that it is very pious to say and prudent to affirm that the holy Bible can never speak untruth—whenever its true meaning is understood. But I believe nobody will deny that it is often very abstruse, and may say things which are quite different from what its bare words signify. Hence in expounding the Bible if one were always to attend to its unadorned grammatical meaning, one might fall into error. Not only contradictions and propositions far from true might thus be made to appear in the Bible, but even grave heresies and follies. Thus it would be necessary to assign to God feet, hands and eyes, as well as corporeal human affections, such as anger, repentance, hatred, and sometimes even the forgetting of things past and ignorance of those to come.[17]

Galileo proceeds to argue that although there is no claim in scripture that is false, it is more profound than any earthly text—for example, by Shakespeare or Yeats. If so, it would be even more difficult to interpret.

26

One cue, Galileo thinks, is that God gave us our senses and our reason, and so the results that these generate must be trustworthy. Otherwise God would be a kind of deceiver:

> I do not feel obliged to believe that the same God who has endowed us with senses, reason, and intellect has intended to forgo their use and by some other means to give us knowledge which we can attain by them. He would not require us to deny

sense and reason in physical matters which are set before our eyes and minds by direct experience or necessary demonstration.[18]

Here Galileo is suggesting that if a clear deduction of our senses and reason appears to contradict a claim in the Bible, that is a clear sign (from God) that the claim requires more than a surface reading. He then cites St Augustine:

> [I]f, against the most manifest and reliable testimony of reason, anything be set up claiming to have the authority of the Holy Scriptures, he who does this does it through a misapprehension of what he has read, and is setting up against the truth not the real meaning of Scripture, which he has failed to discover, but an opinion of his own; he alleges not what he has found in the Scripture, but what he has found in himself as their interpreter.[19]

A criticism of Galileo is that there is not a lot that is completely uncontroversial in the sciences, or that follows with manifest certainty, and so his tool might not be of much help. If the tool is also to help us to interpret scriptural claims about matters of right and wrong, we would need to have access to moral facts that we know with manifest certainty and that thereby inform us that scriptural claims that conflict with these are not to be taken literally. Perhaps we appeal to an objective standard of morality in concluding that there is no way that God could have meant that it is appropriate to kill children who curse their parents. Both the supporter of gay marriage and the opponent of gay marriage might go on to say that there are objective standards of morality to which we can appeal to once-and-for-all interpret the passages about homosexual behavior.

27

Or if we are compelled by the third (and unstated) option of the *Euthyphro* dilemma, we might argue that goodness is just identical to whatever God is or does, and the opposite is bad. Then we would look for signs of antihomosexuality in God's behavior, or His nature. At this point, both sides of the debate might just dig in their heels.

28

The supporter of gay marriage might say that God is neither a heterosexual nor a homosexual, and that we have no business making claims about God's nature in any case. The supporter of gay marriage might also insist that there is no independent standard that tells us that homosexual behavior is bad, and that there are even reasons for thinking that it is good: it is an expression of the emotions of a subset of human beings, and it allows these human beings to inhabit worlds that matter to them. In addition, one might argue that homosexual behavior does occur in nature—for example, in penguins, dolphins, koalas, bison, beetles, warthogs, and macaques, among others.* The argument might continue: any segment of time that homosexual human beings are not using to reproduce or raise their own children can be freed up for other important activities, like assisting with the offspring of others.

29

The opponent of gay marriage might reply that there is a fact of the matter about whether homosexual behavior is wrong, and that we can grasp this fact, just like we can grasp the immorality of the torture of innocent human beings or the burning of innocent puppies. The opponent of gay marriage might then argue that if homosexual behavior is exhibited in nature, the animals that engage in it are still doing something that is wrong. The reasoning might continue: supporters of gay marriage are being reckless and cavalier and flippant about matters divine. The opponent of gay marriage might add: the sight of homosexual behavior causes pain in people who abhor it, and that is a further sign that it is problematic.

30

The supporter of gay marriage might point out that interracial kissing used to induce nausea in a large portion of the public. Perhaps it is a matter of cultural influence that we are disgusted by some behaviors and not others, and our disgust is not automatically an indication of whether a behavior is immoral or wrong. Many also feel disgusted when they find out that they are eating monkey brain or snail, even though for some these are a delicacy. The supporter of gay marriage might then argue that an aversion to homosexual desire is not natural or automatic, and that we should have a second-order desire to get rid of our aversion to homosexual intimacy in the interest of maximizing freedom. This back and forth might go on and on. We are faced with two groups that are each having an impact on the life of the other. Opponents of gay marriage are making the world a place where individuals who engage in homosexual behavior cannot lead the lives that they would find most fulfilling. Supporters of gay marriage want to make the world into a place that most opponents of gay marriage cannot bear to encounter. The latter individuals do not *want* to have a second-order desire to find homosexual behavior acceptable. They do not want to become that sort of person. The idea here is that if we are in the business of respecting freedom, we should not suggest that people go to all the trouble of changing their desires. People should be free to have the desires that they have, and to want what they want.

31

In addition, we might be asking *way too much* in the case of a lot of first-order desires and interests. We would be suggesting that a person should separate from what they identify with and take most seriously, but that would be quite disorienting. In a less extreme sort of example, a person might be a fan of NFL football and get together every week to watch the game with their friends. This person might concede that if they developed an interest in watching IWFL games, and tried to get others to develop such an interest, women would be more free to make a living at professional football. If the person was successful at revising their desires, however, other aspects of their life would probably start to change as well: they would not watch football with their friends on Sunday; they might no longer spend time with these friends at all; and the person might get to the point where they no longer like NFL football at all. If the person used to spend a lot of their time thinking about the games during the week, and talking about the upcoming schedule, they would now experience a loss. Presumably a person's faith is a much more central component of who they are.

32

To return to football once again, some NFL fans might recognize that they have preferences that are contingent on their upbringing and that end up reducing the ability of women to be professional football players. Such a person might refuse (or be unable) to change their desires, but perhaps they could decide to contribute in some other way. For example, the person could continue as a passionate NFL fan, inhabiting the NFL world, but give money to a fund that increases the freedom of the less fortunate. Again, this would be basically the analogue of a carbon-offset credit. Or, returning to some of the issues in Chapter Seven, the person might contribute to organizations that attempt to equalize the amount of corrosion in the interface between decisions and the world. But this would be a person who was voluntarily manifesting an interest in equalizing freedom. If a person is *forced* to make the donations, their freedom is being thwarted.

33

Of course, the NFL fan who changes into an IWFL fan is not the most extreme sort of case that we can imagine. Hume might chime in here (with his view from Chapter Two) and argue that since we (human beings) have a natural inclination to feel pleasure at the well-being of others, we could try to make that inclination more pronounced—to the point where we help others, and that is what predominantly fulfills us. That again would be to have a second-order desire, and to play an autonomous role in crafting our motivations. We might even think that we are *obligated* to alter our desires in this way, if we knew in advance that the world would become a much better place and that eventually we would become as invested in our new pursuits as we are in our current ones. The philosopher Sarah Buss has argued that it is very difficult to deflect this obligation once we think it through: perhaps the best that we can do is to conclude that since we cannot accurately weigh all the different variables and values that are at stake, or the risk to our personhood of attempting the sort of change in question, it is at least possible that our current pursuits are justifiable.[20]

34

A more extreme case still is that of the person who eradicates all of their first-order desires and has second-order desires to better the world as much as possible. This person would look to the world for the most important and pressing problems to address, and then build his life around a concern for them. If there is *this* much plasticity to a person's trajectory, there would be something very impersonal about being a person.[21] In effect, the person would be taking steps to be somebody else, all for the sake of the good.

35

If it is agreed that this is too much to ask, we could return to the issue of gay marriage and ask who should take steps to be somebody else: the individual who is opposed to homosexual behavior and who does not want to compromise on his values, or the homosexual who wants to be able to craft a life that his opponent despises. The faith of an individual who is opposed to homosexual behavior might be an important component of who they are, but a homosexual individual might insist that they are also being told to deny an important component of who they are.

36

Opponents of homosexual behavior might repeat that they do not want to look out and encounter the world to be a certain way, but *their* opponents might say that that is too bad, or they might argue that they find repugnant a world in which people are restricting freedom on the basis of assumptions about God's nature and His deliverances. If homosexual individuals and individuals who are opposed to homosexual behavior cannot lead lives that they fully endorse without getting in each other's way, a question arises about who is supposed to budge.

37

A further wrinkle is that individuals on each side might insist that those on the other side would be better off if they were the ones who budged. An individual opposed to homosexual behavior might say that homosexuals are wrong about what would most fulfill them—that they would be better off repressing their homosexual desires and building a life around a world of activities that are different. Or someone might argue that opponents of homosexual behavior would be better off if they were more humble in their views about an infinite being.

38

A similar analysis might apply to aspects of other societal debates: for example, over abortion, euthanasia, the legalization of drugs, immigration, the rights of transgender individuals, and other issues. A common question in each is who should be entitled to do what, and who should be entitled to intervene. For example, in the case of abortion, some might appeal to a passage in scripture or to their own sense of how horrific the world would be if abortion was permitted. Or, someone might insist that they grasp (and hence know) the truth that personhood begins at conception. Or, someone might insist that they detect an objective standard that says that, other things being equal, we ought protect the life of a fetus if it is more than halfway through its gestation period, or if it is able to survive outside of the womb with the help of machines. A common sort of analogy that comes up in the philosophy classroom, though the details of the analogy will vary, is this. Imagine that we are living in early modern Europe, and by some chain of events a half-finished Rembrandt painting ends up in our house. We might feel an obligation not to discard the painting, so that it can be completed. Or, we might feel obliged to provide it sanctuary until it is completed, if there is nowhere else that it can be safe.

39

Our response to this sort of case might be different if we adjust it to reflect some of the different parameters of the contemporary debate over abortion: for example, we specify that the painting was stashed in our house at gunpoint by a criminal, against our will, or that the painting appeared in our house by accident and through no fault of our own. Perhaps it makes a difference if we had previously installed a security system to keep such things from transpiring, where we would be able to say, "I did all that I could." That is, we should not be burdened to take care of the painting if it ends up in our house despite our best efforts. An opponent might respond that a potential human being is much more valuable than a painting.

40

Or some might have an intuition that the freedom of a pregnant individual is always overriding, or that population concerns can sometimes trump. Maybe it matters that, comparatively speaking, it is not nearly as painful or disruptive to keep the painting in our attic for nine months, and that it is not as emotionally complicated to part with it when the time in fact comes. The parties to the different sides of the debate would appear to place a high value on freedom, among other things, but disagree on how these are best promoted.

41

Here it might be useful to do a brief review of the topics that have been covered and the ways in which we might interconnect them. In Chapter One, there was a discussion of what kinds of things we are in a position to know, and what the criteria are for knowledge. If we have a preferred account of knowledge in hand, we might consider the views and assumptions and arguments of the later chapters and ask when we have knowledge with respect to these, and when we should be more skeptical. In Chapter Two, we addressed the question of the nature of morality and value—the origin and status of these, and the extent to which they have a claim on us. Chapter Three was a discussion of the relation between mind and body. Chapter Four was a discussion of the meaning of life and whether or not the most fulfilling life for a human being is a life that revolves around an experience of satisfaction and pleasure, or if a meaningful life has to incorporate actual value. Chapter Four also included a related discussion of the respective values of mind and body, and the respective values of intellectual versus embodied pursuits. Chapter Five explored arguments for the view that the universe was created by an eternal sophisticated mind and arguments for the view that the universe is eternal and sophisticated on its own. In Chapter Six, we raised the issue of how much control we have over our thinking and decisions, and in Chapter Seven we discussed the question of the extent to which freedom is also a function of the interface between our decisions and the world. We concluded (in this chapter) with a discussion of who if anyone is responsible for intervening. Our approach to any of these topics will presumably depend on our approach to the others—our view of the criteria for knowledge, our view of the status of morality and value, our view of the sophistication of mind and the sophistication of body, our view of the control that we have over our decisions and our trajectory.

42

The issue that we have been discussing in this last chapter is what in fact promotes freedom: whether it is policies that emphasize the exercise of free will and autonomy, or policies that attempt to manage the conditions in which our minds develop and act, or if it is perhaps something else. Philosophers disagree on this issue, as they disagree on a number of the background issues that inform it. We have not settled the disagreements here, but it can be useful to highlight how they might be grounded in larger commitments, and commitments that run deep.

Possible discussion exercises

1   Do you think that Rawls is correct in his assumptions about how we would choose from behind the "veil of ignorance"?

2   Is it an intrusion to suggest that people *should* have second-order desires? Is it sometimes an intrusion on others when we do not have second-order desires? What do you think and why?

3   Offer a Nozickean critique of a specific social welfare program.

4   Do you think that the belief in the importance of autonomy and individual responsibility is due in large part to the belief that there is a Judgment Day for each individual? Might there be some other sources of the belief in the importance of individual responsibility?

5   Offer a Rawlsean critique of a specific aspect of the American penal system—mandatory sentencing laws for drug-related offences, "Stand Your Ground" laws, the death penalty, etc.

6   Should the members of a society only receive social welfare benefits—for example disability—if they are under surveillance or if they do something in return? Would this constitute a good compromise between Rawls and Nozick?

7   What do you think is one specific proposal that would help to equalize the ability of people to lead meaningful lives?

8   Do you think there are such things as objective value and objective morality? How much (if anything) turns on this debate?

9   Come up with an example of a case in which you help another person, but for purely self-interested reasons.

10 What would you do if you were in possession of Gyges' ring?

11 Do you think that Galileo is right that in many cases we cannot read scripture literally? Why or why not?

12 How confident do you think we should be in truths of faith? How confident should we be in truths of reason or truths of the senses?

13 Is there a way for a person of faith to have a meaningful life if they have to compromise on central components of their faith? Why or why not?

14 Do you think a person is ever under an obligation to abandon their first-order desires and try to become the sort of person who is driven by the desire to make the world a better place? What if the person could become just as fulfilled (or almost as fulfilled) as they were before?

15 Do you think that a person could be fulfilled if they modified their desires to the point that they cared less about their own interest than about the interest of others?

16 Should people feel obligated to critique or modify their nausea or their other uncomfortable responses to the behavior of others? Why or why not?

17 Bracketing the question of whether or not homosexual behavior is unnatural, are there any behaviors (in animals or humans) that are natural but that are bad? Are there behaviors that are unnatural but good?

18 Are there cases in which it is acceptable for a majority to vote for laws that inhibit the freedoms of a minority? Is freedom promoted in these cases? Why or why not?

19 Come up with your own everyday example for one of the views or arguments or objections presented in this chapter.

20 Have a debate about the social and political benefits of free markets versus governmental intervention. Or, have a debate on one of the following: the pros and cons of gay marriage; abortion; prison reform; military conscription; affirmative action. Make sure that the debate is informed by the various theses that were considered in Chapters One through Eight.

Notes

1 John Rawls, *A Theory of Justice*, 11–22. Professor Rawls was a philosopher at Harvard University. His views on justice shaped a lot of the academic debate in the late twentieth century and are still actively debated today.

2 Ibid., 14.

3 Ibid., 150–66.

4 Nozick, *Anarchy, State, and Utopia*, 213–14. Nozick and Rawls were colleagues and friends, and worthy adversaries.

5 Ibid., 160–1.

6 Ibid., 161.

7 Ibid., 333–4.

8 Michael Vick was a star quarterback for the Atlanta Falcons for six seasons before he was convicted in 2007 for his involvement in a cruel dogfighting ring. He lost all of his endorsements and was imprisoned for 21 months. He returned to the NFL in 2010 for the Philadelphia Eagles.

9 St Augustine, *On Free Choice of the Will*, 1.

10 Ibid., 20.

11 Cornell West, "Nihilism in Black America," in James A. Montmarquet and William H. Hardy (eds), *Reflections: An Anthology of African American Philosophy*, Belmont, CA: Wadsworth (2000), 284.

12 This is in Book II of Plato's *Republic*, 359a–360d.

13 Translations are from *The Holy Bible: King James Version*.

14 Leviticus 20.9.

15 Leviticus 25.44–5.

16 Hosea 9.14. See also Hosea 9.16, and Numbers 5.27–8.

17 Galileo Galilei, "To the Most Serene Grand Duchess Mother," in Stillman Drake (trans. and ed.), *Discoveries and Opinions of Galileo*, Garden City, NY: Doubleday and Company (1615/1957), 181. Galileo is more famous for his scientific writings, arguing, for example, that two bodies with different mass fall at the same rate, and that the "retrograde" motion of Mars and the moons of Jupiter are evidence that the sun is at the center of our solar system. During his lifetime the Church condemned Galileo for his controversial views, but in 1992 Pope John Paul II declared that the Church had been in error.

18 Ibid., 183–4.

19 Letter 143, "Augustine to Marcellinus, 412 A.D.," in J. G. Cunningham (trans.) and Philip Schaff (trans. and ed.), *From Nicene and Post-Nicene Fathers, First Series, Vol. 1*, Buffalo, NY: Christian Literature (1887). This is cited in Galileo's letter to Christina, 186.

20 Sarah Buss, "Needs (Someone Else's), Projects (My Own), and Reasons," *Journal of Philosophy* 103 (2006), 373–402. Sarah Buss is Associate Professor of Philosophy at the University of Michigan. She works primarily on issues in philosophy of action, autonomy, and ethics.

21 See, for example, Bernard Williams, "Consequentialism and Integrity," in J. J. C. Smart and Bernard Williams (eds), *Utilitarianism: For and Against*, Cambridge: Cambridge University Press (1973), 82–118. Sir Williams was a philosophy professor at Cambridge University and UC Berkeley. He was first and foremost a philosopher, but he thought and wrote about connections with many other disciplines as well. He was knighted in 1999.

REFERENCES

The Holy Bible: King James Version, New York: Harper-Collins (2011).

Adams, Marilyn McCord, "Horrendous Evils and the Goodness of God," *Proceedings of the Aristotelian Society*, Supplementary Volume 63 (1989), 297–310.

Anselm, St, *Proslogion*, in Richard N. Bosley and Martin Tweedale (trans. and ed.), *Basic Issues in Medieval Philosophy*, Orchard Park, NY: Broadview Press (1997), 105–6.

Aquinas, St Thomas, *Summa Theologiae*, in Richard N. Bosley and Martin Tweedale (trans. and ed.), *Basic Issues in Medieval Philosophy*, Orchard Park, NY: Broadview Press (1997), 114–16.

Arendt, Hannah, *Eichmann in Jerusalem: A Report on the Banality of Evil*, New York: Penguin Books (1963).

Armstrong, D. M., *Belief, Truth and Knowledge*, New York: Cambridge (1973).

Armstrong, Louis, "(When We Are Dancin') I Get Ideas," Catalog Number 27720, Decca Records (1951).

Astell, Mary, *A Serious Proposal to the Ladies. Parts I and II*, ed. P. Springborg, Ontario: Broadview Literary Texts (1696/2002).

Augustine, St, *On Free Choice of the Will*, trans. Thomas Williams, Indianapolis: Hackett (395/1993).

—, *Confessions*, trans. Henry Chadwick, Oxford and New York: Oxford University Press (400/1991).

—, Letter 143, "Augustine to Marcellinus, 412 A.D.," in J. G. Cunningham (trans.) and Philip Schaff (trans. and ed.), *From Nicene and Post-Nicene Fathers, First Series, Vol. 1*, Buffalo, NY: Christian Literature (1887).

Baker, Lynne Rudder, "Why Christians Should Not Be Libertarians: An Augustinian Challenge," *Faith & Philosophy* 20 (2003), 460–78.

De Beauvoir, Simone, *The Second Sex*, trans. and ed. H. M. Parshley, New York: Random House, Vintage Books (1989).

Beldecos, Athena, Sarah Bailey, Scott Gilbert, Karen Hicks Lori Kenschaft, Nancy Niemczyk, Rebecca Rosenberg Stephanie Schaertel, and Andrew Wedel, "The Importance of Feminist Critique for Cell Biology," *Hypatia* 3 (1988), 61–76.

Berkeley, George, *A Treatise Concerning the Principles of Human Knowledge*, ed. Kenneth Winkler, Indianapolis and Cambridge: Hackett (1710/1982).

BonJour, Lawrence, "Externalist Theories of Empirical Knowledge," *Midwest Studies in Philosophy* 5 (1980), 53–73.

Brink, David, "Rational Egoism, Self, and Others," in O. Flanagan and A. Rorty (eds), *Identity, Character, and Morality*, Cambridge, MA: MIT Press (1990), 339–78.

Buss, Sarah, "Needs (Someone Else's), Projects (My Own), and Reasons," *Journal of Philosophy* 103 (2006), 373–402.

Camus, Albert, *The Stranger*, trans. Matthew Ward, New York: Vintage (1942/1989).

Cavendish, Margaret, *Bell in Campo*, in *Playes*, London: John Martyn, James Allestrye, and Tho. Dicas (1662). Note that all of the Cavendish texts are available at the Early English Books Online site through the University of Michigan. Search keyword: Newcastle, Margaret.

—, *The Description of a New World, Called the Blazing World*, in *Margaret Cavendish: Political Writings*, ed. Susan James, Cambridge: Cambridge University Press (1666/2003).

—, *Grounds of Natural Philosophy*, ed. Collette V. Michael, West Cornwall, CT: Locust Hill Press (1668/1996).

—, *Nature's Pictures*, London: printed by A. Maxwell (1671).

—, *Observations Upon Experimental Philosophy*, Printed by A. Maxwell (1666).

—, *Philosophical and Physical Opinions*, London: Printed for William Wilson (1663).

—, *Philosophical Letters*, London (1664).

—, *Poems and Fancies*, London: Printed by T. R. for J. Martin and J. Allestrye (1653).

—, *The World's Olio*, London: printed for J. Martin and J. Allestrye (1655).

—, *Youth's Glory and Death's Banquet*, in *Playes*, London: John Martyn, James Allestrye, and Tho. Dicas (1662).

Churchland, Paul, *Matter and Consciousness*, Cambridge, MA: MIT Press (1984).

Cruse, Harold, *Plural but Equal*, New York: William Morrow (1987).

Cudworth, Ralph, *A Treatise Concerning Eternal and Immutable Morality*, ed. Sarah Hutton, Cambridge: Cambridge University Press (1731/1996).

—, *The True Intellectual System of the Universe*, Stuttgard-Bad Cannstatt: F. Fromann Verlag (1678/1964).

Darwin, Charles, *The Origin of Species*, Oxford and New York: Oxford University Press (1859/1996).

Descartes, Rene, *The Philosophical Writings of Descartes, Volume I,* trans. and ed. John Cottingham, Robert Stoothoff, and Dugald Murdoch, Cambridge: Cambridge University Press (1985). In the text this is "CSM 1."

—, *The Philosophical Writings of Descartes, Volume II,* trans. and ed. John Cottingham, Robert Stoothoff, and Dugald Murdoch, Cambridge: Cambridge University Press (1984). In the text this is "CSM 2."

Dreyfus, Hubert, *Being-in-the-World,* Cambridge, MA: MIT Press (1991).

—, *On the Internet,* London: Routledge (2008).

Dylan, Bob, "Ballad of a Thin Man," *Highway 61 Revisited,* Columbia Records (1965).

Einstein, Albert, Foreword to Max Jammer, *Concepts of Space,* Cambridge: Harvard University Press (1954).

Elisabeth of Bohemia, "Princess Elisabeth of Bohemia to René Descartes, 16 May 1643," in Andrea Nye (ed.), *The Princess and the Philosopher,* New York: Roman and Littlefield (1999).

Epictetus, *Encheiridion,* trans. and ed. Nicholas White, Indianapolis: Hackett (2010).

Epicurus, "To Monoeceus," in Cyril Bailey (trans. and ed.), *Epicurus: The Extant Remains,* New York: Georg Olms Verlag (1975), 82–93.

—, *Principal Doctrines,* in Cyril Bailey (trans. and ed.), *Epicurus: The Extant Remains,* New York: Georg Olms Verlag (1975), 94–105.

Foot, Phillipa, "Morality as a System of Hypothetical Imperatives," *The Philosophical Review* 81 (1972), 305–16.

Frankfurt, Harry, "Freedom of the Will and the Concept of a Person," *The Journal of Philosophy* 68 (1971), 5–20.

Galilei, Galileo, "To the Most Serene Grand Duchess Mother," in Stillman Drake (trans. and ed.), *Discoveries and Opinions of Galileo,* Garden City, NY: Doubleday and Company (1615/1957), 175–216.

Gines, Kathryn, "Fanon and Sartre 50 Years Later: To Retain or Reject the Concept of Race," *Sartre Studies International* 9 (2003), 55–67.

Goldman, Alvin, "A Causal Theory of Knowing," *Journal of Philosophy* 64 (1967), 357–72.

Gowans, Chris, "Moral Relativism," *The Stanford Encyclopedia of Philosophy* (Spring 2012 Edition), Edward N. Zalta (ed.), URL = <http://plato.stanford.edu/archives/spr2012/entries/moral-relativism/>.

Harding, Sandra, *The Science Question in Feminism,* Ithaca, NY: Cornell University Press (1986).

Haslanger, Sally, "What Knowledge Is and What it Ought to Be," *Philosophical Perspectives* 13 (1999), 459–80.

Heidegger, Martin, *Basic Problems of Phenomenology*, trans. and ed. Albert Hofstadter, Bloomington: Indiana University Press (1927/1988).

—, "The Environmental Experience," in Günter Figal (ed.) and Jerome Veith (trans.), *The Heidegger Reader*, Bloomington: Indiana University Press (1922/2007), 33–7.

—, "The Question Concerning Technology," in William Lovitt (trans. and ed.), *The Question Concerning Technology and Other Essays*, New York: Harper & Row (1962/1977), 3–35.

Hobbes, Thomas, *Leviathan*, ed. Edwin Curley, Indianapolis: Hackett (1651/1994).

Hume, David, *Dialogues Concerning Natural Religion*, in J. C. A. Gaskin (ed.), *David Hume: Principle Writings on Religion*, Indianapolis: Hackett (1779/1993).

—, *An Enquiry Concerning Human Understanding*, ed. Tom L. Beauchamp, Oxford: Oxford University Press (1748/1999).

—, *An Enquiry Concerning the Principles of Morals*, ed. Tom L. Beauchamp, Oxford: Oxford University Press (1998).

—, "To Gilbert Elliot of Minto, 10 March 1751: A Letter Concerning the Dialogues," in *David Hume: Principle Writings on Religion*, 25–6.

—, *A Treatise of Human Nature*, ed. David Fate Norton and Mary J. Norton, Oxford: Oxford University Press (1739/2011).

Jackson, Frank, "Mind and Illusion," in Anthony O'Hear (ed.), *Minds and Persons*, Cambridge: Cambridge University Press (2003), 251–71.

—, "What Mary Didn't Know," *The Journal of Philosophy* 83 (1986), 291–5.

Jeske, Diane, *Rationality and Moral Theory: How Intimacy Generates Reasons*, New York: Routledge (2008).

Johnston, Daniel, "Life in Vain," *Fun*, Atlantic Records (1994).

Kant, Immanuel, *The Critique of Pure Reason*, trans. and ed. Paul Guyer and Allen Wood, Cambridge: Cambridge University Press (1998).

Kierkegaard, Søren, *Fear and Trembling*, trans. Sylvia Walsh, Cambridge: Cambridge University Press (2006).

—, *Practice in Christianity*, ed. and trans. Howard V. Hong and Edna H. Hong, Princeton: Princeton University Press (1991).

—, *The Present Age*, trans. Alexander Dru, ed. Walter Kaufmann, New York: Harper & Row (1962).

Kim, Jaegwon, "Epiphenomenal and Supervenient Causation," *Midwest Studies in Philosophy* 9 (1984), 257–70.

Lackey, Jennifer, "Testimonial Knowledge and Transmission," *The Philosophical Quarterly* 49 (1999), 471–90.

Langton, Rae, *Kantian Humility: Our Ignorance of Things in Themselves*, Oxford: Oxford University Press (1998).

—, *Sexual Solipsism: Philosophical Essays on Pornography and Objectification*, Oxford: Oxford University Press (1998).

Leibniz, G. W., *Discourse on Metaphysics*, in Roger Ariew and Daniel Garber (trans. and eds), *G. W. Leibniz: Philosophical Essays*, Indianapolis: Hackett (1984), 35–68.

—, *Monadology*, in Roger Ariew and Daniel Garber (trans. and eds), *G. W. Leibniz: Philosophical Essays*, 213–24.

Lucretius, *On the Nature of Things*, trans. and ed. Anthony M. Esolen, Baltimore: Johns Hopkins University Press (1999).

Mackie, John, *Ethics: Inventing Right and Wrong*, London: Penguin Books (1977).

Maddy, Penelope, *Realism in Mathematics*, New York: Oxford University Press (1992).

Malebranche, Nicolas, *Dialogues on Metaphysics and on Religion*, trans. and ed. Nicholas Jolley and David Scott, Cambridge: Cambridge University Press (1688/1997).

—, *The Search After Truth*, trans. and ed. Thomas Lennon and Paul Oscamp, Cambridge: Cambridge University Press (1674–5/1997).

Mallon, Ron, "Passing, Traveling and Reality: Social Constructionism and the Metaphysics of Race," *Nous* 38 (2004), 644–73.

McGrath, Sarah, "Moral Disagreement and Moral Expertise," *Oxford Studies in MetaEthics* 3 (2008), 87–107.

de la Mettrie, Julien Offray, *Machine Man*, in Ann Thomson (trans. and ed.), *Man Machine and other Writings*, Cambridge: Cambridge University Press (1748/1996).

Mills, Charles, "Alternative Epistemologies," *Social Theory and Practice* 14 (1988), 237–63.

Moore, G. E., "Proof of an External World," in G. E. Moore (ed.), *Philosophical Papers*, New York: Collier Books (1962), 144–8.

Moss, Jeff, and Damar Fehlau, *I Don't Want to Live on the Moon*, New York: Random House Books for Young Readers (2001).

Moss-Racusin, Corinne A., John F. Dovidio, Victoria L. Brescoll, Mark J. Graham, and Jo Handelsman, "Science Faculty's Subtle Gender Biases Favor Male Students," in *Proceedings of the National Academy of the Sciences* (2012), www.pnas.org/cgi/doi/10.1073/pnas.1211286109.

Nadler, Steven, *Spinoza: A Life*, Cambridge: Cambridge University Press (1999).

Nagel, Thomas, "The Absurd," *The Journal of Philosophy* 68 (1971), 716–27.

—, "What's it Like to Be a Bat?," *The Philosophical Review* 83 (1974), 435–50.

Nietzsche, Friedrich, *On the Genealogy of Morality*, ed. Keith Ansell-Pearson, trans. Carol Diethe, Cambridge: Cambridge University Press (1997).

—, *The Will to Power*, trans. Walter Kaufman and R. J. Hollingdale, New York: Vintage (1968).

Nozick, Robert, *Anarchy, State and Utopia*, New York: Basic Books (1975).

Paley, William, *Natural Theology, Volume I*, London: Charles Knight (1802/1839).

Pascal, Blaise, "The Wager," in *Pensées*, trans. A. J. Krailsheimer, London: Penguin Books (1966), 149–54.

Plato, *Apology*, in G. M. A. Grube (trans. and ed.), *Five Dialogues*, Indianapolis and Cambridge: Hackett (1981), 21–44.

—, *Euthyphro*, in G. M. A. Grube (trans. and ed.), *Five Dialogues*, Indianapolis and Cambridge: Hackett (1981), 1–20.

—, *Phaedo*, in G. M. A. Grube (trans. and ed.), *Five Dialogues*, Indianapolis and Cambridge: Hackett (1981), 93–154.

Plotinus, "On Beauty," in Elmer O'Brien (trans. and ed.), *Essential Plotinus: Representative Treatises from the Enneads*, Indianapolis: Hackett (1975).

Preston, John, and Mark Bishop (eds), *Views into the Chinese Room: New Essays on Searle and Artificial Intelligence*, Oxford: Clarendon Press (2002).

Russell, Bertrand, "The Faith of a Rationalist," in Al Seckel (ed.), *Bertrand Russell on God and Religion*, Amherst, NY: Prometheus Books (1947/1986), 87–94.

—, *What I Believe*, New York: E. P. Dutton and Company (1925).

Sartre, Jean-Paul, *Being and Nothingness*, trans. Hazel E. Barnes, New York: Washington Square Press (1956).

—, "The Humanism of Existentialism," in Charles Guignon and Derk Pereboom (eds), *Existentialism: Basic Writings*, Indianapolis: Hackett (2001).

Searle, John, *Minds, Brains and Science*, Cambridge, MA: Harvard University Press (1984).

—, *The Rediscovery of the Mind*, Cambridge, MA, and London: MIT Press (1992).

Smart, J. J. C., "Sensations and Brain Processes," *The Philosophical Review* 68 (1959), 141–56.

Sosa, Ernest, *Reflective Knowledge: Apt Belief and Reflective Knowledge, Volume II*, Oxford: Oxford University Press (2007).

Sowaal, Alice, "Mary Astell's *Serious Proposal*: Mind, Method, and Custom," *Philosophy Compass* 2 (2007), 227–43.

Spinoza, Baruch, *Ethics*, in Samuel Shirley (trans.) and Michael
    Morgan (ed.), *Spinoza: Complete Works*, Indianapolis: Hackett
    (1677/2002).
—, *Short Treatise on God, Man and His Well-Being*, in Samuel Shirley
    (trans.) and Michael Morgan (ed.), *Spinoza: Complete Works*,
    Indianapolis: Hackett (1662/2002), 33–107.
Stroud, Barry, *The Significance of Philosophical Skepticism*, Oxford:
    Oxford University Press (1984).
Struhl, Kartsen J., "No (More) Philosophy Without Cross-Cultural
    Philosophy," *Philosophy Compass* 5 (2010), 287–95.
Turing, Alan, "Computing Machinery and Intelligence," *Mind* 59
    (1950), 433–60.
Van Inwagen, Peter, "The Powers of Rational Beings: Freedom of the
    Will," in John Perry, Michael Bratman, and John Martin Fischer
    (eds), *Introduction to Philosophy: Classical and Contemporary
    Readings*, Fifth Edition, Oxford and New York: Oxford University
    Press (2010), 400–11.
West, Cornell, "Nihilism in Black America," in James A. Montmarquet
    and William H. Hardy (eds), *Reflections: An Anthology of African
    American Philosophy*, Belmont, CA: Wadsworth (2000), 281–5.
Williams, Bernard, "Consequentialism and Integrity," in J. J. C.
    Smart and Bernard Williams (eds), *Utilitarianism: For and Against*,
    Cambridge: Cambridge University Press (1973), 82–118.
Wolf, Susan, "The Meanings of Lives," in John Perry, Michael Bratman,
    and John Martin Fischer (eds), *Introduction to Philosophy: Classical
    and Contemporary Readings*, Fifth Edition, Oxford and New York:
    Oxford University Press (2010), 794–805.
Yancy, George, *Black Bodies, White Gazes: The Continuing
    Significance of Race*, Lanham, MD: Rowman and Littlefield (2008).
Zack, Naomi, "Reparations and the Rectification of Race," *The Journal
    of Ethics* 7 (2003), 139–51.
Zagzebski, Linda, "An Agent-Based Approach to the Problem of Evil,"
    International Journal for Philosophy of Religion 39 (1996), 127–39.

INDEX